Medieval Women in their Communities

Medieval Women
in their
Communities

Edited by

DIANE WATT

UNIVERSITY OF TORONTO PRESS
TORONTO BUFFALO

© The Contributors, 1997

First published in North America in 1997
by University of Toronto Press Incorporated,
Toronto Buffalo.

ISBN 0-8020-4289-9 (cloth)

ISBN 0-8020-8122-3 (paper)

Canadian Cataloguing in Publication Data

Main entry under title:

Medieval women in their communities

ISBN 0-8020-4289-9 (bound)   ISBN 0-8020-8122-3 (pbk.)

1. Women – Europe – History – Middle Ages, 500-1500-
1. Watt, Diane.

HQ1147.E85M42 1997   305.4'094'0902   C97-930623-X

Printed on acid-free paper

Typeset in Great Britain at The Midlands Book Typesetting Company, Loughborough
Printed in Great Britain by Dinefwr Press, Llandybïe

I Jane Aaron
ac i Gymru

Ei diffinio rown
ar fwrdd glân,
rhoi ffurf i'w ffiniau,
ei gyrru i'w gororau
mewn inc coch;
ac meddai myfyriwr o bant,
'It's like a pig running away';
wedi bennu chwerthin,
rwy'n ei chredu;
y swch gogleddol
yn heglu'n gynt
na'r swrn deheuol
ar ffo rhag y lladdwyr.

Menna Elfyn, o 'Siapiau o Gymru'

Contents

Illustrations

Acknowledgements

In 1995, 'community' was taken as the theme of the annual meeting of the Gender and Medieval Studies Group, which met at Gregynog, the conference centre of the University of Wales. The topic was chosen because it was generally felt to be one which needed opening out for discussion, and the meeting proved so stimulating that the decision was made to publish some of the research. Thanks are owed to all who took part, especially Ruth Evans, Jane Gilbert, E. Kay Harris, Kirsten Hill, Richard Ireland, Rhiannon Purdie and Catherine Williams. My own introduction is particularly indebted to the papers by Ruth Evans and Jane Gilbert, and to the discussions provoked by their sessions. I would like to thank Alison Yarnold (Flora Hadfield) for her invaluable assistance at the conference, and also Patricia Duncker, Andrew Hadfield and John Watts for their help. I am grateful to the administrators of the University of Wales Aberystwyth College Research Fund for generously supporting this project, to Ned Thomas of the University of Wales Press for his encouragement, and to the reader appointed by the publisher for such informed and constructive advice. I am indebted to Bill Watts for recovering data from a damaged disk, and to Jean Matthews from the Computer Unit, UWA, and to Joan Crawford and June Baxter from the English Department, who all helped with the typing. Patricia Watt read through the proofs with painstaking care. Finally, this book would never have come into being without the efforts of its contributors, whose cheerful co-operation made its editing a surprisingly painless process.

Editor and Contributors

DIANE WATT is Lecturer in British Medieval Literature in the Department of English, University of Wales Aberystwyth. She gained her D.Phil. from the University of Oxford in 1993. Her book, *Secretaries of God: Women Prophets in Late Medieval and Early Modern England* will be published by Boydell and Brewer in 1997, and she has published several articles on medieval and Renaissance writing. Her main research interests are English women writers before 1700, feminist theory and gender studies, and Middle English and Middle Scots literature.

JANE CARTWRIGHT is Lecturer in the Department of Welsh, Trinity College Carmarthen. Formerly she held the position of Lecturer in the Celtic Studies Department at the Catholic University of Lublin, Poland. She has recently completed a doctoral thesis entitled 'Y Forwyn Fair, Santesau a Lleianod: Agweddau ar Wyryfdod a Diweirdeb yng Nhgymru'r Oesoedd Canol', at the University of Wales, Cardiff. She is interested in the Virgin Mary, female saints and nuns in medieval Welsh literature, Welsh hagiography, feminine sanctity, virginity and chastity tests, and women's history generally.

SUSANNAH MARY CHEWNING has recently completed her doctoral thesis on medieval mysticism at Drew University, Madison, New Jersey. She has published a number of articles and reviews on medieval and Renaissance literature and is working on an edition entitled *A Talkyng of the Loue of God*, to be published by Cornell University Press. She currently teaches in the English Department, Kean College of New Jersey.

MARIE-LUISE EHRENSCHWENDTNER studied Latin and Theology at the University of Munich. From 1986 to 1991 she was a research assistant in the Protestant Faculty of Theology at the University of Tübingen. She currently lives in Cambridge and is completing a Ph.D. thesis on the education of Dominican nuns in southern Germany from the thirteenth to fifteenth centuries. Her special interests are the theology and spirituality of medieval religious communities, on which she has published a number of articles.

PENELOPE GALLOWAY is a research student and Snell Exhibitioner at Balliol College, Oxford. She is writing her doctoral thesis on the beguine communities of northern France, 1200–1500. Her principal interests are nuns and religious lay women and their communities in medieval Europe, and she plans to develop her current research project into a comparative study of beguine communities in Germany.

CYNTHIA KRAMAN is a Ph.D. candidate at Queen Mary and Westfield College, University of London. Her research interests include landscape description and women's issues in the late Middle Ages. She currently teaches at the College of New Rochelle, New York. She is a member of the MLA and NEMLA and is biographically listed in *Contemporary Authors and Poets and Writers*. Her previous publications include *Taking on the Local Color* (Middleton, 1977) and *The Mexican Murals* (San Francisco, 1986). Her poetry has appeared most recently in *Antaeus, Poetry Flash* and *The Paris Review*.

PATRICIA SKINNER is Lecturer in Humanities in the Department of Adult Continuing Education, University of Southampton. She held research fellowships at the University of Birmingham and the Wellcome Institute for the History of Medicine, London. Her main area of interest is the social history of medieval southern Italy. Her book, *Family Power in Southern Italy*, was published by Cambridge University Press in 1995, and she has published several articles focusing on family structures and women. Her current projects include a book on medieval southern Italian healthcare. Patricia acts as medieval editor for two series published by Longman: the *Longman History of European Women* and *Women and Men in History*. She is writing a history of Italian women for the latter series.

J. A. TASIOULAS is Lecturer in the Department of English at Stirling University. Previously she held a junior research fellowship at New College, Oxford. She has recently completed a doctoral thesis on childhood in the Middle Ages, submitted to the University of Oxford. She has published articles on Old and Middle English literature and is working on an edition of Middle Scots poetry.

ROSALYNN VOADEN is a Research Fellow in Medieval Literature at St Anne's College, Oxford. She received her doctorate from the University of York in 1994. Her principal interests are the writings of late medieval women visionaries, and the effects of gender on mystical experience in the Middle Ages. She is the editor of *Prophets Abroad: The Reception of Continental Holy Women in Medieval England* (Cambridge, 1996). For light relief she works on modern romance and detective fiction.

JENNIFER C. WARD is Senior Lecturer in History at Goldsmith's College, University of London, specializing in medieval British History, c.1066–c.1550. Her major recent publications include *English Noblewomen in the Later Middle Ages* published by Longman in 1992, and *Women of the English Nobility and Gentry, 1066–1500,* published by Manchester University Press in 1995. Her main research interests are Elizabeth de Burgh and the Clare family, medieval women in England and Europe, and the regional history of eastern England.

JANET WILSON teaches Medieval English and New Zealand Literature at the University of Otago, and during 1995–6 was on an exchange at Oxford Brookes University. In addition to articles on Middle English and Renaissance literature, she has published *Preaching in the Reformation: An Edition of Roger Edgeworth's Sermons Very Fruitfull, Godly and Learned* (Woodbridge, 1993). She is currently working on a study of the culture of the court of Mary I. In 1994 she founded the New Zealand Studies Research Centre at the University of Otago.

Introduction:
Medieval Women in their Communities

DIANE WATT

T HE resolution to produce a volume of essays on the subject of
women in the Middle Ages requires little justification. It is
impossible to deny that the growth disciplines of women's and gender
studies have had their impact on research and teaching on the Middle
Ages. This fact is attested to by the constantly expanding circulation of
the journal *Medieval Feminist Newsletter*, and by the existence of both
the Society for Medieval Feminist Scholarship (a US based
organization) and the Gender and Medieval Studies Group (largely,
although not entirely, made up of British academics).[1] As Allen Frantzen
states in an article which appeared in 1993 in a special issue of the
periodical *Speculum* devoted to studying medieval women, 'If writing
about women was once an innovation, it is now an imperative.'[2] Four
years before the publication of Frantzen's piece, the growing interest in
the connected subjects of medieval women and communities was
illustrated when *Signs: A Journal of Women in Culture and Society*
brought out an issue headed *Working Together in the Middle Ages:
Perspectives on Women's Communities.*[3] That volume includes studies of
women in religious communities, fictive chivalric communities, brothels,
craft and trade communities and guilds, and in the medical profession.
It provides an extremely useful starting point for those interested in the
topic of medieval women and their communities, but clearly there is
scope for much more work to be done. The present book is a further
contribution to this developing field.

1. Community and its Implications

'Community' is often used in very specific contexts and the significance
given to the word should warn us against using it without fully considering

its implications. To give just some examples of its recent applications: Benedict Anderson has formulated the expression 'imagined political community' to explain the phenomenon of nationalism;[4] Stanley Fish talks about 'interpretive communities' when he theorizes about the source of meaning;[5] and Brian Stock has coined the phrase 'textual communities' in his account of the transformation of oral and written traditions in the eleventh and twelfth centuries.[6] Despite such specialized usages, community is still often taken more generally by historians of the medieval and early modern periods to mean a group of people living in a given locality, often, but not necessarily, tied by bonds of kinship – the population of a village, town, region or country. Yet, as the historian Miri Rubin explains, even in its most general application, 'community' also carries certain connotations:

> Community, like all coins for social and political explanation is and has always been discursively constructed and is always laden with aspirations and contests over interpretative power. Community is neither obvious nor natural, its boundaries are loose, and people in the present, as in the past, will use the term to describe and to construct worlds, to persuade, to include and to exclude.[7]

Even beyond the specific usages mentioned above, 'community' has ideological implications which go both hand in hand with and beyond its socio-economic and geographic senses.

For Rubin, one of the principal difficulties with the word 'community' is that it carries with it certain implications of social unity: 'community conjures a moral economy based on close interaction and clear attitudes between small and great, through deference, patronage, or struggle. Thus community operates as a measure of well-being . . .'[8] While, as Jennifer C. Ward's essay on English noblewomen in this volume rightly stresses, feudal bonds, hospitality and patronage all functioned to draw together local communities, Rubin is surely correct to suggest that such an image of rural harmony is often artificial – competition and conflict are inevitable characteristics of any community, modern or medieval. Communities are marked by exclusion as well as inclusion, and some communities in western Christendom, such as Jewish communities, can in fact be characterized as communities of outsiders – a point made by Cynthia Kraman in her chapter on the *Merchant's Tale* and *Song of Songs*.

Membership of a community is often seen to imply a shared identity, but a point which Rubin emphasizes is that 'identity can never be

Illustration from MS Peniarth 28, f.17 (by permission of the National Library of Wales). This illustration appears at the start of the section on women in a Welsh law book. The existence of a separate code for women suggests that they were perceived as marginal to their community.

constituted through a single or overarching affinity – whether gender, class, or age – but rather at the intersection and the changing dynamic negotiation of these and other positions in the world.'[9] To put this another way, identities are sites of complex and sometimes conflicting differences; and consequently they are constructed not through a single static community but through the overlap and interaction of networks of communities. The example of Margery Kempe illustrates this point quite clearly: in her *Book*, Kempe's identity emerges from various aspects of her life which are often at odds with one another, such as her sex, economic position, race, and vocation. Kempe is woman, wife, tradesperson, English pilgrim and visionary, and not only her *Book*, but also the little we know of her history, indicate the sheer diversity of the communities of which she was part. We might also note that in her imitation of Christ, Kempe deliberately associated herself with those on the margins of the community or in marginal communities, such as the mad, the poor, and lepers.

Margery Kempe's *Book* might also be described as indicating a very different sort of community altogether, and one which might be seen as a specifically female 'textual community'. Stock has shown that both heretics and reformers used literacy 'to structure the internal behaviour of the groups' members and to provide solidarity against the outside world'.[10] In order to vindicate her often controversial piety, parallels are drawn, by Kempe and her scribe, between her life and devotions and those of St Bridget of Sweden and Mary of Oignies, and references are also made to mystical texts like Walter Hilton's *Scale of Perfection*, Richard Rolle's *Incendium amoris*, and the pseudo-Bonaventuran *Stimulus amoris* or Nicholas Love's translation of the *Meditationes vitae Christi*, and to authorities such as Elizabeth of Hungary and Julian of Norwich. These works are part of a literary culture which, although not exclusively female, is, as Felicity Riddy has argued, shared by nuns, anchoresses and pious gentlewomen; 'a textuality of the spoken as well as the written word'.[11] It might be extended to include devotional works written specifically for a female audience, for example *þe Wohunge of Ure Lauerd* (discussed here by Susannah Mary Chewning), *Ancrene Wisse* and *Sawles Warde*, and also texts like the N-Town Mary Play, which would, as J. A. Tasioulas suggests, have had a particular appeal to women. The secular and ecclesiastical communities in which Janet Wilson's study locates *The Book of Margery Kempe* are not, however, dominated by women, but by men. Indeed, only the first five essays in the volume are concerned primarily with communities of women as such.

The relationship between these medieval communities and modern feminist notions of collectivity is one which should be considered, before more general conclusions can be drawn about women's position within medieval society as a whole.

2. Feminisms / Women / Communities

The editorial of the special issue of *Signs* on women's communities in the Middle Ages opens with the statement, 'For modern feminists, community is a valued concept and an acknowledged goal. In our decision making, we work towards consensus; in our world-view, we strive for inclusiveness; in our social lives, we seek group support and comfort. In all these actions, those of us who are Western feminists move against the individualism of our culture.'[12] This view is reiterated in the introduction to a recent volume of essays, *Feminist Readings in Middle English Literature*, in which the editors, Ruth Evans and Lesley Johnson claim that 'it remains the case that a feminist politics must ground itself in some sort of idea of collective identity.'[13] Evans and Johnson point out that twentieth-century feminism had as its foundation 'an essentialist notion of "sexual identity": an identity which would allow women to organise themselves politically as a unified group to combat male oppression'.[14] Collectives played key roles in the formative early years of Women's Liberation in particular, and the importance of community has been emphasized by feminist theorists, historians, critics and writers.[15]

One basic problem with a feminist rejection of hierarchy and individualism as patriarchal instruments of oppression seems to be that even, or perhaps especially, the most separatist of notions of women's collectivity define women in terms of sexual sameness, and consequently also in terms of sexual difference: women are still defined in relation to men. More recently, feminist theorists have started to wonder just how useful it is to assume that women constitute a unified group, a 'natural' community, simply because they are women. Can we take it as read that women have a common identity? In her important study *Gender Trouble*, in which she attacks the reductive opposition of biological sex to socially-constructed gender, Judith Butler stresses the limitations of an approach which essentializes or naturalizes the category of 'woman'.

> If one 'is' a woman, that is surely not all one is; the term fails to be exhaus-
> tive . . . because gender is not always constituted coherently or consistently
> in different historical contexts, and because gender intersects with racial, class,
> ethnic, sexual and regional modalities of discursively constituted identities.
> As a result, it becomes impossible to separate out 'gender' from the politi-
> cal and cultural intersections in which it is invariably produced and main-
> tained.[16]

In other words, the assumption that 'woman' is a transhistorical,
transcultural category, is one which can and should be questioned.
Concerning the matter of women's communities and women's
collectives, Butler further contends that 'identity categories often
presumed to be foundational to feminist politics, that is, deemed
necessary to mobilize feminism as an identity politics, simultaneously
work to limit and constrain in advance the very cultural possibilities that
feminism is supposed to open up.'[17] From a political perspective, it seems
that it is crucial that feminists attempt to acknowledge and accommodate
difference.

If feminists have themselves critiqued the problematic utopianism of
women's collectivity, it is none the less valid to ask if there is any
evidence of similar idealism in the Middle Ages. Certainly, women
religious, whether nuns or anchorites, lived in all-female and sometimes
isolated communities, yet even the most autonomous of these (such as
the convent of Helfta, the subject of Rosalynn Voaden's essay in this
volume) remained under the authority of monks and priests. Other
medieval women came together in religious groups such as beguinages,
studied in this collection by Penelope Galloway, which were not under
the direct control of the Church. Galloway describes the beguine
communities as 'a unique system of female solidarity', but they enjoyed
only a certain degree of independence. In secular society the situation
seems to have been much the same. Even the outspoken and fiercely
independent laywoman Margery Kempe was answerable to her spiritual
fathers. As Evans and Johnson observe, there is no historical evidence
to suggest that there was in the Middle Ages any sort of 'political
programme committed to a struggle against all forms of female
subordination'.[18] It follows therefore that, if the women's groups of the
late twentieth century had medieval foremothers, there were nevertheless
no women's communities in the radical feminist sense. Of course this
does not mean that medieval women did not either form or play
important parts in other sorts of collective groups and it is the purpose
of this volume to explore more fully some of the complex and diverse

relationships between women and their communities in pre-modern Europe.

3. Notions of the Community in the Middle Ages

Clearly, recent scholarship such as that by Rubin, challenges Jacob Burckhardt's assertion that in the Middle Ages people had no sense of themselves as individuals, that medieval man was 'conscious of himself only as a member of a race, people, party, family, or corporation – only through some general category'.[19] Just as it would be a mistake to think of the Middle Ages as a unified and discrete period in history, so it is naïve to assume that medieval people had no conception of individuality, subjectivity, and identity.[20] None the less, the editorial of the 1989 special issue of *Signs* seems to reveal the influence of Burckhardt's thinking when it argues for continuity between the community experience of medieval people and that of modern feminists:

> In the medieval West, people sought association with one another through a wide variety of communities; monasteries for men and women seeking the contemplative life, guilds for persons engaged in the same craft or trade, parishes for Christian worshippers, nucleated villages for rural dwellers, and many other such forms of public association. For medieval people of all ranks and regions, cooperation and association with others was a basic fact of life . . . Even medieval writings – philosophical, literary, and religious – emphasised community. Political commentators spoke of the community of the realm (*communitas regni*), and social commentators conceived of their entire world as a community, dividing their 'Christendom' into three co-operating groups of those who pray, those who fight, and those who work (*oratores, bellatores, labores*) . . . By examining the history of women's communities during an age that strongly espoused ideals of community, we have sought to gain insights for our own very different, but also very similar struggles . . . But all of these stories and experiences reflect on the abilities of women in the past to form sustained, autonomous, strong communities, and in so doing, they speak to modern feminists working towards new forms of women's community and women's cooperation.[21]

The assumption that medieval people had a much stronger sense of their communities is in itself dubious, reflecting as it does both the naïve preconception of idyllic social harmony attacked by Rubin, and the optimism expressed by early feminist writers. However my primary concern here is whether we should accept without question the assumption that women were included unproblematically within medieval communities.

An enquiry into the status of women within medieval communities might begin with medieval definitions of community.[22] According to the MED the vernacular word *communite* was more restricted in meaning than its modern equivalent.[23] The Middle-English *communite* has a range of political, socio-economic, legal and metaphorical definitions which include, amongst others, 'the people of a country, city', 'the third estate', 'the House of Commons', 'a religious community or brotherhood', and 'a guild'. All of the citations given date to the late fourteenth century or the fifteenth century; prior to that period the Latin term *communitas* was widely used, especially in formal, technical contexts.[24] Evidently women might theoretically be included in certain usages, for example in phrases such as *the communite of the peple* ('the totality of the people, all the people'); *the communite of mankinde, of the worlde* ('all of mankind'). Furthermore, communities of women certainly existed, convents and beguinages being the female equivalents of male religious brotherhoods.

None the less, many of these medieval usages, including some of the most general, may actually exclude women altogether. To give an example, recent scholarship has debated the extent to which women professionally involved in the trades and crafts were granted guild membership. Galloway's point that the guilds decreased the labour opportunities for women is relevant here. While some were admitted to the franchise, it seems that this was largely because they were wives or widows of guild members, and even in those areas of production dominated by women, such as silk working, they only rarely seem to have formed their own professional bodies.[25] Even when women were included in medieval notions of community, their position was often completely subordinate. To take another example, the earliest citation recorded in the OED of *community* meaning 'the body of those having common or equal rights or rank, as distinguished from the privileged classes; the body of commons; the commonalty' is Barbour's *Bruce*, the Scottish historical chronicle written *c.*1375. In the *Bruce*, all Scots, no matter their class, ethnicity, ages or gender, are portrayed as part of a 'fictionally unified "community of the realm"'.[26] In the imaginary world of the text, political conflict *within* Scotland does not exist. The text functions to persuade the masses, serfs as well as freemen, of the importance of defending Scotland's independence, yet the peasants in

particular stood to gain very little from this cause. Likewise, the poem
constitutes women as political subjects, but only within the patriarchal
system in Scotland. Their rights and interests as women are certainly not
defined in the *Bruce* or furthered by the poem's ideology. The idea that
women are included in the 'community of the realm' is illusory.

A point which is made by both Jane Cartwright and Patricia Skinner
is that the circumstances of many women, such as members of impoverished communities like the Welsh convents, or widows and lone
mothers who found themselves marginalized in the community as a result of economic hardship, are seldom fully or reliably documented. As
Cartwright notes, had it not been for the bishop's licence of 1530 grant-
ing a nun from an Augustinian house in England permission to transfer
to the 'stricter' Cistercian house of Llanllugan in order to lead a more
holy life, one might have formed quite a different and much more negative impression of religious communities in Wales. The strength of the
hostile reactions of men, both lay and religious, was evidently a factor
in determining the success of some of the communities of women discussed here. In contrast with the situations described by Cartwright and
Skinner, the cluster of essays in this volume focusing on the Norfolk area
reflects the considerable amount of evidence which has survived from
this region: Ward and Tasioulas give us telling insights into aspects of
secular life in East Anglia at the end of the Middle Ages, while Wilson
characterizes the locality as one riven by controversy in which Kempe's
singular piety was regarded with ambivalence. To sum up then, we must
not only weigh up the usefulness of various types of sources, and be
careful to avoid sliding between modern and medieval usages, but also
be aware that women may often have been perceived as marginal to or
outside medieval communities.

4. Medieval Women in their Communities

The subject of this book is a large one. The title chosen for it, *Medieval
Women in their Communities*, is in many ways over-optimistic. The
volume does not provide, or attempt to provide, an account or overview
of women in every sort of community in the known world, or even
throughout Christendom, in the period 500–1500. Rather, this anthology
of interdisciplinary essays is intended to fill in some of the gaps in our
knowledge by providing detailed small-scale studies of women as
members of a whole range of different types of communities. In this

collection a wide variety of communities and women from a range of backgrounds are discussed: in terms of regionality, women from the geographical areas which correspond roughly to modern Wales, England, France, Italy, and Germany are included; in terms of religious beliefs, Jews as well as Christians; in terms of social and economic conditions, rich and poor, religious and secular, noblewomen and commoners are represented. Although one study looks at evidence from as early as the ninth century, for the most part the book concentrates on the period between 1200 and 1500. These essays all consider women's historical experience to be distinct from men's, but they are not restricted to a single theoretical perspective or methodological approach. Certainly, not all the contributors to this book would necessarily describe themselves as feminist, although it might well be argued that any current scholarship about women is informed, either directly or indirectly, by feminism. The two main academic disciplines are history and literature, but in a number of the essays these two fields of study overlap considerably. The contributors are all specialist researchers in their own fields: they use different methodologies, ask different questions, and formulate their conclusions from their own points of view.

While research on women's religious life in the Middle Ages has flourished in recent years, Jane Cartwright's essay on medieval Welsh nuns covers an area which has previously been neglected by scholars. Cartwright examines the surviving historical and literary evidence of convent life in Wales, arguing that the relative dearth of establishments for religious women (there seem to have been only four convents at most) may be an indication of national patterns of female devotion: rather than seeking a life of virginity and claustration, Welsh women tended to express their piety within a domestic context. There is reason to think that few noblewomen in Wales were in a position to found convents or offer extensive patronage to their inmates, and it is unlikely that other less formal alternatives, such as beguinages, hospitals, and anchorites' cells were available to those who felt drawn to a religious vocation. In other words, women in Wales would have had less opportunity to join a religious community than women elsewhere. Cartwright cites examples of *Cywyddwyr* poetry, which illustrate that Welsh poets perceived nuns as a corruptible commodity, as evidence of the low esteem in which the convents and their inhabitants were held. Unfortunately no writings by medieval Welsh nuns themselves survive, so the picture which we receive is necessarily distorted: very little is known about their education, social status, or devotional life.

Fortunately the convent experiences of religious women in other parts of Europe are better documented. Marie-Luise Ehrenschwendtner's study, while narrower in scope than Cartwright's, concentrates on one crucial and much disputed aspect of life within a women's religious community – the level of education of nuns. Ehrenschwendtner restricts her analysis to the Dominican convents in the former German province of Teutonia. Her research reveals that although divine services were sung or read in Latin, outside the church the everyday language spoken by the nuns was German. Many nuns may not have understood the services, and the surviving records indicate that there were only a few Latin books in the convents and that many liturgical texts were translated into the vernacular. While the nuns were not denied the opportunity to become literate in Latin, it was not deemed necessary. This situation contrasts with that of the Blackfriars, with whom they had close contact, who had responsibilities in terms of preaching and pastoral care (the former activity being forbidden to the sisters), and who were constitutionally required to learn Latin so that they could study theology. Yet despite these apparent limitations on their education, the Dominican nuns were learned in the vernacular and some wrote devotional works; thus they played an important role in the development of a tradition of vernacular spirituality.

The subject of Rosalynn Voaden's chapter, the community which flourished at the convent of Helfta, near Eisleben in Saxony, in the closing decades of the thirteenth century, takes up the theme of the prevalence of the vernacular in women's communities, but reveals a rather different situation to that described by Ehrenschwendtner. The Helfta community, a centre of women's spirituality and education, was evidently much more autonomous than the Dominican convents in Teutonia, and within it some of the nuns appropriated roles traditionally restricted to the male priesthood. It was in Helfta that the three visionaries, Mechtild of Magdeburg, Mechtild of Hackeborn and Gertrude the Great, composed accounts of their visions; works which comprise some of the most vivid and influential writings by medieval women. These texts are the more remarkable because no male scribes were involved in their production; instead the nuns seem to have worked together offering each other inspiration and emotional sustenance as well as practical assistance. Voaden contends that the mystical discourse of Mechtild of Hackeborn and Gertrude the Great, with its focus on the Sacred Heart in particular, is distinctive both in its incorporation of images of biological femaleness (as opposed to the more common devotional idealization of socially-constructed feminine characteristics, found for example in the metaphor of Jesus as mother), and also in its emphasis on the importance of the community as a sanctuary and a place of mutual support. Mechtild of Magdeburg, in contrast with the other two visionaries, was not raised in Helfta but entered the convent late in life after living as a beguine. Her different background may explain her more conventional humility, her greater dependence on male spiritual advisors, and the greater sense of isolation conveyed in her visionary writing.

The beguinages of northern France in the period 1200–1500, especially Douai and Lille, are discussed by Penelope Galloway. The beguines, who took no vows, did not live a strictly cloistered existence or follow a single rule, and often continued to hold property; they cannot be described as a single movement, and the problem of definition is such that it is often difficult to decide on the basis of the historical records whether or not a given establishment should be described as a beguinage. Galloway is particularly interested in the interaction between the beguinages and the religious and secular communities in which they were located, and she suggests that their popularity (which is so remarkably greater than the popularity of convents in medieval Wales) is related to the development of urban society. None the less, Galloway questions the assumption made by some historians that the interventionist role played by the rulers of Flanders and Hainault indicates that the beguine convents were fostered as a practical solution to the problems faced by urban communities containing large numbers of single women and widows. While they were also important as a means of maintaining civic obedience and preventing itinerancy, beguinages were undoubtedly founded primarily for spiritual reasons. Although beguinages may have provided refuges from the sort of 'conjunctural' poverty discussed later in this volume by Patricia Skinner, many of the women entering them seem to have been far from destitute. Looking at the social backgrounds of those who joined the beguine houses, it becomes clear that members of the ruling families were amongst their recruits. None the less, although the involvement of noble lay patrons such as the countesses Jeanne and Marguerite, of Flanders and Hainault, is particularly significant in their growth, beguinages relied on the support of members of the lower orders in the communities in which they arose, and on the championship of men as well as women: therefore gender appears not to be such a crucial factor in the patronage of women's communities as it is often thought.

Informal communities of religious women of a somewhat different

nature are the subject of Susannah Mary Chewning's chapter on the
anonymous thirteenth-century Middle-English devotional text *þe
Wohunge of Ure Lauerd.* The context of the *Wohunge,* like that of the
more well-known *Ancrene Wisse,* is almost certainly one of anchoritic
piety. According to Chewning, those who joined these semi-formal,
semi-secluded communities were discouraged from forming close
relationships with other religious, whether men or women, and
encouraged instead to direct their thoughts and emotions towards God
alone. The mystical content of the *Wohunge* places it in the continental
tradition of women's writing to which the nuns of Helfta made such
an important contribution. Chewning does not contend that the *Wohunge*
was authored by a man – indeed in her view the sex of the author is
incidental – but rather that the voice of the text, and the very mode of
mystical expression itself, is feminine. In her analysis of language and
subjectivity in the *Wohunge,* Chewning draws on post-structuralist ideas
and terminology, and in particular the work of Judith Butler and of the
French feminists Julia Kristeva, Luce Irigaray and Monique Wittig. The
seemingly conflicting desires of the mystic to experience obliteration
of the self in order to achieve union with the divine and to express in
writing that which is by its very nature inexpressible – the mystical
experience – and the potentially transgressive nature of such a project
are explored with reference to theories of the *chora, l'écriture féminine,*
abjection, and the lesbian.

A combination of traditional medieval scholarship and post-
structuralist theories of sexuality (in particular the work of Kristeva and
Jacqueline Rose) similarly inform Cynthia Kraman's reading of
Chaucer's *Merchant's Tale.* The most strikingly original aspect of
Kraman's approach is her discussion of the influence of the rabbinical
commentary on *Song of Songs* on Chaucer's text. Despite the
prevalence of anti-semitism and widespread 'ethnic cleansing' in
Western Europe in the Middle Ages, the Christian and Jewish
intellectual communities were not isolated from one another – Kraman
points out that in the twelfth century Troyes was the seat of one of the
most prominent medieval scholars, Rabbi Rashi, as well as of the
Cistercians, and that the latter consulted Rashi's school on theological
questions. Kraman posits the notion of 'communities of otherness' –
communities not necessarily of individuals connected by geographical,
vocational or ideological identity, but of marginalized 'representations,
texts, concepts, cultural groups'. She suggests that the others in the
Merchant's Tale are the female body, the sexual body, the landscape,

and the *Song of Songs* and its Jewish commentaries, and that these others function in the *Tale* to simultaneously define and destabilize the Christian world-view with its emphasis on the inferiority and subjugation of women and the idealization of virginity. In brief, Kraman argues that the Christian world consigned the body to marginal communities (women, Jews) which then fed back into the centre.

The notion of marginality is again crucial in Janet Wilson's analysis of the fifteenth-century *Book of Margery Kempe*. Wilson contends that the *Book* constructs Kempe as a figure who enjoys a marginal status in the ecclesiastical and secular communities with which she comes into contact. Through Wilson's sensitive negotiation of its dual perspective, our attention is also drawn to the marginal status of the *Book* itself as both socio-historical document and literary text. While the text testifies that Kempe's religious devotion caused social disruption, polarizing both churchmen and the devout laity into those who opposed her and those who gave her their support, external sources indicate that within Kempe's home county of Norfolk there existed an underlying tradition of tolerance of religious diversity; a tolerance which may have manifested itself in lenient attitudes towards issues such as women's teaching. Certainly Kempe herself seems to have become something of a focus of dissent amongst her supporters, some of whom may have been radical clerics, and the *Book* was clearly written in response to her own experiences of persecution. If the *Book* represents Kempe's followers as showing an interest in mystical revelations as a means of personal reformation within existing social and ecclesiastical structures, the possibility remains that Kempe's ambiguous status within East Anglian society may reflect something of a full-scale crisis of faith in that area.

Eastern England in the later Middle Ages is examined again in Jennifer C. Ward's chapter on the relationship of the English noblewoman with the community in which she lived. For her purposes, Ward defines community as 'the village or town where the noblewoman resided and over which she often exercised lordship', but as Ward notes, in this context community can also be understood both in the narrower sense of the household, and more broadly to mean either the localities surrounding the lady's residence, or to indicate social circles and groupings. Rather than simply exploiting the land and the labourers, the nobility had a vital role to play in providing business for traders and purveyors and employment for local people. Hospitality was an important responsibility for the nobility, and they were significant benefactors of religious houses, parish churches and charities. The part played by noblewomen within the community is less a reflection of their gender than of their social status; none the less, in their husbands' absences or after their deaths, noblewomen often acted as the head of the household, and certain community activities such as almsgiving and intercession seem to have been expected of them *as women*.

Drawing in particular on her findings from southern Italy in the period 800–1200, Patricia Skinner reassesses the stereotype of the impoverished woman, reliant on the charitable donations of her community for her survival. As was noted earlier, Cartwright's scepticism about the transparency of her source material is shared by Skinner. Once more, it is difficult to get a clear picture when the community or sector of the community in question (in this case the poor) was not thought to be significant enough to have its existence documented. In questioning the assumption, shared by modern historians and medieval biographers of kings and church leaders alike, that widows and lone mothers in particular were more likely than men to experience poverty, Skinner proposes that a variety of factors, social, economic and legal, contributed to depriving women of the means on which to live. Like Ward, Skinner notes the importance of almsgiving as an appropriate activity for the devout noblewoman, but (again like Ward, and also Cartwright), she has discovered little evidence to suggest that women were particularly concerned to provide specifically for other women rather than for the community as a whole. Skinner's findings illustrate the extent to which women were not only subordinate, inferior and vulnerable, but also a case apart. They reflect one social reality – the lack of power, the lack of control over their own lives which women often experienced within medieval communities.

J. A. Tasioulas's contribution to this volume centres on the portrayal of the Virgin Mary's childhood in the N-Town Marian Plays, a late medieval mystery cycle which probably originated in East Anglia. Medieval drama provided an important focal point for community activity in late medieval urban societies. Although the pageants and plays of the later Middle Ages were presented by the male-dominated guilds (and might thus be seen as an expression of masculine supremacy), women would certainly have made up a large proportion of the audience, and female types do appear in some of the narratives. The Virgin Mary, of course, represents the cultural construct of ideal womanhood. Explaining the complex and often contradictory traditions about the Blessed Virgin's birth and childhood which were in circulation in the Middle Ages, and which also reflect contradictions inherent in medieval notions of women, sex and childbirth, Tasioulas shows that Mary is depicted in these plays as the *puella senex* ('aged female youth'). The significance of the Virgin Mary as a role-model for women is an area of contention in medieval scholarship, but Tasioulas believes that as a child who possesses all feminine virtue and adult gravity, women of all ages might identify with the N-Town Mary. While emphasizing the didactic function of the N-Town Plays, Tasioulas disputes the suggestion made by previous scholars that they were written for a women's religious community. The Virgin Mary is not equated with one single aspect of society and unlike *Ancrene Wisse* or *þe Wohunge of Ure Lauerd*, the N-Town Plays do not confine their appeal to cloistered or enclosed women.

Women themselves formed a community of outsiders or otherness in so far as they were often *perceived* as outside or marginal to their communities. If women were often excluded from medieval concepts of community, or seen as both 'other' to the community and part of a community of otherness, it is something of a paradox that one woman, the Blessed Virgin Mary, should stand apart in Christian thought as an exemplar for the community, and indeed for humanity as a whole. Yet this paradox lies at the heart of another: the paradox that women were both *marginal to* and *essential to* medieval communities. Women represented half the population and half of the work force in medieval Europe, and, as the studies in this volume show, they had vital roles to play in the communities in which they lived.

Notes

1. Information about the *Medieval Feminist Newsletter*, the Society for Medieval Feminist Scholarship, and the Gender and Medieval Studies Group can be obtained from Lesley Johnson, School of English, University of Leeds, Leeds, LS2 9JT. In the USA, information about the *Medieval Feminist Newsletter* and the Society for Medieval Feminist Scholarship can be obtained from Regina Psaki, Department of Romance Languages, University of Oregon, Eugene, OR 97403.
2. Frantzen, 'When women aren't enough', 445.
3. *Signs* 14.2 (Winter 1989).
4. Anderson, *Imagined Communities*, 6.
5. Fish, *Is There a Text in This Class?*
6. Stock, *Implications of Literacy*, especially 88–92.
7. Rubin, 'Small groups', 134.

[8] *Ibid.*, 132.

[9] *Ibid.*, 141.

[10] Stock, *Implications of Literacy*, 90.

[11] Riddy, 'Women talking about the things of God', 111.

[12] *Signs*, 255.

[13] Evans and Johnson, *Feminist Readings*, 3.

[14] *Ibid.*

[15] See, for example, Fairbairns *et al.*, *Tales I Tell My Mother*, 3.

[16] Butler, *Gender Trouble*, 3. See also Scott, 'Gender', and the essays in *Speculum* 68 (1993).

[17] Butler, *Gender Trouble*, 147.

[18] Evans and Johnson, *Feminist Readings*, 3.

[19] Burckhardt, *Civilization of the Renaissance*, 81.

[20] See, for example, Aers, *Community, Gender and Individual Identity*, especially 1–19; Aers, 'A whisper in the ear of early Modernists'; Benton, 'Consciousness of self'; Bynum, 'Did the twelfth century discover the individual?; Eco, 'Living in the new Middle Ages'; Morris, *Discovery of the Individual*; Patterson, *Negotiating the Past*; and Patterson, 'On the margin'.

[21] *Signs*, 255–6.

[22] For a full discussion of medieval notions of community, see Reynolds, *Kingdoms and Communities*.

[23] MED, s.v. *communite*; c.f. OED, s.v. *community*.

[24] *Dictionary of Medieval Latin*, s.v. *communitas*, Reynolds comments that 'Just as the word *communitas* and its derivatives were used very widely, with a range of meanings which apparently needed little or no definition, so the values they embodied were too fundamental to need much spelling out.' Reynolds, *Kingdoms and Communities*, 3.

[25] See Kowaleski and Bennett, 'Crafts, gilds, and women in the Middle Ages'; and Goldberg, *Women, Work and Life Cycle*.

[26] Goldstein, *Matter of Scotland*, 192. See also Watt, 'Nationalism in Barbour's *Bruce*,' especially 104–6.

Bibliography

Aers, D., *Community, Gender and Individual Identity: English Writing 1360–1430* (London, 1988).

Aers, D., 'A whisper in the ear of early modernists; or, reflections on literary critics writing the "history of the subject"', in D. Aers (ed.), *Culture and History 1350–1600: Essays on English Communities, Identities and Writing* (London, 1992), 177–202.

Anderson, B., *Imagined Communities: Reflections on the Origin and Spread of Nationalism* (rev. edn., London, 1991).

Benton, J. F., 'Consciousness of self and perceptions of individuality', in R. L. Benson and G. Constable (eds.), *Renaissance and Renewal in the Twelfth Century* (Oxford, 1982), 263–95.

Burckhardt, J., *The Civilization of the Renaissance*, trans. S. G. C. Middlemore (London, 1944).

Butler, J., *Gender Trouble: Feminism and the Subversion of Identity* (London, 1990).

Bynum, C. W., 'Did the twelfth century discover the individual?', *Journal of Ecclesiastical History* 31 (1980), 1–17.

Chaucer, G., *The Riverside Chaucer*, gen. ed. L. D. Benson (3rd edn., Oxford, 1988).

Dictionary of Medieval Latin from British Sources, comp. R. E. Latham (London, 1981).

Eco, U., 'Living in the new Middle Ages', in *Travels in Hyperreality: Essays*, trans. W. Weaver (London, 1987), 73–85.

Evans, R., and Johnson, L. (eds.), *Feminist Readings in Middle English Literature: The Wife of Bath and All Her Sect* (London, 1994).

Fairbairns, Z., Maitland, S., Miner, V., Roberts, M., and Wandor, M., *Tales I Tell My Mother: A Collection of Feminist Short Stories* (London, 1978).

Fish, S., *Is There A Text In This Class? The Authority of Interpretive Communities* (Cambridge, Mass., 1980).

Frantzen, A. J., 'When women aren't enough', *Speculum* 68 (1993), 445–71.

Goldberg, P. J. P., *Women, Work, and Life Cycle in a Medieval Economy: Women in York and Yorkshire c.1300–1520* (Oxford, 1992).

Goldstein, R. J., *The Matter of Scotland: Historical Narrative in Medieval Scotland* (London, 1993).

Kowaleski, M., and Bennett, J. M., 'Crafts, gilds and women in the Middle Ages: fifty years after Marian K. Dale', *Signs* 14 (1989), 474–501.

Morris, C., *The Discovery of the Individual, 1050–1200* (London, 1972).

Patterson, L., *Negotiating the Past: The Historical Understanding of Medieval Literature* (Madison WI, 1987).

Patterson, L., 'On the margin: postmodernism, ironic history, and medieval studies', *Speculum* 65 (1990), 87–108.

Reynolds, S., *Kingdoms and Communities in Western Europe, 900–1300* (Oxford, 1984).

Riddy, F., 'Women talking about the things of God': a late medieval sub-culture', in C. M. Meale (ed.), *Women and Literature in Britain, 1150–1500* (Cambridge, 1993), 104–27.

Rubin, M., 'Small groups: identity and solidarity in the late Middle Ages', in J. Kermode (ed.), *Enterprise and Individuals in Fifteenth Century England* (Stroud, 1991), 132–50.

Scott, J. W., 'Gender: a useful category in historical analysis', *American Historical Review* 91 (1986), 1053–75.

Signs: Journal of Women in Culture and Society 14.2 (Winter 1989). Special issue on *Working Together in the Middle Ages: Perspectives on Women's Communities.*

Speculum: A Journal of Medieval Studies 68 (1993). Special Issue on *Studying Medieval Women: Sex, Gender, Feminism.*

Stock, B., *The Implications of Literacy: Written Language and Models of Interpretation in the Eleventh and Twelfth Centuries* (Princeton, 1983).

Watt, D., 'Nationalism in Barbour's Bruce', *Parergon* 12 (1994), 89–107.

1

The Desire to Corrupt: Convent and Community in Medieval Wales[1]

JANE CARTWRIGHT

H ERE the aim is to investigate the possible roles women played in relation to religious life in medieval Wales. The objective is not to present any definitive conclusions, but to explore tentative interpretations in the light of the extant sources. Little is known about communities of religious women in medieval Wales. Although Wales boasts a wealth of native female saints (from the fifth to the seventh centuries), the importance of contemporary holy women in medieval Wales appears to have been negligible. Indeed, there were remarkably few formal communities of religious women. An attempt will be made here to shed some light on the convents of medieval Wales, by examining the documentary and literary evidence, and suggestions will be proposed to explain their scarcity. This will involve studying and attempting to interpret possible social and cultural attitudes, within the wider community, concerning nuns and female religious activity more generally. In particular the focus will be on *Cywyddwyr* poetry and the poets' perception of the female religious as corruptible virgin. *Cywyddwyr* poetry forms a vital source as it represents a tradition that lies outside of the direct province of religious activity and, thus, may provide some insight into a more secular mentality. The Bardic Grammars suggest that nuns should be praised for their devotion to God and their holy way of life, yet *Cywyddwyr* poetry reflects nothing but a desire to pollute the brides of Christ. More frequently it is the secular Christian wife who is praised for her piety and Christian virtue. Women may have been too important within the social, political and economic concerns and interests of the secular community to have been actively encouraged to retreat to more isolated and rarefied religious environments. This essay examines the possibility that private devotion rather than claustration was the mode of religious expression preferred for Welsh women.

If we are to begin to build up a picture of the nature of female monasticism and the kind of religious opportunities available to Welsh women, it is necessary to review the data relating to the number and type of religious establishments within medieval Wales. It is informative to compare and contrast this evidence with that available for England, Ireland and Scotland. It has often been noted by medieval historians that there were fewer monastic establishments for women than there were for men.[2] It is not surprising, then, that there were less nunneries than monasteries in medieval Wales.[3] Yet the lack of provision made for women wishing to follow a religious vocation in Wales is quite astonishing. Whilst there were approximately one hundred and fifty nunneries in late medieval England,[4] about sixty-four in Ireland[5] and fifteen in Scotland,[6] there appear to have been only three enduring nunneries in post-Conquest Wales: two Cistercian abbeys and a Benedictine priory.

Let us consider the evidence for these Welsh nunneries in greater depth. The Cistercian abbey for women at Llanllŷr in Ceredigion was founded before 1197 by the Lord Rhys as a daughter-house to Strata Florida Abbey. There was another Cistercian house for women at Llanllugan in Cydewain (now Powys), founded by Maredudd ap Rhobert probably sometime between 1170 and 1190, although possibly later. It appears that there were strong links between the Cistercian nunneries of Wales and particular male abbeys. Llanllugan was placed under the jurisdiction of Strata Marcella. Before 1135 Richard de Clare settled Benedictine nuns at Usk and Richard Strongbow later granted an important charter to the priory which was confirmed in 1330 by Elizabeth de Burgh.[7]

The above nunneries seem to be safely vouched for by contemporary documentary and/or material evidence. However, further contenders are less reliable. Leland, writing *c.*1536–9, notes a ruined building at Llanrhystyd and suggests that this may have been a nunnery.[8] However, it appears that he was referring to the ruins of Llanrhystyd castle and buildings that had belonged to the Knights Hospitallers.[9] He also, incorrectly, suggests that Llansanffraid Cwmdeuddwr[10] was the location of another nunnery mentioned by Gerald of Wales. According to Gerald of Wales there was a Cistercian nunnery at Llansanffraid-yn-Elfael. In three different works he recounts the tale of how Enoc, abbot of Strata Marcella, assembled a community of virgins at Llansanffraid-yn-Elfael. Tempted by the beauty of one of the nuns, Enoc entered into a 'sordid' affair and eloped with the nun, only to regret bitterly his 'misdemeanour' and return repentant to his abbey.[11]

The three versions of the Enoc story, given by Gerald of Wales, vary in detail. Only in *Speculum Ecclesiae* is it stated that the nunnery was at Llansanffraid-yn-Elfael:[12] the other two versions do not mention the location of the nunnery. Whilst according to *Itinerarium Kambriae* Enoc is abbot of Strata Marcella, *Gemma Ecclesiastica* suggests that he is abbot of Whitland and *Speculum Ecclesiae* mentions only that he was an abbot from Powys. All these variations and vagaries do not enhance the confidence which we can place in Gerald's account as a historically rigorous record. As D. H. Williams points out, a Cistercian nunnery at Llansanffraid-yn-Elfael would probably have come under the auspices of Cwmhir Abbey – not Strata Marcella.[13] There are also other contradictions in the tale which lead to a questioning of its historical utility. Whilst in the *Itinerarium* and *Speculum* Enoc elopes with a nun, in *Gemma Ecclesiastica* he also manages to impregnate a number of virgins at the convent, before throwing off the ecclesiastical habit:

> There is a story about an abbot Enoc who gathered together in Wales during our own time a group of virgins for the service of Christ. He at length succumbed to temptations and made many of the virgins in the convent pregnant. Finally, he ran around in a comical manner, throwing off the religious habit, and fled with one of the nuns. After he had spent many years in the service of the devil, he at last returned to his Order and the mother-house from which he had fled. The monastery [he returned to] was called Whitland. He was taken back, not without great compunction, and performed his penance with fitting devotion, according to the rigors of the Cistercian rule.[14]

The context of the Enoc tale within Gerald's texts should also be taken into account, as should the possible motives and meanings of Gerald's writings in relation to his social and cultural context. In *Itinerarium Kambriae* it is used to illustrate the wizard Meilyr's psychic powers, since he knew of the scandal before anyone else. In *Gemma Ecclesiastica* it is recounted amidst a number of other 'stories relevant to these matters of not fixing your gaze on and not living with women'.[15] In one such 'story' Gerald relates how Eliah, chaplain and steward of a community of women, was tempted with carnal desires and had to flee from the convent he had founded. Having witnessed three angels sever his testicles in a dream, he returned to the convent untroubled by lust. Gerald notes that his successor had the good sense not to live with the nuns, but to instruct them through the window of his cell. In this context, the narrative in which the Llansanffraid nunnery features can be seen as yet another example serving to illustrate the dangers felt to be involved in caring for a community of women. It is, perhaps, more indicative of male prejudice and of the fear felt by medieval clergy that religious women were a threat to their reputation, than it is of an eagerness to record the history of an otherwise unknown nunnery. Is it not plausible that sometimes fictional or semi-fictional characters and places were preferable within such tales of scandal and criticism? This is particularly likely if such criticism were too close to the mark for comfort and primarily designed to warn and instruct rather than aggravate.

It is also possible that Gerald aimed to entertain rather than offend. Tales of sexually active nuns and pregnant abbesses were immensely popular in the Middle Ages, for example: the tale of the abbess who dons her lover's trousers on her head instead of her veil in Boccacio's *Decameron* and the history of the nun of Watton (although the latter does draw on historical events).[16] The tale of the pregnant abbess who was comforted by the Virgin Mary was translated into Welsh and included in *Gwyrthyeu e Wynvydedic Veir* (*The Miracles of the Blessed Virgin*). The earliest extant Welsh text is in NLW Peniarth MS 14 (second half of the fourteenth century).[17] Angell points out that the tale of the pregnant abbess was one of the most popular of the Virgin's miracles and is included in almost every collection.[18]

It is possible to interpret the 'history' of the Llansanffraid nunnery as belonging to a particular tale type. Whilst not wishing to state categorically that there was never a nunnery at Llansanffraid-yn-Elfael, it is worth questioning the validity of Gerald's tale and pointing out the contradictions within it. It has, perhaps, been too frequently recounted by modern historians who amalgamate the three versions into a neat tale of sexual scandal and avoid highlighting any of the contradictions in this unique source for another Welsh nunnery. It is recounted by J. E. Lloyd in his classic *History of Wales*[19] and Helen Fulton quotes Lloyd's version in her article on medieval Welsh poems to nuns, thus giving the impression that this particular interpretation can be accepted as historical fact.[20] Saunders Lewis built up a complete picture of how a Dafydd ap Gwilym poem, which expresses the desire to corrupt one of the nuns of Llanllugan, was sung to the monks of Strata Marcella, where the tale of the errant abbot and the nun from Llansanffraid was still fresh in the memory.[21] Somehow, this weaving together of sources and speculation produces a picture that is too simplistic and, possibly, quite inaccurate.

The discussion so far has demonstrated that there were very few nunneries in post-Conquest Wales: probably only three long-standing establishments and possibly a fourth short-lived community. Let us now turn to a closely related feature of our evidence that also has a strong bearing upon our attempt to build up a picture of female monasticism in medieval Wales and the nature of provisions made and opportunities provided for female religious activity. Not only were Welsh nunneries few in number, but there appear to have been relatively few nuns in these communities despite the fact that Llanllugan and Llanllŷr are, rather surprisingly, given the status of abbeys.[22] It is possible that this can be attributed to the notion that all Cistercian houses were designated as abbeys.[23] However, this certainly does not seem to have been the case in England where only two Cistercian nunneries, Marham and Tarrant, were officially recognized as abbeys. The others, although sometimes described as abbeys in early charters, appear to have been priories.[24] This blurred categorization in relation to status can, perhaps, be attributed to the lack of official cognizance of the Cistercian nunneries. At any rate, regardless of their status, the Cistercian nunneries of Wales do not appear to have been large communities.

At the time of the suppression there were only three nuns at Llanllugan. Although the number of inmates at the suppression is usually substantially lower than the actual number reached at an earlier period, an assessment of 1377 reveals that there were only four nuns and an abbess at Llanllugan at that time.[25] Knowles and Hadcock suggest that there were sixteen nuns at Llanllŷr and about eight at the suppression, but, unfortunately, do not list documentary sources.[26] According to Dugdale's *Monasticon* the priory at Usk was founded for five nuns, but there certainly appear to have been more inmates than this at the time of Archbishop Peckham's Visitation in 1284.[27] If we take Knowles and Hadcock's more optimistic estimate of thirteen, then we can precariously suggest that there were, at most, roughly thirty-five women living in religious communities in medieval Wales. Obviously, because of the paucity of primary sources, exact numbers are impossible to calculate. However, it is interesting to compare this rough estimate of the number of female religious in Wales with Eileen Power's estimate of the number of nuns in England at the Dissolution – between 1,500 and 2,000.[28] Before the end of this essay we will examine why there were so few nunneries in Wales and suggest possible reasons for the lack of provision made for Welsh religious women.

Not only was female monasticism neglected in medieval Wales, the resultant paucity of sources has a legacy. Hence, nuns have also been neglected within much modern Welsh scholarship. Recent studies on the female religious highlight previous neglect of nunneries in more general studies of medieval monasticism – noting that the role of religious women has frequently been ignored or marginalized.[29] Gilchrist points out that the nunneries have often been dismissed as poor or failed monasteries and that, because of this, they have received little attention.[30] This is certainly true of the Welsh nunneries. Gerald of Wales describes Llanllŷr as a small and poor house and Leland refers to Llanllugan as 'a veri little poore nunneri'.[31] In the nineteenth century Morris Charles Jones dismisses Llanllugan as 'an insignificant establishment'[32] and in the 1920s Eileen Power includes Usk in her list of medieval English nunneries and only mentions Llanllŷr and Llanllugan in her corrigenda.[33] Significant contributions to the study of the Welsh nunneries have been made by D. H. Williams and Helen Fulton who have published articles on the history of the nunneries and medieval Welsh poems to nuns respectively.[34] R. Morgan has also published an early Llanllugan charter.[35] Whilst there is nothing to compare with Gilchrist's study of the archaeology of religious women in England, some recent excavation has taken place at Usk.[36] Nevertheless, the Welsh nunneries, on the whole, have attracted little research – possibly because there were so few and possibly because poverty has been considered a sign of insignificance.

The Welsh nunneries do appear to have been relatively poor. The net incomes of the convents of Llanllugan, Llanllŷr and Usk c.1535 were £22, £57 and £55 respectively.[37] Of the thirteen Cistercian abbeys in Wales whose net income c.1535 has been recorded, eight had incomes of £100–£200 and only two had incomes of less than £50.[38] This is constant with Gilchrist's findings concerning net incomes of Benedictine nunneries and monasteries in England c.1535: nunneries were generally poorer than monasteries for men.[39] Adequate endowment was, no doubt, difficult to sustain over long periods – in particular during times of political and economic upheaval. It is likely that nunneries were better endowed at certain periods than at others. War damage affected the Welsh nunneries, as it did other monastic establishments. In 1284 Llanllŷr was awarded forty marks' compensation for damage done to the nunnery during the Edwardian Conquest. Two Latin letters confirm that the abbess acknowledges receipt of the reparation.[40] Interestingly one of the letters is written on her behalf by John of Caeau, a monk of Strata Florida, and sealed with the seals of the abbots of Strata Marcella and Valle Crucis, because John of Caeau did not have the seal of the abbess with him at the time. Adam of Usk notes that 'none but virgins of noble birth' were received at the Priory of Usk and that, before the Glyndŵr Uprising, the priory had been sufficiently endowed.[41] However, in 1404 Adam of Usk petitioned the pope requesting that indulgences be granted in order to attract alms at St Radegund's chapel in the Benedictine priory of Usk. He states that:

> owing to the burnings, spoilings and other misfortunes which have been caused by the wars which raged in those parts, or otherwise, this same monastery hath come to such want that, unless ready help be forthwith found by your holiness, the sisterhood will be forced to beg for food and clothing, straying through the country, or to stay in the private houses of friends; whereby it is feared that scandals may belike arise.[42]

Interestingly, the success of his petition rests on the pope's desire for strict active enclosure and fear of scandal (again highlighting male preconceptions concerning the female religious).[43]

One of the complaints in Archbishop Peckham's visitation record in 1284 was that the nuns of Usk were wandering outside the confines of the nunnery and staying with layfolk. Other criticisms are mainly to do with economic affairs and he suggested the appointment of two Treasuresses.[44] In 1299 the abbess of Llanllŷr was acquitted by Queen Margaret of a fine for illegally felling an oak.[45] Criticism for felling trees appears in the visitation records of some of the English nunneries described by Eileen Power.[46] Once again it is likely that this illegal activity was brought about by financial hardship. John Nichols warns of the dangers of depending too heavily upon visitation records when building up a picture of life in the convent. As he points out, it is very easy to use the visitation records to create a negative impression of monastic standards, since the purpose of episcopal visitations was to criticize and suggest improvements – not to document achievements.[47]

So far we have considered evidence relating to the number of nunneries in medieval Wales, their population and economic status. We have also found it increasingly necessary to refer to social and cultural attitudes and relations of power when attempting to construct a picture of female monasticism. Let us now focus much more directly upon these social and cultural attitudes and the possible motives and purposes they represent, both within the religious and secular communities of Wales, communities which were, of course, dominated by male concerns and power structures. It is easy to use the extant information available on the Welsh nunneries to build up a very negative picture of the few religious communities of women in medieval Wales; small communities of women who failed to manage their financial affairs, who chopped down trees illegally, wandered outside the convent, caroused with layfolk, eloped with abbots and, as we shall see, kept exotic pets, revealed one of the most erotic part of their bodies – their foreheads – and agreed to make love in Welsh woodlands! Yet were the Welsh nunneries really this morally lax? What of the spiritual nature of their religious vocation – their contemplative lifestyle and their devotion to God? One of their saving graces is a bishop's licence which granted permission, as late as 1530, for an Augustinian nun of Limebrook (Katherine Dodd) to transfer to Llanllugan because she wished to lead 'a holier life'. The rule at Llanllugan was said to be 'stricter' and the religious life 'better and [more] frugal'.[48] This document, although late, provides a rare glimpse of a genuinely monastic lifestyle.

Sadly there are no descriptions of monastic life recorded by the nuns themselves. All extant evidence appears to have been recorded by men: the *vox feminae* is non existent. This perhaps explains why so much of the extant evidence throws little light on the devotional nature of the nunneries. No devotional literature or mystical works by Welsh women have survived and it is quite possible that none were ever composed. It is not known whether the female religious received any kind of education – whether formal or informal, written or oral. It is not known whether nuns in Wales were Latin-literate or indeed literate at all. It is worth recalling that one of the letters sent to acknowledge the receipt of reparation for damage done to the nunnery at Llanllŷr, was written by a monk (John of Caeau) on behalf of the abbess.[49] It is not clear whether the other letter was written by the abbess herself or by someone else on her behalf. However, it appears to have been standard practice for a proctor to write letters of acquittal for war damages on behalf of abbots and abbesses. A comparison of John of Caeau's letter with a similar letter, written on behalf of the abbot of Strata Florida, reveals the formulaic nature of this form of correspondence.[50]

The only reference to religious literature being translated from Latin into Welsh for a Welsh woman is found at the beginning of the thirteenth-century Welsh translation of *Quicumque Vult (Credo Athanasius Sant).* Brother Gruffudd Bola notes that he is translating the text into Welsh for Efa ferch Maredudd so that she may read and understand it and that it might be spiritually beneficial to her.[51] Although she was not Latin-literate, Efa certainly seems to have been able to read. It is not known whether Efa was a nun, but interestingly, she was a descendant of the Lord Rhys who founded the nunnery at Llanllŷr.

Whilst there are no poems written by nuns in Wales and there are no *chansons de nonnes,* there are a number of *cywyddau* written to nuns and one fifteenth-century *cywydd gofyn* supposedly written on behalf of the abbess of Llanllŷr. *Cywyddau Gofyn,* poems requesting gifts from patrons and Welsh nobility, occur frequently in the poetry of *Beirdd yr Uchelwyr (The Poets of the Gentry).*[52] One such poem by Huw Cae Llwyd requests a pet ape from Sir William Herbert, earl of Pembroke, as a gift for Annes, abbess of Llanllŷr. This particular *cywydd gofyn* is very unusual in that rather than praise the gift requested (as usually happens in a *cywydd gofyn*) the poet heaps scorn and derision on the animal:

> Cythraul llwyd, crinllwyd yw'r croen,
> Cleiriach gruddgrach, garweiddgroen.
> Gwrach foel yw goruwch y fainc,
> Gyrrai ofn i'r gwŷr ifainc.
> Gwar ymylgrach gŵr moelgryg,
> Ac ysbryd llun gwas brawd llyg.
> Mynach brwnt gyfeillach breg,
> Iddew heb gael ei oddeg.
> Lledryn o bryf, lleidryn brwnt,
> Lledrith goesfrith atgasfrwnt . . .
> . . . Bryntach, anafach na neb,
> Byr einioes ys bo i'r wyneb![53]

[Grey/brown[54] devil with crinkly brown skin, old man with scabby cheeks and rough skin. A bald witch above the bench, used to frighten the young men. Tonsured man with scabby sides on the nape of his neck, with a spirit that resembles a lay brother's serving boy. Foul monk, false friend, Jew who hasn't been loved. Infested animal skin, dirty petty thief. Odious, foul apparition with mottled legs . . . Dirtier and more blemished than anyone. May his face have a short life!]

Rather than wishing the animal a long life, as is customary in a *cywydd gofyn*, the closing line wishes him a short life. Although the poem is unusual within its genre, it is not unique. A similar poem by Robert ap Gruffudd Leiaf requests a pet ape for Huw Lewys and contains a similar derogatory description of the animal.[55] It appears, then, that the poem belongs to a particular topos and is, perhaps, satirical. It seems unlikely that Annes was present at the court of Sir William as Leslie Harries suggests: '. . . rhaid mai rywbryd rhwng 1461 a 1469 yr ymwelodd y lleian o ddyffryn Aeron â'r marchog enwog hwn yn ei lys ym Mrycheiniog . . .'[56] [. . . it must have been sometime between 1461 and 1469 that the nun from the Aeron valley visited this famous knight at his court in Breconshire . . .]. Not only would it have been inappropriate for an abbess to be visiting Sir William's court at Rhaglan – since she would have been breaking the rule of strict claustration – but it would also have been unseemly for her to request such a pet. Nevertheless, exotic pets, such as apes, do seem to have been popular in the Middle Ages and nuns were reprimanded for keeping them.[57] One needs to ask whether the abbess of a poorly endowed nunnery would have been in a position to sponsor poetry, and, if she was, whether she would have condoned a *cywydd* that cast her in such a negative light. However, since both William Herbert and the abbess are named, it is unlikely that the poem is purely a piece of fabrication on behalf of the poet. There must have been some connection between Sir William and Annes or her family. Since the abbess of a nunnery would have been of gentle birth, one can easily imagine that William Herbert, who was, no doubt, acquainted with Abbess Annes's family, would have appreciated the humour of the *cywydd* – regardless of whether Annes genuinely expected to receive a pet ape.

A number of *cywyddau gofyn* written on behalf of men of the church request gifts such as a goshawk, bows, a book on the Holy Grail and a poem praising God.[58] However, the majority of *cywyddau gofyn* written in connection with religious men request gifts from them. The most heavily requested gifts are horses and no less than eight *cywyddau* are extant which request horses from Dafydd ab Owain, abbot of the Cistercian abbey of Aberconwy.[59] No poems are extant which request gifts from abbesses or nuns. Considering how few nuns there were in Wales, this is not at all surprising. Furthermore, it is unlikely that they would have had the financial stability to offer gifts. Although the Bardic Grammars suggest that nuns should be praised in much the same way as religious men, vast differences exist between Welsh poetry to nuns and to men of the church. Whilst at least a hundred *awdlau* and *cywyddau* praise specific, named churchmen,[60] hardly any of the poems to nuns name their subjects – thus failing to identify them as historical characters.

According to the Bardic Grammars a nun should be praised for her holiness and pure way of life, her chastity and heavenly love of God and other spiritual virtues, just as a religious man is praised.[61] However, rather than praising nuns for their religious virtues, the *cywyddau* to nuns reflect only a desire to corrupt the brides of Christ. In the Dafydd ap Gwilym *cywydd,* mentioned above, the poet attempts to entice the abbess or one of the nuns into the leafy grove.[62] The poem is usually interpreted as seeking out the abbess, but Helen Fulton suggests that the real target is the chantress – one practised in the art of love.[63] Considering that there were so few nuns at Llanllugan in the fourteenth century, it is, of course, possible that Dafydd was happy to entice any one of them. He refers to the sisters as 'Chwiorydd bedydd bob un i Forfudd' [god-sisters are they every one to Morfudd]. Dafydd ap Gwilym mentions Morfudd, a married woman who appears frequently in his poetry.[64] Thus we are reminded that the poet is not merely eager to commit adultery against *Y Gŵr Eiddig (The Jealous Husband),* but that in this poem Dafydd's blasphemy increases in magnitude: he wishes to adulterate the brides of Christ.

Another *cywydd* which belongs to the Dafydd ap Gwilym apocrypha attempts to persuade a female religious to give up her monastic lifestyle:

> Er Duw, paid â'r bara a'r dŵr
> A bwrw ar gasau'r berwr.
> Er Mair, paid â'r paderau main
> A chrefydd mynaich eryfain.
> Na fydd lân yn y gwanwyn,
> Gwaeth yw lleianaeth na llwyn,
> Gwarant Morwyn, â mantell
> A gwerdd wisg, a urddai well.
>
> Dyred i'r fedw gadeiriog,
> I grefydd y gwŷdd a'r gog –
> . . . Duw a fyn, difai annerch,
> A saint roi pardwn i serch.

[For God's sake give up the bread and water and strive to hate cress. For Mary's sake, dispense with stone beads and the religion of carousing monks. Do not be chaste in the spring-time, a nun's life is worse than the grove: the Virgin's guarantee, with mantle and green gown, would confer greater honour. Come to the spreading birch trees, to the religion of the trees and the cuckoo – God and the saints will want, perfect greeting to give pardon to love.][65]

The nun here is not so much an object of praise as the object of the poet's lust. In true courtly love tradition she is enticed into the woodland to make love. As Helen Fulton points out, the nuns' vows 'are not taken seriously by secular poets and they are wooed with offers of romantic love into abandoning their virginity, abandoning what amounts to a separatist position, and serving the patriarchy instead'.[66] Some late manuscript versions of the poem quoted above include the phrase '*gwra oedd well*' ['it were better to marry'] thus promoting married life rather than a life of claustration.[67] In some manuscripts the poem ends by suggesting that the poet and the nun have had sexual relations whilst on pilgrimage to Rome and Santiago de Compostella.[68]

Other *cywyddau* suggest that the nuns are already sexually active. The Dafydd ap Gwilym *cywydd* mentions a nun with forehead revealed, friend of some sixty other darlings, and another poem from the Dafydd ap Gwilym apocrypha uses the rhetorical device of *occupatio* to deny that the poet has been having sexual relations with a nun. The more frequently that this is denied the stronger the suggestion that it is true.[69] Another poem attributed to Hywel ap Dafydd ab Ieuan ap Rhys in some manuscripts plays on the juxtaposition of black and white in a nun's colouring – her black veil and her white skin suggesting both purity and potential sinfulness.[70] The poem consists mainly of a detailed description of the girl's face, framed by her black clothing. The poet laments that she has been blackened around her face and that he cannot see her forehead. Nowhere in the poem is it specifically stated that the girl is a nun, one can only infer this from the description of her clothing.

Clothing is all important when identifying the subjects of other more ambiguous *cywyddau* which may, or may not, describe women who belong to religious orders. The main problem here is to establish to what extent uniformity of religious habit was current within the Cistercian and Benedictine orders and within what period. Whilst the Benedictines are traditionally thought of as wearing black, the Cistercian habit is usually described as white – '*rhai lliwgalch*' ['chalk-white ones'] according to Dafydd ap Gwilym.[71] However, Thompson points out that nuns described as *moniales albae* [white nuns] do not necessarily belong to the Cistercian order. One could add that women described as wearing black are not necessarily Benedictine nuns. Some attempts to establish uniformity of habit are apparent in the thirteenth century when the Cistercian General Chapter decreed that a cowl should be worn, or a cloak, but not both and that nuns' veils must be black.[72] A stained glass window at Llanllugan, which may be late medieval, depicts a female religious wearing a white gown and wimple and a blue hooded cloak – presumably blue represents black.[73]

A complex poem attributed to Dafydd ab Edmwnd describes a woman, called Gwenonwy, dressed in pure black.[74] The poet, who is pining for the woman's love, laments the woman's choice of black clothing (as in

the poem mentioned above) and suggests that it would be better if she
wore green. This particular idea is reminiscent of one of the poems in
the Dafydd ap Gwilym apocrypha: *'A gwerdd wisg, a urddai well'*
['green gown would confer greater honour']. However, the fact that the
woman is dressed in black does not necessarily mean that she is a nun.
Another possible interpretation of this rather ambiguous poem is that it
may describe a widow who is unobtainable because she is still mourning
her husband.[75]

Gilbert Ruddock suggests that a *cywydd* by Iolo Goch, *'I Ferch'*,
describes a nun.[76] Although she wears a pale headdress and carries a
rosary it does not necessarily follow that she is a nun. Headdresses,
wimples and veils were all worn by secular noblewomen, who also
possessed rosaries.[77] The remaining description of her attire – scarlet
gown,[78] fur trimmed garment, golden sleeves and rings – certainly seems
to suggest that she is not a member of a religious order. As Gilbert
Ruddock points out, nuns were often criticized for wearing their own
clothing, but the unorthodoxy of this attire does little to suggest that the
young girl described here is a nun. No phrase in the poem implies that
this shy girl, with lowered eyes, is sexually experienced or rebellious,
as one might expect if she were wearing clothing unsuited to her
vocation.[79] The fact that she has never known a man implies only that
she is a virgin:

> Brwynengorff heb rin ungwr . . .
> . . . Duw a'i gwnaeth, arfaeth eurfab,
> Myn delw Bedr, ar fedr ei Fab.
> Pentyriais gerdd, pwynt dirym,
> Puntur serch, pond trahaus ym
> Dybio cael, bu hael baham,
> Gytgwsg â'm dyn lygatgam?

[Reed-like body which no man has ever known . . . God made her, golden
son's purpose, by Peter's image, for His son. I have heaped up poetry, help-
less state, pencil of love, is it not presumptuous of me to imagine getting, it
was a noble reason, to sleep with my girl with the lowered eyes?][80]

The suggestion that God made her especially for His son is more
suggestive of a bride of Christ, but again this may simply refer to her
pure, virginal state.

'Pererindod Merch', another Dafydd ap Gwilym poem, describes a
pilgrimage from Anglesey to St David's.[81] The girl in this poem is

referred to as a nun and, whilst this is a strong possibility, it may also be interpreted as metaphor. In the same way that the girl has not literally killed the poet, she is, perhaps, not literally a nun. As with many of these ambiguous poems, it is virtually impossible to decide with any authority whether the girl referred to actually belongs to religious orders; nor, perhaps, is it important to do so since the poet may not have a particular female in mind. Since most of the 'nuns' described in Welsh poetry belong to the *Canu Serch* tradition rather than *Canu Mawl*,[82] they are not identifiable as particular individuals. Instead, they pertain to a virginal type: pure and potentially corruptible, yet often unobtainable.

The corruptibility of virginity is depicted not only in poems to nuns (or possible nuns) but in *cywyddau* to young devout virgins. In a fifteenth-century *cywydd* by Hywel Dafi the poet looks through a keyhole and sees a young girl reciting psalms, kneeling in front of a statue of the Virgin Mary. The blasphemous nature of the imagery is startling:

> Rhwng dwy lenlliain feinon
> och fis haf na chefais hon,
> a'i bwrw rhwng dau bared
> i'r llawr a'i dwyfraich ar lled;
> offrwm, liw blodau effros,
> ar dalau y gliniau'n glos,
> a hon o'i bodd yn goddef,
> a rhoddi naid rhyddi a nef;
> disgyn rhwng ei dwy esgair,
> addoli fyth i'r ddelw Fair.

[Between two fine bed-curtains if only I could have her in a summer month, and throw her between two walls to the ground with her arms outstretched; I'd offer, colour of euphrasy flowers, on my knees up close, and she'd let me willingly, and I'd leap between her and heaven; coming down between her legs I'd worship forever Mary's image.][83]

The type of religious location in which the girl is viewed is not clear. Does Hywel Dafi see the girl through the keyhole of a convent church, a parish church or a private chapel? The reference to 'her speech in a golden book' possibly suggests that she is holding a psalter or a Book of Hours often used by women for private devotion.[84] However, despite the fact that much of the contents of Books of Hours was translated into Welsh in the Middle Ages, no Books of Hours in the vernacular are extant.[85] The *Llanbeblig Hours,* a Latin Book of Hours associated with north Wales, appears to have belonged to Isabella Godynogh whose obit, 1413, is recorded on 23 April. Her name suggests that she was not Welsh.[86]

Bearing in mind that there were so few nunneries in medieval Wales, it seems likely that private devotion rather than claustration was the mode of religious expression generally preferred for Welsh women. Although Welsh poetry to nuns does not take their religious vocation seriously, a number of praise poems and elegies to married noblewomen, for example, Elsbeth Mathau, Mabli ferch Gwilym, Gwladus ferch Syr Dafydd Gam and Annes of Caerleon praise their Christian virtues, their generosity, chastity and religious devotion.[87] Many are compared to female saints and from some are requested gifts that would have been considered appropriate gifts for women of the church to offer. For example, Lewys Glyn Cothi requests a curtain depicting the Virgin Mary, Christ, the twelve apostles and both male and female saints from Annes of Caerleon and in an *awdl* he thanks Efa ferch Llywelyn for a rosary.[88]

Two *marwnadau,* or elegies, to Welsh noblewomen – Nest Stradling and Gwenllian ferch Rhys – seem to suggest that they retired to the convent after the death of their husbands.[89] Nest, the wife of Siôn Stradling from Westplas, is described as a nun from Gwent and it is emphasized that she was chaste when she passed away. No mention is made of any particular religious house and the reference to her as a nun may be taken to mean that she remained chaste – that is, that she did not remarry – after the death of her husband. In her *marwnad* her body is described as going to join her husband's but, rather confusingly, in Siôn's *marwnad* Nest is also described as being in heaven.[90] There seems to be some confusion, then, over who died first. It seems likely that Nest died shortly after her husband and if she did spend any time in religious orders, it is unlikely to have been for long. The elegy places great emphasis on her Christian beliefs, her charity work and her importance as a wife and mother. It is probable that most of her charitable acts took place whilst she was married and religious devotion and marriage are portrayed as compatible and harmonious. Gwenllian, like Nest, is described as joining her husband after death[91] and both elegies link the women with St Non. Although it is said that Gwenllian ascends to the rank of virgins (presumably as a bride of Christ), she is also mentioned as joining Non's choir in heaven. Non, the mother of St David, is one of the few female saints who was not a virgin, since her sanctity was closely related to her maternity.[92] By comparing these women with Non, the poets place emphasis on both their holiness and their maternity.

Pious noblewomen are frequently compared to female saints in Welsh poetry – often to Non and Elen, the mother of Constantine, who is accredited with finding the true cross.[93] Women who are described as healing the poets, or their husbands, are frequently compared to Mary Magdalene – *'meddyges Iesu'* (Christ's physician).[94] For example, in two separate *cywyddau* Guto'r Glyn compares both Elen wraig Hywel o Foelyrch and Siân wraig Syr Siôn Bwrch to Mary Magdalene. Elen is praised for her special healing ointment which will heal her husband's injured knee and Siân's hospitality is said to work wonders in alleviating the poet's physical ailments.[95] Guto'r Glyn appears to have turned either to married noblewomen or to Welsh abbots for healthcare, but not to the female religious. When the poet breaks a rib he turns to Dafydd ab Ieuan, abbot of Valle Crucis, for support and it was to this abbey that Guto'r Glyn retired in old age.[96] Although he wrote a number of poems to men of the church, none of his works are addressed to specific religious women. Gwenllian ferch Rhys (mentioned above) is praised for healing the poet Lewys Glyn Cothi – probably in her capacity as a married noblewoman, rather than a nun, since the main objective of the poem is to praise her son Rhys ap Dafydd and the household at Blaen Tren and there is no indication in this poem that she is a nun.[97]

Gilchrist observes that in medieval England hospitals offered a more flexible religious life to a wider spectrum of women: some were semi-monastic and more akin to the *via media* of the beguines.[98] Whilst women's contributions to the healing of the sick are apparent in medieval England, there is, as yet, no evidence of similar institutions in Wales being run specifically by religious women.[99] Many of the native Welsh saints are associated with healing: the holy wells of Gwenfrewi and Dwynwen, for example, were popular places of pilgrimage for the sick. However, the role of healer is not recorded as being performed by medieval Welsh nuns and the poets turn either to the hospitality of male abbots or married noblewomen for their healthcare.

It appears that the vast majority of Welsh women were encouraged to lead chaste but not celibate religious lives within marriage, whilst a few retired to the convent after the death of their husbands, having reached the end of their reproductive careers. On the whole, though, there does not seem to have been much encouragement for Welsh women to devote their virginity to Christ and retire to the convent at an early age – for virginity was both a precious and a saleable commodity.

One must exercise great caution when dealing with native Welsh law. It is not certain to what extent it reflects actual practice and it is also difficult to date with any accuracy, since late manuscripts contain archaic elements.[100] However, it is worth noting that according to the tractate *Cyfraith y Gwragedd* (The Law of Women) a fee, called *amobr*, was payable to a woman's lord on loss of virginity.[101] This fee varied according to the woman's status:

Amobyr merch maer kyghella6r, punt. Amobyr merch maer, chweugeint. Amobyr merch penkenedyl, chweugeint a phunt. Amobyr merch uchel6r, chweugeint. Amobyr merch mab eillt, pedwar ugeint. Amobyr merch alltut, pedeir ar ugeint. Amobyr merch pob penns6yda6c, herwyd rei punt, herwyd ereill chweugeint. Amobyr merch pob un o'r s6ydogyon ereill, herwyd rei chweugeint, herwyd ereill tri ugeint. Amobr merch kaeth, deudec k*einya6c*.

[The *amobr* of a *maer cynghellor's* daughter, a pound. The *amobr* of a *maer's* daughter, six score pence. The *amobr* of the daughter of the head of a kindred, a pound and six score pence. The *amobr* of an *uchelwr's* daughter, six score pence. The *amobr* of a villein's daughter, four score. The *amobr* of a foreigner's daughter, twenty-four. The *amobr* of the daughter of any chief official, according to some a pound, according to others six score. The *amobr* of the daughter of any of the other officials, according to some six score, according to others three score. The *amobr* of a slave's daughter, twelve pence.][102]

It is probable that *amobr* was payable more than once – for illicit sexual relations as well as loss of virginity.[103] R. R. Davies suggests that this became a lucrative source of income for the territorial lord. If this really were the case, then it is little wonder that Welsh lords were reluctant to establish foundations in which women could remain perpetual virgins. In 1334 the surveyor of Denbigh calculated the return on *amobr* at £41 annually and in 1395 in Kidwelly it was calculated at £21. 6s. 8d.[104] These sums are substantial – especially considering that the net incomes of the nunneries at Llanllugan, Llanllŷr and Usk in 1535 were £22, £57 and £55 respectively.[105]

Women were instrumental in the founding of a number of medieval English nunneries.[106] Wealthy widows seem to have been particularly fond of patronizing religious houses: often retiring to the convent after the death of their husbands. Thompson notes that several nunneries founded jointly by husband and wife were, in fact, located on land that had formed part of the wife's dowry.[107] Although women in England had minimal rights to inheritance, according to feudal law daughters could inherit land and property in the absence of male heirs. In 1317 Elizabeth de Burgh inherited one-third of the Clare lands in the partition of her brother's inheritance.[108] Elizabeth de Burgh, who confirmed an important charter to Usk Priory in 1330, is also recorded as entertaining the Benedictine nuns of Usk.[109] According to Welsh law women could not inherit land nor could they receive a dower in land on their husbands' death.[110] The Welsh equivalent of dowry – *argyfrau* – appears to have consisted of moveable goods, rather than land and property. Despite the fact that some families managed to circumvent the laws of inheritance,[111] it seems likely that Welsh women, on the whole, were not in a position to offer land for the founding of nunneries. Jennifer Ward's essay in the present volume proposes a variety of relationships that existed between English noblewomen and religious houses. She suggests that whilst women of the higher nobility often preferred to exercise patronage over religious houses, women of the lower nobility and of the gentry turned their attention to their parish churches.[112] Given that there were so few wealthy women of the higher nobility and so few nunneries in medieval Wales, one could speculate that the parish church rather than the convent was more likely to receive religious patronage. Women who wished to share in the spiritual benefits of religious endowment and arrange, for example, for prayers or requiem masses to be said for their souls or for their families' souls may well have made donations to their parish churches, given gifts, set up or been included in chantries. Sustained endowment of religious houses was, perhaps, out of reach of most Welsh women's capabilities.

Many reasons can be proffered as to why there were so few nunneries in medieval Wales. The order most favoured by the Welsh princes and the Welsh nobility was the Cistercian order and Cistercian hostility towards the creation of new foundations for women has frequently been noted by medieval historians.[113] In 1220 and 1225 the Cistercians attempted to ban the admission of existing nunneries to the order and in 1228 the building of entirely new Cistercian nunneries was forbidden.[114] Communities of religious women were dependant upon the services of a priest for Mass and confession and there were strong links between the Cistercian nunneries of Wales and the male abbeys responsible for them. In 1222 Cistercian abbots petitioned the pope requesting that they should not be forced to send monks to live at women's houses, as this endangered both their souls and the reputation of their order.[115] No doubt, the tale of the Llansanffraid nunnery did little to promote the establishment of further communities of women in Wales. In 1216 the Cistercians laid down restrictions on how near a nunnery could be to a male abbey and how near it could be to another nunnery.[116]

The accumulation of land was also an important feature of the
Cistercian order and the creation of more nunneries would have meant
greater competition for land and appropriated churches. Gerald of
Wales records that Strata Florida stole some of the property of Llanllŷr
after the death of Lord Rhys.[117]

The Benedictine order, popular in England, does not seem to have
been favoured by the native Welsh princes and nobility. It is quite likely
that the Benedictine nuns of Usk were of Norman rather than of Welsh
descent. In Wales there was not the same diversity of orders open to
women as there was elsewhere. Ironically, one of the few Welsh women
we know of who joined another order was Gwenllian, daughter of
Llywelyn the last Prince of Wales.[118] According to *Brut y Tywysogyon*
(The Chronicle of the Princes) after her father was killed she was sent,
against her will, to a convent in England. In fact, this was the Gilbertine
order at Sempringham (the only order to have originated in England):

> Ac yna y gwnaethpwyt priodas Lywelin ac Elienor yg Kaer Wynt, ac Edwart,
> vrenhin Lloegyr, yn costi y neithawr ehun yn healaeth. Ac o'r Elienor honno
> y bu y Lywelin verch a' elwit Gwenlliant. A'r dywededic Elienor a uu varw
> y ar etiued; ac y hagkladwyt ymanachloc y Brodyr Troetnoeth yn Llann Vaes
> yMon. A'r dywededic Wenlliant, gwedy marw y that, a ducpwyt yg
> keith[i]wet y Loeger; a chynn amser oet y gwnaethpwyt ynn vanaches o'e
> hanuod.

> [And then the marriage of Llywelyn and Eleanor was solemnized at Win-
> chester, with Edward, king of England, himself liberally defraying the costs
> of the wedding banquet. And by that Eleanor Llywelyn had a daughter called
> Gwenllïan. And the said Eleanor died in childbirth; and she was interred in
> the monastery of the Barefooted Friars at Llan-faes in Anglesey. And the said
> Gwenllïan, after the death of her father, was taken into captivity to England;
> and before coming of age she was made a nun against her will.][119]

As of yet no evidence exists to suggest that Welsh women followed
less orthodox religious vocations such as those of the beguine, the sister
in a hospital, the hermit or the anchorite. Considering that medieval
Wales had a thriving tradition of Welsh women saints (for example
Dwynwen, Gwenfrewi, Melangell, Non, Tegfedd and Eluned),[120] most
of whom were consecrated virgins, astonishingly little provision was
made for those who wished to follow in their footsteps. All of these
female saints were purported to have been alive in the fifth, sixth and
seventh centuries and the tradition of making *mulieres sanctae* did not

continue in Wales into the Middle Ages. Elsewhere holy women such as Christina of Markyate (*c*.1097–*c*.1161), Mafalda of Portugal (1184–1257), Margaret of Hungary (1242–70) and Juliana Falconieri (1270–1341) continued to be regarded as saints.[121] Nor in Wales are there any famous medieval religious women such as Julian of Norwich (1342–1416) and Margery Kempe (*c*.1373–*c*.1440).[122] Whilst numerous men of the church are named in Welsh praise poetry, the religious vocation of the nebulous nuns is not taken seriously. Nuns – the ultimate in forbidden fruit – made excellent subjects for Welsh courtly love poetry because not only did they remain anonymous, but they barely existed. They belonged more to the erotica of the imagination, than to any social reality. It can be postulated that Welsh women were encouraged to worship within the confines of marriage, rather than in a community of religious females. Unless new evidence is uncovered to suggest alternative, less institutionalized forms of religious activity in Wales – such as anchoritic activity – then it appears that the monastic life was rarely a genuine vocation for Welsh women.

Notes

1 I would like to thank Sioned Davies, my supervisor, for her support during the past few years during which time I have been compiling my Ph.D. thesis. This article is closely related to one chapter in the thesis, 'Y Forwyn Fair, Santesau a Lleianod: Agweddau ar Wyryfdod a Diweirdeb yng Nghymru'r Oesoedd Canol' (University of Wales Ph. D. thesis, 1996).

2 For example, Gilchrist, *Gender and Material Culture,* 61, notes that in later medieval England monasteries for men and friaries outnumbered nunneries by six to one.

3 Knowles and Hadcock, *Medieval Religious Houses,* list sixty-three monastic establishments for men in Wales (including abbeys, priories, alien priories, friaries and cells). G. Williams, *The Welsh Church,* 347, notes that there were forty-seven religious houses left in Wales by the beginning of the Tudor period (including the three nunneries). He points out that there were far fewer monasteries in Wales than in England and that Wales was probably supporting as many monastic houses as it could manage due to economic and geographical constraints.

4 Gilchrist, *Gender and Material Culture,* 36–9. There were also eighteen double houses, six nuns' cells attached to male houses and four 'quasi-double' houses. In all, Knowles and Hadcock, *Medieval Religious Houses,* 251–89, list 184 entries under 'Houses of Nuns' and thirteen double houses. Some houses were ephemeral and others may be counted several times since they were attributed

to more than one order. Often no one official order was adhered to, as some nunneries swapped allegiance between Benedictine and Cistercian. Of the many female houses in England which claimed to be Cistercian, only two were officially recognized by the order: Thompson, *Women Religious,* 99.

[5] Carville, 'Cistercian nuns in medieval Ireland', 65. Gilchrist, *Gender and Material Culture,* 40, states that there were sixty-two. More are listed in Gwynn and Hadcock, *Medieval Religious Houses: Ireland,* 307–26. Again, some were short-lived. The vast majority of female houses in Ireland were Arrouasian and followed the Augustinian Rule.

[6] Easson, 'Nunneries of medieval Scotland', 22. More are listed in Easson, *Medieval Religious Houses: Scotland,* 120–30, and Gilchrist, *Gender and Material Culture,* 39, states that there were thirteen.

[7] D. H. Williams, 'Cistercian nunneries', 157, 163: *Welsh Cistercians,* I, 11; 'Usk Nunnery', 44; Cowley, *Monastic Order in South Wales,* 37–8; Fulton, 'Medieval Welsh poems to nuns', 94. Morgan suggests *c.*1216–17 as a date for Maredudd ap Rhobert's charter. Maredudd's charter may have acted as confirmation of Llanllugan's lands rather than as a foundation charter: Morgan, 'An early charter of Llanllugan Nunnery', 117–19.

[8] Leland, *Itinerary,* 123–4.

[9] G. Owen, *Description of Penbrokshire,* IV, 459.

[10] Also known as Llansanffraid Cwmteuddwr, E. Davies, *Gazetteer of Welsh Place-Names,* 68.

[11] Cambrensis, *Opera,* II, 248; IV, 168–9; VI, 59.

[12] Cambrensis, *Opera,* IV, 168–9. I am grateful to Professor John Percival for his translation of *Speculum Ecclesiae.*

[13] D. H. Williams, 'Cistercian nunneries', 156.

[14] Hagen, *Jewel of the Church,* 188–9. For the Latin text see Cambrensis, *Opera,* II, 248.

[15] Hagen, *Jewel of the Church,* 185–9.

[16] For details on the former, see Power, *Medieval English Nunneries,* 522–3 and on the latter, see Constable, 'Nun of Watton', 205–26.

[17] There is also a complete copy of the thirty-two miracles in NLW Peniarth MS 5 and incomplete copies in Llanstephan MS 27 and Hafod MS 16. For the Welsh version of the tale see Angell, *'Gwyrthyeu',* 66–7.

[18] Angell, *'Gwyrthyeu',* 15. Mittendorf, 'The Middle Welsh Mary of Egypt', 205–18, suggests that the Welsh version of *Gwyrthyeu e Wynvydedic Veir* derives from the Latin text found in Oxford, Balliol College MS 240.

[19] Lloyd, *History of Wales,* II, 599.

[20] Fulton, 'Medieval Welsh poems to nuns', 95.

[21] S. Lewis, 'Dafydd ap Gwilym', 205–6.

[22] D. H. Williams, 'Cistercian nunneries'; *Welsh Cistercians,* I, 10–11. They are listed as priories in Knowles and Hadcock, *Medieval Religious Houses,* 272.

[23] Fontette, *Les Religieuses*, 34.

[24] Thompson, *Women Religious*, 97–100.

[25] Thomas, *St Asaph*, I, 485; D. H. Williams, 'Cistercian nunneries', 158.

[26] Knowles and Hadcock, *Medieval Religious Houses*, 274.

[27] Dugdale, *Monasticon*, IV, 591. See also Knowles and Hadcock, *Medieval Religious Houses*, 267. On Peckham's visitation, see Martin, *Registrum Epistolarum*, III, 805–6; D. H. Williams, 'Usk Nunnery', 44; Power, *Medieval English Nunneries*, 223–4.

[28] Power, *Medieval English Nunneries*, 3. For an estimate of the number of Welsh clergy, 1377–81, see Russell, *British Medieval Population*, 326 and for details of the number of monks in Wales at the end of the Middle Ages, see G. Williams, *The Welsh Church*, 561–3.

[29] Thompson, *Women Religious*, 1; Johnson, *Equal in Monastic Profession*, 3; Burton, *Monastic and Religious Orders in Britain*, 85.

[30] Gilchrist, *Gender and Material Culture*, 22–5.

[31] Cambrensis, *Opera*, IV, 152–3; Leland, *Itinerary*, 55.

[32] M. C. Jones, 'Llanllugan Nunnery', 301.

[33] Power, *Medieval Nunneries*, 692.

[34] D. H. Williams, 'Cistercian nunneries'; 'Usk Nunnery'; Fulton, 'Medieval Welsh poems to nuns'.

[35] Morgan, 'An early charter of Llanllugan Nunnery'.

[36] See, Maylan, 'Excavations at St Mary's Priory'; Mein, 'Usk Priory'.

[37] Knowles and Hadcock, *Medieval Religious Houses*, 255, 272.

[38] Knowles and Hadcock, *Medieval Religious Houses*, 112–15, Abbey Dore on the medieval ecclesiastical boundary between England and Wales could also be considered. Its income *c*.1535 was £101.

[39] Gilchrist, *Gender and Material Culture*, 41–4, 61.

[40] Edwards, *Littere Wallie*, 89, 132–3. I am grateful to Professor John Percival for translating these letters.

[41] Adam of Usk, *Chronicon*, 268.

[42] *Ibid.*

[43] On strict claustration see, Schulenburg, 'Strict active enclosure', 51–86.

[44] Martin, *Registrum Epistolarum*, III, 805–6; Power, *Medieval English Nunneries*, 223–4, 348; D. H. Williams, 'Usk Nunnery', 44.

[45] D. H. Williams, 'Cistercian nunneries', 164.

[46] Power, *Medieval English Nunneries*, 205.

[47] Nichols, 'Medieval Cistercian nunneries', 245.

[48] Bannister, 'Registrum', 241–2; D. H. Williams, 'Cistercian nunneries', 159.

[49] Edwards, *Littere Wallie*, 89, 132–3.

[50] S. W. Williams, *Strata Florida*, xlviii–l; Edwards, *Littere Wallie*, 90–1. Compare also, Edwards, *Littere Wallie*, 76, 84, 96–7, 174.

[51] S. J. Williams, 'Rhai Cyfieithiadau', 304–5.

[52] On the *cywydd gofyn* see Huws, 'Astudiaeth o'r Canu Gofyn a Diolch'.

[53] C. T. B. Davies, 'Cerddi'r Tai Crefydd', I, 95. See also Harries, *Gwaith Huw Cae Llwyd*, 69–71.

[54] *Llwyd* can mean grey or brown. It can also mean sacred and the poet, aware of this ambiguity, is perhaps hinting at its rather ironic religious connotations.

[55] Huws, 'Astudiaeth o'r Canu Gofyn a Diolch', 394–6.

[56] Harries, *Gwaith Huw Cae Llwyd*, 17.

[57] For example, Archbishop Peckham forbade the abbess of Romsey to keep monkeys or dogs in her chamber. Power, *Medieval English Nunneries*, 306.

[58] C. T. B. Davies, 'Cerddi'r Tai Crefydd', I, 132–3, 142–4, 223–4, 247.

[59] *Ibid.*, 64–77, 81–2; Huws, 'Astudiaeth o'r Canu Gofyn a Diolch', 82.

[60] See C. T. B. Davies, 'Cerddi'r Tai Crefydd'.

[61] Williams and Jones, *Gramadegau'r Penceirddiaid*, 16, 35, 56.

[62] Parry, *Gwaith Dafydd ap Gwilym*, 298–9; Fulton, 'Medieval Welsh poems to nuns', 105–7.

[63] Fulton, 'Medieval Welsh poems to nuns', 88–9.

[64] See, for example, Parry, *Gwaith Dafydd ap Gwilym*, 216–17, 227–9, 266–7.

[65] Fulton, 'Medieval Welsh poems to nuns', 107–8.

[66] *Ibid.*, 103.

[67] *Ibid.*, 101, n.30.

[68] Parry, *Oxford Book of Welsh Verse*, 106–7; Williams and Thomas, *Cywyddau Dafydd ap Gwilym a'i Gyfoeswyr*, 10–11.

[69] Fulton, 'Medieval Welsh poems to nuns', 93–4.

[70] *Ibid.*, 103.

[71] This may refer to the colour of their skin rather than their habit.

[72] Thompson, *Women Religious*, 100.

[73] M. Lewis, *Stained Glass*, 68. It is possible that the figure represents the donor of the window. I am grateful to David O'Connor for his comments on photographs of the window.

[74] BL Add. MS 14999 fo. 104^{r-v}.

[75] I am grateful to Graham Thomas of the National Library of Wales for his help in transcribing the poem. I am also grateful to Professor Dafydd Johnston for sharing with me his ideas on this poem and for many helpful comments on other aspects of the poetry discussed in this article.

[76] Ruddock, 'Cywydd i Grefyddes?'; D. R. Johnston, *Gwaith Iolo Goch*, 101–3.

[77] See, Truman, *Historical Costuming*, 41–2; Sichel, *Costume Reference*, 1. Numerous references are made to rosaries in Welsh poetry. Lewys Glyn Cothi thanks Efa ferch Llywelyn for providing him with a rosary and Syr Dafydd Trefor composed a *cywydd gofyn* requesting a rosary for Marged ferch William ab William, D. Johnston, *Gwaith Lewys Glyn Cothi*, 406–7; George, 'Syr Dafydd Trefor', 145–7.

[78] *Ysgarladwisg* may refer to the type of material rather than its colour, D. R. Johnston, *Gwaith Iolo Goch*, 325, n.42, but see also D. Johnston, *Canu Maswedd*, 589.

[79] Compare the reference to *dyn eglur dâl* – the nun with forehead revealed – in the Dafydd ap Gwilym *cywydd*, Fulton, 'Medieval Welsh poems to nuns', 106.

[80] D. Johnston, *Iolo Goch Poems,* 100–3.

[81] Parry, *Gwaith Dafydd ap Gwilym,* 269–70.

[82] I use *Canu Serch* to refer to love poetry and *Canu Mawl* to refer to the more formal praise poetry.

[83] D. Johnston, *Canu Maswedd,* 58–61.

[84] See also Jennifer Ward's essay in the present volume, p. 195.

[85] See, for example, Roberts, *Gwassanaeth Meir,* and Roberts, 'Pymtheg Gweddi San Ffraid'.

[86] Warner, *Descriptive Catalogue,* I, 59–60. I am grateful to Ceridwen Lloyd-Morgan of the National Library of Wales for providing me with information on the *Llanbeblig Hours.*

[87] For these poems see, Williams and Rowlands, *Rhisiart ap Rhys,* 50–2; D. Johnston, *Gwaith Lewys Glyn Cothi,* 137–9, 247–8, 268–9.

[88] D. Johnston, *Gwaith Lewys Glyn Cothi,* 268–9, 406–7.

[89] Williams and Rowlands, *Rhisiart ap Rhys,* 34–6; D. Johnston, *Gwaith Lewys Glyn Cothi,* 107–8.

[90] The poem to her husband is described as a praise poem, rather than an elegy, in the manuscript, Williams and Rowlands, *Rhisiart ap Rhys,* 33–4, 77, n.53–5.

[91] D. Johnston, *Gwaith Lewys Glyn Cothi,* 108.

[92] On St Non see Cartwright, 'Non – Mam Dda Ddinam'.

[93] On the Welsh version of St Helen and the Holy Cross see T. G. Jones, '*Val a Cauas Elen y Grog*'. In Welsh tradition Elen is a composite saint.

[94] Williams and Williams, *Gwaith Guto'r Glyn,* 119.

[95] *Ibid.,* 118–19, 123–5.

[96] C. T. B. Davies, 'Cerddi'r Tai Crefydd', I, 130–1; Williams and Williams, *Gwaith Guto'r Glyn,* xvi.

[97] D. Johnston, *Gwaith Lewys Glyn Cothi,* 100–2.

[98] Gilchrist, *Gender and Material Culture,* 172–6.

[99] For a list of hospitals in medieval England and Wales see Knowles and Hadcock, *Medieval Religious Houses,* 313–410.

[100] M. E. Owen, 'Y Cyfreithiau (1)', 200–1, 212–13. A list of the manuscripts (twelfth–fifteenth century) is provided by M. E. Owen, 'Y Cyfreithiau (1)', 201–2.

[101] For a definition of *amobr* see Jenkins and Owen, *The Welsh Law of Women,* 190; see also 73–5.

[102] Jenkins and Owen, *The Welsh Law of Women,* 172–3.

[103] At least, this certainly seems to have been the case in the March, where *amobr* was paid for each sexual encounter until the woman's family declared her a common prostitute, R. R. Davies, *Lordship and Society,* 137. See also Jenkins and Owen, *The Welsh Law of Women,* 88–90.

[104] R. R. Davies, *Lordship and Society,* 137.

[105]Knowles and Hadcock, *Medieval Religious Houses,* 255, 272.

[106]See details given in Thompson, *Women Religious,* 167–76; Gilchrist, *Gender and Material Culture,* 50; Burton, *Monastic and Religious Orders in Britain,* 91–3. For a discussion of English noblewomen and religious patronage see Jennifer Ward's essay in the present volume, pp. 192–3.

[107]Thompson, *Women Religious,* 177.

[108]Ward, *English Noblewomen,* 6. Edward I arranged that the Clare estates be held jointly by husband and wife when his daughter, Joan of Acre, married Gilbert, earl of Gloucester, in 1290, Ward, *English Noblewomen,* 26–7.

[109]PRO E101/93/4, m. 5. I am grateful to Jennifer Ward for this reference. Ward's essay in the present volume discusses Elizabeth de Burgh's relationship with other religious houses, such as the Minoresses' convent in London. Elizabeth had a house built in the outer precinct of the convent and it appears that this became the home of a number of other noblewomen.

[110]R. R. Davies, 'The status of women', 100–2.

[111]R. R. Davies, 'The status of women', 100–1; Carr, *Medieval Anglesey,* 156–60.

[112]Ward, 'English noblewomen and the local community', this volume, 196.

[113]Thompson, *Women Religious,* 213; 'Why English nunneries had no history'; Fulton, 'Medieval Welsh poems to nuns', 96–7.

[114]D. H. Williams, 'Cistercian nunneries', 155.

[115]Thompson, 'Why English nunneries had no history', 134.

[116]D. H. Williams, 'Cistercian nunneries', 155.

[117]Cambrensis, *Opera,* IV, 152–3; Lloyd, *A History of Wales,* II, 603. On Cistercian lands owned by the different religious houses, see D. H. Williams, *Atlas of Cistercian Lands.*

[118]Her cousin, Gwladus, was sent to the Gilbertine priory of Sixhill: S. Davies, 'Y Ferch', 23. Efa, daughter of William Marshal, earl of Pembroke, may have retired to the priory of Augustinian nuns at Cornworthy in Devon after her husband, William de Braose, was hanged in 1230 by Llywelyn ap Iorwerth: Thompson, *Women Religious,* 172.

[119]T. Jones, *Brut y Tywysogyon,* 262–5.

[120]According to William Worcestre (1415–*c*.1485) the body of St Elvetha (Eluned?), one of the daughters of Brychan Brycheiniog, lay in the priory church at Usk: Worcestre, *Itineraries,* 155.

[121]On these saints see Farmer, *Dictionary of Saints,* 97, 274, 312, 319–20.

[122]Wales had to wait until the eighteenth century for its next prominent religious woman – Ann Griffiths (1776–1805).

Bibliography

Adam of Usk, *Chronicon Adae de Usk A.D. 1377–1421,* trans. Edward Maunde Thompson (2nd edn., London, 1904).

Angell, L. H., *'Gwyrthyeu e Wynvydedic Veir:* astudiaeth gymharol ohonynt fel y'u ceir hwynt yn llawysgrifau Peniarth 14, Peniarth 5 a Llanstephan 27' (Univ. of Wales MA thesis, 1938).

Bannister, A. T., *'Registrum Caroli Bothe', Canterbury and York Series* 28 (1921), 241–2.

Bradney, A. J., *A History of Monmouthshire,* III, i (London, 1993).

Burton, J., *Monastic and Religious Orders in Britain 1000–1300* (Cambridge, 1994).

Cambrensis, Giraldus, *Giraldi Cambrensis Opera,* I–VIII, eds. J. S. Brewer, J. F. Dimock and G. F. Warner (London, 1861–91).

Carr, A. D., *Medieval Anglesey* (Llangefni, 1982).

Cartwright, J., 'Non – Mam Dda Ddinam', *Barn* 374 (1994), 57–9.

Carville, G., 'Cistercian nuns in medieval Ireland: Plary Abbey, Ballymore, County Westmeath', in J. A. Nichols and L. T. Shank (eds.), *Medieval Religious Women. III, Hidden Springs: Cistercian Monastic Women* (Kalamazoo, 1995), 63–84.

Constable, G., 'Ailred of Rievaulx and the nun of Watton: an episode in the early history of the Gilbertine order', in D. Baker (ed.), *Medieval Women* (Oxford, 1978), 205–26.

Cowley, F. G., *The Monastic Order in South Wales* (Cardiff, 1977).

Davies, C. T. B. (ed.), 'Cerddi'r Tai Crefydd', I–II (Univ. of Wales MA thesis, 1972).

Davies, E. (ed.), *A Gazetteer of Welsh Place-Names* (Cardiff, 1957).

Davies, R. R., *Lordship and Society in the March of Wales 1282–1400* (Oxford, 1978).

Davies, R. R., 'The status of women and the practice of marriage in late-medieval Wales', in D. Jenkins and M. E. Owen (eds.), *The Welsh Law of Women* (Cardiff, 1980), 93–114.

Davies, S., 'Y Ferch yng Nghymru yn yr Oesoedd Canol', *Cof Cenedl 9* (1994), 3–32.

Dugdale, W., *Monasticon Anglicanum,* I–VI, eds. J. Caley, H. Ellis and B. Bandinel (London, 1655–73; 1817–30 edn.).

Easson, D. E., 'The nunneries of medieval Scotland', *Scottish Ecclesiological Society Transactions* 13.2 (1940–1), 22–38.

Easson, D. E., *Medieval Religious Houses; Scotland* (London, 1957).

Edwards, J. Goronwy (ed.), *Littere Wallie* (Cardiff, 1940).

Farmer, D. H., *The Oxford Dictionary of Saints* (3rd edn., Oxford, 1992).

Fontette, M., *Les Religieuses à l'âge classique du droit canon. Recherches sur les structures juridiques des branches féminines des ordres* (Paris, 1967).

Fulton, H., 'Medieval Welsh poems to nuns', *Cambridge Medieval Celtic Studies* 21 (1991), 87–112.

George, S. E. I., 'Syr Dafydd Trefor ei Oes a'i Waith' (Univ. of Wales MA thesis, 1929).

Gilchrist, R., *Gender and Material Culture: The Archaeology of Religious Women* (London, 1994).

Gwynn, A. and Hadcock, R. N., *Medieval Religious Houses: Ireland* (Dublin, 1988).

Hagen, J. J. (trans.), *Gerald of Wales: The Jewel of the Church, a translation of Gemma Ecclesiastica* (Leiden, 1979).

Harries, L. (ed.), *Gwaith Huw Cae Llwyd ac Eraill* (Cardiff, 1953).

Huws, B. O., 'Astudiaeth o'r Canu Gofyn a Diolch Rhwng *c.*1350 a *c.*1630' (Univ. of Wales Ph.D. thesis, 1994).

Jenkins, D. and Owen, M. E. (eds.), *The Welsh Law of Women* (Cardiff, 1980).

Johnson, P. D., *Equal in Monastic Profession: Religious Women in Medieval France* (Chicago, 1991).

Johnston, D. (ed.), *Gwaith Iolo Goch* (Cardiff, 1988).

Johnston, D. (ed. and trans.), *Canu Maswedd yr Oesoedd Canol/Medieval Welsh Erotic Poetry* (Cardiff, 1991).

Johnston, D. (ed. and trans.), *Iolo Goch: Poems* (Llandysul, 1993).

Jones, M. C., 'Some account of Llanllugan Nunnery', *Montgomeryshire Collections* 2 (1869), 301–10.

Johnston, D. (ed.), *Gwaith Lewys Glyn Cothi* (Cardiff, 1995).

Jones, T. (ed. and trans.), *Brut y Tywysogyon or The Chronicle of the Princes* (Cardiff, 1955).

Jones, T. G., *'Ystorya Addaf a Val a Cauas Elen y Grog:* tarddiad, cynnwys ac arddull y testunau Cymraeg a'u lledaeniad' (Univ. of Wales MA thesis, 1936).

Knowles, D. and Hadcock, R. N., *Medieval Religious Houses: England and Wales* (London, 1953).

Leland, J., *The Itinerary in Wales,* ed. L. T. Smith (London, 1906).

Lewis, M., *Stained Glass in North Wales up to 1850* (Altrincham, 1970).

Lewis, S., 'Dafydd ap Gwilym', *Llên Cymru* 2 (1953), 199–208.

Lloyd, J. E., *A History of Wales,* I–II (London, 1911).

Martin, C. T. (ed.), *Registrum Epistolarum Fratris Johannis Peckham Archiepiscopi Cantuariensis (1279–92),* I–III (London, 1882–5).

Maylan, N., 'Excavations at St Mary's Priory, Usk', *The Monmouthshire Antiquary* 9 (1993), 29–41.

Mein, G., 'Usk Priory; an unrecorded excavation', *The Monmouthshire Antiquary* 9 (1993), 43–5.

Mittendorf, I., 'The Middle Welsh Mary of Egypt and the Latin source of the *Miracles of the Virgin Mary*', in E. Poppe and B. Ross (eds.), *The Legend of Mary of Egypt in Medieval Insular Hagiography* (Blackrock, 1996), 205–36.

Morgan, R., 'An early charter of Llanllugan Nunnery', *Montgomeryshire Collections* 73 (1985), 116–19.

Nichols, J. A., 'Medieval Cistercian nunneries and English bishops', in J. A. Nichols and L. T. Shank (eds.), *Medieval Religious Women, 1; Distant Echoes* (Kalamazoo, 1984), 237–49.

Owen, E., 'The Cistercian nunnery of Llanllugan', *Montgomeryshire Collections* 37 (1915), 1–13.

Owen, G., *The Description of Penbrokshire*, I–IV, ed. H. Owen (London, 1892–1936).

Owen, M. E., 'Y Cyfreithiau – (1) Natur y testunau', in G. Bowen (ed.), *Y Traddodiad Rhyddiaith yn yr Oesau Canol* (Llandysul, 1974), 196–219.

Owen, M. E., 'Y Cyfreithiau – (2) Ansawdd y rhyddiaith', in G. Bowen (ed.), *Y Traddodiad Rhyddiaith yn yr Oesau Canol* (Llandysul, 1974), 220–44.

Parry, T. (ed.), *Gwaith Dafydd ap Gwilym* (Cardiff, 1979).

Parry, T. (ed.), *The Oxford Book of Welsh Verse* (Oxford, 1989).

Power, E., *Medieval English Nunneries c. 1275 to 1535* (Cambridge, 1922).

Richards, R., *Church and Priory of S. Mary, Usk* (London, 1904).

Roberts, B. F. (ed.), 'Pymtheg Gweddi San Ffraid a'r Pardwn', *Bulletin of the Board of Celtic Studies* 16 (1956), 254–68.

Roberts, B. F. (ed.), *Gwassanaeth Meir sef Cyfeithiad Cymraeg Canol o'r Officum Parvum Beatae Mariae Virginis* (Cardiff, 1961).

Ruddock, G., 'Cywydd i Grefyddes?', *Llên Cymru* 12.1 and 12.2 (1972), 117–20.

Russell, J. C., *British Medieval Population* (Albuquerque, 1948).

Schulenburg, J. T., 'Strict active enclosure and its effects on the female monastic experience (500–1100)', in J. A. Nichols and L. T. Shank (eds.), *Medieval Religious Women, 1: Distant Echoes* (Kalamazoo, 1984), 51–86.

Sichel, M., *Costume Reference 1: Roman Britain and the Middle Ages* (London, 1977).

Thomas, D. R., *The History of the Diocese of St Asaph*, I–III (Oswestry, 1908–13).

Thompson, S., 'The problem of the Cistercian nuns in the twelfth and early thirteenth centuries', in D. Baker (ed.), *Medieval Women* (Oxford, 1978), 227–52.

Thompson, S.,'Why English nunneries had no history: A study of the problems of the English nunneries founded after the Conquest', in J. A. Nichols and L. T. Shank (eds.), *Medieval Religious Women, 1: Distant Echoes* (Kalamazoo, 1984), 131–49.

Thompson, S., *Women Religious: The Founding of English Nunneries after the Conquest* (Oxford, 1991).

Truman, N., *Historical Costuming* (London, 1936; 1966 ed.).

Ward, J. C., *English Noblewomen in the Later Middle Ages* (London, 1992).

Ward, J. C., 'Elizabeth de Burgh, Lady of Clare (d. 1360)', in C. M. Barron and A. F. Sutton (eds.), *Medieval London Widows 1300–1500* (London, 1994), 29–45.

Warner, G. F., *Descriptive Catalogue of Illuminated Manuscripts of C. W. Dyson Perrins*, I–II (Oxford, 1820).

Williams, D. H., 'Cistercian nunneries in medieval Wales', *Citeaux* 26.3 (1975), 155–74.

Williams, D. H., 'Usk Nunnery', *The Monmouthshire Antiquary* 4 (1980), 44–5.

Williams, D. H., *The Welsh Cistercians* (Caldey Island, 1984).

Williams, D. H., *Atlas of Cistercian Lands in Wales* (Cardiff, 1990).

Williams, G., *The Welsh Church From Conquest to Reformation* (Cardiff, 1976).

Williams, G. J. and Jones, E. J. (eds.), *Gramadegau'r Penceirddiaid* (Cardiff, 1934).

Williams, I. and Thomas, R. (eds.), *Cywyddau Dafydd ap Gwilym a'i Gyfoeswyr* (Bangor, 1914).

Williams, J. L. and Williams, I. (eds.), *Gwaith Guto'r Glyn* (Cardiff, 1961).

Williams, J. M. and Rowlands, E. I. (eds.), *Gwaith Rhys Brydydd a Rhisiart ap Rhys* (Cardiff, 1976).

Williams, S. J., 'Rhai Cyfieithiadau', in G. Bowen (ed.), *Y Traddodiad Rhyddiaith yn yr Oesau Canol* (Llandysul, 1974), 303–11.

Williams, S. W., 'Architectural notes upon Usk Church, Monmouthshire', *Archaeologia Cambrensis* 3, 5th ser. (1886), 90–3.

Williams, S. W., *The Cistercian Abbey of Strata Flórida: Its History and an Account of the Recent Excavations made on its Site* (London, 1889).

Worcestre, W., *Itineraries,* ed. J. H. Harvey (Oxford, 1969).

2

Puellae litteratae:
The Use of the Vernacular in the Dominican Convents of Southern Germany[1]

MARIE-LUISE EHRENSCHWENDTNER

I N 1286 or 1287, Hermann of Minden, in his capacity as head of the German Province of the Dominican order, found it necessary to remind the Dominican sisters that 'Every week the constitutions should be publicly read in the vernacular in the refectory.'[2] Among the Dominican monks, Latin was the principal language,[3] but I will argue in this paper that virtually from the foundation of their order the nuns used the vernacular as well. Latin was, of course, the language of the divine service and as such it had to be read and sung by all nuns except the lay sisters. It was also the language of prayer, although recitation of the *Pater noster* was often enough to fulfil their duties in this respect.[4] Outside the chapel, however, Latin faded in importance compared to the use the friars made of it. The instruction of Hermann of Minden illuminates this point – it is significant that having realized that not all of the nuns would understand the constitutions if they were to be read in Latin, he does not insist that measures be taken to improve their knowledge of it. This paper will not only consider the extent to which the sisters could understand Latin, but also examine the role played by the vernacular in the Dominican convents. I will then explore why the practices of the male and the female branches of the order differed so greatly in respect of their use of language. The sources I have used are legislative documents of the order, works of Dominican sisters and theologians, and remnants of convent libraries in the former German province of Teutonia.

1. Latin and the Vernacular in Dominican Convents

The first Dominican convent, founded in 1206 by Dominic himself, was Prouille in southern France. In 1220, Dominic accepted the guidance of

St Sisto in Rome, and during the following years a large number of convents were incorporated into the order. In Germany the female branch grew faster than that of the friars: by the beginning of the fourteenth century there were about forty-six priories compared to approximately seventy convents.[5] In the southern German province there were nearly as many convents as in all the other Dominican provinces put together.[6] There, and above all in the dioceses of Basel, Constance and Strasbourg, far more women joined the Dominican order than in the lower Rhine valley and the Low Countries, where the convents had for the most part been established by the Cistercians. The Dominican friars first arrived in the upper Rhine valley in the early 1220s, and came across many women who wished to live a religious life and were not satisfied simply to follow a monastic rule, but wanted to imitate the earthly lives of Christ and the Apostles, and particularly their renunciation of worldly goods.[7] Despite numerous attempts by the order's hierarchy to rid itself of their pastoral care,[8] these women found that the Dominican friars were interested in their spirituality and offered them encouragement and support.[9] None the less, as there were more women who wanted to join the order than could be admitted, the friars who were responsible for them had to restrict the numbers allowed to live in each convent.[10] In 1237, for example, it was noticed that approximately three hundred nuns were living in the five Strasbourg convents, but only one hundred women could be supported by their incomes.[11]

Since women were not allowed to be itinerant preachers – as such they would have been denounced as heretics – early Dominican nuns pursued their purpose by living in voluntary poverty within their communities. Although the situation changed in the fourteenth and fifteenth centuries (when the nuns were much better off), in the first century of their history, life in the convents was often extremely harsh. For example, in contrast with the situation in the convents of the Benedictine or Cistercian nuns, the Dominican sisters often endured a shortage of food. The *Schwesternbuch* of Ötenbach celebrates the poverty of the convent in its account of the meals served to the first sisters: they enjoyed a meagre diet, and because there was always so little food many of the sisters starved.[12] Yet as the convent chronicles show, this was not considered something to complain about, but just the opposite. Some sisters tried, as the *Schwesternbuch* of Unterlinden reveals, to eat or drink less than was given to them, while others deliberately spoilt their food by adding unsavoury ingredients.[13] In following Christ, the early Dominican nuns were equally rigorous in other forms of asceticism and self-discipline.[14]

They attempted to overcome the demands of the body and to mortify their desires, which explains in part why they regarded chastity as an outstanding virtue. Sometimes their pastoral guides interfered. Heinrich Seuse for example forbade Elsbeth Stagl, whom he called his '*geischliche tohter*', his 'spiritual daughter', to continue tormenting her body in imitation of the desert fathers because he wanted to prevent her from doing physical harm to herself.[15] The Dominicans of the fifteenth century were much more cautious as far as practical asceticism was concerned, but because they preserved the records their predecessors had left, they were very well aware of the past harshness of convent discipline.[16]

Dominican convent life was further characterized by the strong link between the first and second orders. The Dominican convents did not share the relative autonomy the nuns of the older monasticism had enjoyed,[17] and they were much more under the control of their spiritual guides. Furthermore, the male and female branches shared parts of the constitutions, and the liturgy in both houses was the same. There were only two fields from which the sisters were excluded: the apostolate towards the public, and, connected with that, study.[18] Yet even with regard to these activities it was assumed among Dominicans that the sisters did have a role to play: because the monks were busy with their pastoral or academic duties, it was the sisters' part to offer prayers on their behalf.[19] Thus, the second master general wrote to his friend Diana d'Andalo, who lived in the convent of Bologna, 'often pray for me to the Lord since I need it because of my shortcomings. I seldom pray',[20] and he describes the sisters as '*laboris nostri participes*', 'participating in our labours'.[21]

In his book on the religious movements of the twelfth and thirteenth centuries, originally published in 1935, Herbert Grundmann pointed out the coincidence of a strong tradition of female spirituality and the emergence of religious writings in the vernacular, not only in southern Germany but in the Low Countries and Belgium too;[22] and it was he who first suggested that the Dominican order was at the centre of this development. Grundmann contended that the Dominican friars, confronted with a large number of their sisters who did not know enough Latin to read for themselves or even follow the readings, were forced to provide them with texts which they would be able to understand.[23] This would suggest that the friars were responding to a decline in the standard of education of the nuns, since the foundation of the first convents. However, Grundmann was working on the assumption that in the early history of the order, because many of the Dominican nuns were able to write, they must have had a good knowledge of the Latin language.[24] Subsequent generations of scholars have accepted these arguments without questioning, and so a reconsideration of the surviving evidence is long overdue.[25]

As has been already noted, Latin was the language of the divine service; during the time the sisters spent in chapel everything was read or sung in that language.[26] The only exceptions were the sermons which, to facilitate understanding, were held in German.[27] Many sermons by famous mystics and theologians like Master Eckhart or Johannes Tauler were addressed to the female communities of their order and then written down by the sisters to preserve them.[28] Outside the chapel, the importance of Latin decreased over time – the quotation from Hermann of Minden which began this paper reveals that the constitutions were already read in the vernacular by the end of the thirteenth century. Yet it seems likely that the table readings were still often held in Latin, even if there were sisters who did not understand them. In the so-called *Schwesternliteratur* of the late thirteenth and early fourteenth centuries we find records of sisters suddenly and miraculously comprehending what had been read in the refectory. Sister Tuoda from Unterlinden, for example, who entered the convent when she was an old woman, had never learnt Latin, but her short *vita* in the *Schwesternbuch* records that on some days she was able to understand the Latin texts of the divine service and table readings.[29] Margarethe Ebner, in her *Offenbarungen*, says the same about herself: she was very surprised when she suddenly realized that she had followed the table readings even though she too had never been taught Latin.[30] However, the chronicle of Engelthal reports on table readings in German before the convent was incorporated in the Dominican order; this might have changed afterwards but it indicates the women's original distance from the traditional monastic way.[31] At the beginning of the fifteenth century, supporters of the Dominican reform movement finally institutionalized table readings in the vernacular: emphasizing the need for strict adherence to the rule and constitutions, they tried to deepen the sisters' comprehension of the Dominican religious life. The Dominican convent of Nuremberg originally had permission to have table readings partly in the vernacular,[32] but the extant catalogues of table readings of St Catharine's reveal that the nuns actually abolished the Latin table readings.[33] The decision to allow table readings in the vernacular offered a solution to a problem which was also being experienced by other orders: around the same time the Poor Clares of Nuremberg complained about Latin table readings they did not understand.[34]

Latin as the language of the divine service was imposed on the sisters by ecclesiastical legislation, and as the language of the table readings it had been inherited as a time-honoured custom,[35] but the evidence suggests that in other areas of religious life, the nuns often chose the vernacular. The Dominican nuns preferred their mother tongue when they said their private prayers, as is shown by a great number of extant texts which were used by Dominican sisters.[36] Exceptions were, of course, the most important liturgical prayers, not only the *Pater noster*, but also the *Ave Maria*, the *Te deum* or the Psalms which were recited during the services and therefore very familiar to nuns.[37] The majority of the books the nuns owned were, as far as we can see, written in the vernacular: in addition to the large number of original texts, there were numerous translations of liturgical texts, of the Bible, and of prayers and legislative texts in many Dominican convent libraries by the fifteenth century.[38] Only a few books possessed by the nuns or convents are in Latin, mostly those for liturgical use. Since many convents had enough copyists to produce their own books in order to enlarge their libraries, we can only conclude from this that they were not particularly interested in Latin books for daily use.[39] Furthermore, the fact that the sisters were busy with copying books, often in order to increase their incomes,[40] does not, as Grundmann believes, necessarily indicate a deep knowledge of Latin, since reading and transcribing do not invariably entail word for word comprehension.

A relatively large number of Dominican sisters of the late thirteenth and early fourteenth centuries (until *c.*1360) were authors. Since their spirituality was strongly influenced by the tendencies of the age and many of them had mystical experiences themselves, they wrote down their own spiritual experiences and visions or collected and edited those of fellow sisters. With only one exception – the *Schwesternbuch* of Unterlinden, Colmar, which is the earliest example of this kind of literature – all these works are written in the vernacular.[41] Other sisters wrote German poems containing mystical instructions, insights, or summaries of teachings of mystical theologians.[42] As far as we can see, the letters exchanged between those sisters who had mystical experiences and their pastoral guides were also written in German. Unfortunately, with very few exceptions, only the letters of the friars have survived, for example one letter from Johannes Tauler to Margarethe Ebner,[43] and some from Heinrich Seuse.[44] Since the Dominican monks would have been Latin-literate, it must be concluded that their correspondence was written in the vernacular for the benefit of the nuns. Hermann of Minden, who was a theologian but not a mystic, wrote letters in Latin to Agnes of Bonlanden, the prioress of St Lambert, but at the same time provided a translator.[45]

The final category of evidence I intend to consider here is that of the official documents which the convents received and made out. During the thirteenth and fourteenth centuries, most of these were written in Latin, especially those which came from the ecclesiastical authorities. However, towards the end of the thirteenth century the first deeds made out by Dominican convents and written in the vernacular begin to appear, for example in Adelhausen, near Freiburg/ Breisgau,[46] or Pettendorf near Regensburg.[47] In the fifteenth century, the documents dealing with secular matters as well as many official instructions produced on behalf of the order's representatives were written in German, whereas Latin remained the language of the documents pertaining to the male branch.[48]

2. The Education of a Dominican Sister

If Latin was not a great concern of the Dominican nuns, to what extent did they need to be acquainted with it? This section will consider in some detail the education which they received. The Dominican authorities ordered that no girl younger than twelve should be admitted to a convent,[49] although this rule was often flouted.[50] When they entered the community, they were supposed to be, as it is put, *puellae litteratae*, that is, 'educated girls'.[51] While this term is never defined, resulting in some speculation among scholars,[52] a re-examination of the sources does provide some clear pointers to its meaning.

Humbert de Romanis, the fifth master general of the Dominican order (died 1277), in a sermon directed to secular girls, advises them as follows: they should learn to read the Psalter and the most important of the liturgical prayers so that they might be fully prepared should they want to enter a convent. He even recommends a further study of the Holy Scriptures according to the example of some saints of the early church.[53] Similarly, Christine Ebner of Engelthal (born 1277), whose *Offenbarungen* have survived, tells us that she learnt to read the Psalter before she reached the age of ten, when she was still at home.[54] Nevertheless, she calls herself *illitterata* when she says: 'ich . . . kan dar zu der schrift niht'. The only explanation for this testimony – if we do not want to dismiss it as a phrase of humility[55] or assume that the author was not able to write despite composing two books[56] – is to take it as a formula literally translated from Latin: '*litteratus/a non sum*'. The term *litteratus* designated a person who had substantial knowledge of Latin.[57] This explanation ties in with other information which can be gleaned from the *Offenbarungen*: when she refers to books she has read, Christine quotes German titles;[58] and she mentions occasions on which she would have liked to understand the Latin liturgy.[59] Christine Ebner uses the translation of '*litteratus/a non sum*' in the traditional way in depicting herself as someone who had not learnt to speak or write Latin. About two hundred years later, the prioress of St Catharine's, Nuremberg, wrote in a letter to the prioress of a Swiss convent that she too wanted the girls entering the convent to be able to read the Latin Psalter.[60] In some respects, these nuns were not *illitteratae*, since they could read Latin even if they did not understand it. These examples reveal the most likely meaning of the phrase *puella litterata*: a Dominican nun was *litterata* because she performed all liturgical duties in Latin even if she was *illitterata* according to the traditional standard which would have included the understanding of this language. Christine Ebner satisfied the requirements for a girl to enter a Dominican convent – she was a *puella litterata* because she could read the Psalter. How many of the novices had made further studies of the Bible and its language, as recommended by Humbert, is difficult to tell.

After entering the convent, the novices had to learn how to live according to the rules and constitutions. One has to differentiate between the educated sisters, '*moniales litteratae*',[61] and the lay sisters, '*sorores illitteratae et laicae*',[62] who were not expected to be able to read, and just supposed to know a few prayers, like the *Pater noster* or the *Ave Maria*, by heart.[63] The first aim of the constitutions was to ensure that the nuns adopted forms of behaviour appropriate to the religious life. The second was to ensure that they learnt how to fulfil their religious duties and take part in the divine service as choir members. In order to do this the novices had to learn how to read and sing the Latin texts, but Latin grammar was still not proposed as an appropriate subject of study.[64] Only the constitutions for the French convent Montargis, written around 1250, mention the possibility of learning Latin: 'After the sisters have learnt how to perform the divine service perfectly, they may learn as much Latin as they need to understand what is read.'[65] Later constitutions do not adopt this passage: in 1259, Humbert de Romanis took the constitutions of Montargis as a model when he wrote the constitutions which were binding for the Dominican convents of all provinces of the order, but in doing so he omitted this part.[66]

The evidence suggests it was supposed that the Dominican sisters could satisfy their spiritual needs simply by understanding their mother tongue. If the nuns wished to follow what was read or sung in chapel or in earlier times in the refectory, they often had to ask for help from a trained companion. To give just one example: one day, Margarethe Ebner wanted to hear the story of the Passion of Christ in the vernacular. Since she did not understand Latin, she had to ask a fellow sister to translate it for her.[67] According to its extant catalogue, at least one convent, St Catharine's in Nuremberg, established the translations of liturgical texts as part of the table readings, so that every sister would be able to follow the services.[68] The list of St Catharine's prescribes, for example, the following readings on the first Advent Sunday:[69] the German translation of the Mass, Epistle and the Gospel;[70] a sermon 'von der zukunft unsers herrn' by Albrecht Fleischmann, which the sisters had probably preserved by writing it down;[71] the explanation of the Mass of the day according to William Durandus' *Rationale divinorum officiorum*, a text which is counted among the works of the *Deutsche Scholastik*;[72] and another sermon 'von den IIII zukunft unsers herren'.[73] All Sunday table readings followed this pattern, and on saints' days their legends were read, sometimes supplemented by sermons.

Yet while the sisters were not forced to learn Latin, neither were they forbidden to study grammar, and some of their confessors may have actively encouraged them to do so. As an unknown spiritual adviser of the early fifteenth century puts it: 'With regard to eternal salvation it does not matter whether you understand Latin, but it would be useful if you did.'[74] Consequently it is not surprising that some of the Dominican sisters were extremely learned and Latinate women. The convent of Unterlinden in particular always seems to have had a comparatively large number of nuns who were able to read, write and translate Latin, as is shown by the *Schwesternbuch*, written in Latin by Katharina of Gebersweiler; it is extremely unlikely that it would have been written in a language which the sisters to whom it was addressed would have been unable to understand.[75] The *Schwesternbuch* also mentions other sisters with a good knowledge of Latin. Sister Hedwig of Steinbach is one such nun. She changed over to the convent of Unterlinden, having been given by her parents into a Benedictine convent as a child, and was something of a scholar,[76] 'tradens nobis primum sanctarum scienciam scripturarum'.[77] Not only did she teach her fellow sisters theology, but she also instructed them how to perform the liturgy properly.[78] Gertrude of Rheinfelden must have been educated in the convent,[79] but was similarly well trained in Latin; she was also an experienced copyist of liturgical manuscripts and other kinds of books.[80] In the same convent in the fifteenth century we find sister Elisabeth Kempf who could not only read, write and translate Latin but also speak it.[81] Sometimes the knowledge of the Latin language was connected with strong theological interests: according to her biographer, sister Claranna of Hochenburg (died 1423), the first prioress of the reform convent Schönensteinbach in Alsace, read many works of theology, among them the 'libri beati Dionysii'.[82] Elisabeth Kempf preferred the works of St Augustine to those of all other theologians.[83] But all these Latin-literate sisters are classified as exceptions, and often, even in texts written by fellow-sisters, the authors express their astonishment at their abilities.[84]

3. Gender and Language?

When Jordan of Saxony, the second master general of the Dominican order, was asked which rule he followed, he answered: 'The Rule of the Friars Preachers. And this is their rule: to live virtuously, to learn and to teach.'[85] From the beginning, the aims of the order were seen as preaching and pastoral care; study was made an 'essential duty of the Dominican religious life' and learning was considered 'an indispensable requirement of its apostolate'.[86] Novices were only admitted if they showed sufficient intelligence and knowledge.[87] Half of the second part of the constitutions of the friars deals with matters of learning,[88] whereas in those of the female branch of the order the directions concerning learning and study are eradicated. It was because of the emphasis laid on erudition, which always meant the study of theology,[89] that the predominant language in Dominican priories was Latin. As has been seen, the sisters only seem to have been *encouraged* to learn Latin but they were never *urged* to do so.

In the Dominican order, study was never considered as an aim in itself. Humbert de Romanis wrote in his Exposition of the Constitutions of the Friars Preachers (*Expositio super constitutiones fratrum Praedicatorum*): 'Study is not the purpose of the Order but it is exceedingly needful for the ends . . . namely preaching and working for the salvation of souls, for without study we can achieve neither.'[90] Study which is not directed towards the fulfilment of these principal objectives is dismissed as curiosity and vanity, and can in no way be tolerated.[91] As has been said, women were not allowed to be preachers or to exercise pastoral care outside their convents.[92] They were denied all public activity and lived, as their constitutions prescribed, in strict enclosure.[93] It follows therefore that the regular study of theology would have been considered useless for them, since they had no opportunity to exercise the duties which were necessary to justify erudition. To fulfil their tasks, which consisted of divine service, and prayer for those in the world and for the dead,[94] it was sufficient simply to be able to read and sing in Latin. This probably explains why many of the Dominican sisters did not bother to acquire a deeper knowledge of this language.

In this the Dominican nuns differed substantially from the sisters in the more conservative convents of the older monastic tradition. During the twelfth and thirteenth centuries there were many learned women in such houses, as is indicated by the example of Hedwig of Steinbach from Unterlinden who started her religious life as a Benedictine nun. Another highly-educated nun was Gertrude the Great of Helfta (died 1302) who belonged to a community which was autonomous but followed Cistercian customs and had Dominican friars as spiritual directors.[95] She entered the convent as a five-year-old girl – her community is discussed in this volume in the essay by Rosalynn Voaden. Not only was she able to read and write Latin (she was able to textualize her religious experiences in Latin without having to rely on an intermediary),[96] but she also studied the *artes liberales*[97] and gained great pleasure from it.[98] These skills seem to have been quite common in Helfta, as is illustrated by the fact that her biographer[99] – herself a nun in the convent – quotes Bede, Augustine, Jerome, Bernard of Clairvaux, Gregory the Great and Hugh of Saint-Victor.[100] Mary J. Finnegan notes that Gertrude's own principal literary sources included 'the Scriptures, liturgical books, the writings of Augustine, and Bernard's sermons on the *Song of Songs*';[101] as a result of her studies she had direct access to texts which had not yet been translated. Gertrude castigated herself for being too involved in her studies: 'she then realized that she had been far from God, in a land of unlikeness, for while clinging too closely to the liberal arts, she had until that moment failed to adjust the eye of her mind to the light of spiritual understanding. By attaching herself too eagerly to the pleasure of human wisdom, she had deprived herself of the most delightful taste of true wisdom.'[102] However, Gertrude always appreciated the education she had received, even after she had adopted new priorities.

The main difference between the majority of Dominican sisters and a nun like Gertrude of Helfta is that the latter had been brought up in a traditional monastic environment where education was still seen as a precondition for contemplation,[103] and where as Jean Leclercq puts it 'monastic knowledge' was 'determined by the end of monastic life: the search for God.'[104] Of course, Gertrude's mind was also shaped by the tendencies of the period in which she lived. She was not content with the kind of worship offered through the community's prayer and liturgy alone, and her religious experiences are deeply influenced by Bernard's sermons on the *Song of Songs*. She found, in the Christocentric and bridal mysticism of Bernard's works, a model for her spirituality. In their imitation of the suffering of Christ in a cloistered community which was itself poor, the Dominican nuns followed a somewhat different tradition, and in their spiritual and physical environment it was only natural that the Latin language lost its importance.

The most powerful influences on the devotional life of the Dominican nuns were, without doubt, the bible and liturgy. The nuns spent up to eight hours a day in chapel performing their liturgical duties, and all their writings show that the ecclesiastical year and its liturgy were the landmarks of their lives.[105] It comes then as no surprise that their libraries contained many translations and explanations of biblical and liturgical texts intended for private prayer and contemplation.[106] Although the sisters rarely had access to works of theology written in Latin, the works in the vernacular, often written by theologians, were derived from the Latin tradition and mediated 'high' theology, in its scholastic as well as in its monastic form.[107] Like the nuns of Helfta, they would have been very familiar with Bernard of Clairvaux, because so many vernacular texts adopted his ideas, even though they may never have read his works in the original.[108] Indeed the impact on the spirituality of the Dominican sisters of Bernard's teaching, especially that which revealed his positive attitude to suffering, should not be underestimated.[109] The nuns used short pieces which had been extracted from his writings, or which were attributed to him, for their daily prayer and contemplation.[110] They were also familiar with the works of Hugh of Saint-Victor, Thomas Aquinas, Augustine, and many other writers of the ecclesiastical tradition. In the convent libraries there were texts in the vernacular, which were ascribed to them, and which, authentic or not, often contained some of their thoughts.[111] In addition, the sisters possessed texts which belong to the tradition of the *Deutsche Scholastik*;[112] writings which supplied scholastical material in the translation, and were explicitly composed for people whose Latin was not sufficient to read such literature in the original.[113] The nuns' knowledge of the fathers was also derived from a variety of other sources: their preachers were trained theologians, who took up a range of learned topics in their sermons;[114] and in the confessional the nuns could discuss religious questions. The relationship between these women and their spiritual guides was not, however, one way: the so-called 'great German mystics', Master Eckhart, Heinrich Seuse and Johannes Tauler, were in their turn highly indebted to the spirituality of nuns.[115]

From the beginning then, the friars accepted the preponderance of the vernacular in the convents, and, to a certain degree, supported it by translating material for the use of the women. As early as 1242, at the time when the order's hierarchy wanted to cut off the female branch, it forbade the production of such texts, but without much success.[116] But even if they favoured some women's efforts to learn Latin, it seems that the friars never tried to introduce the *artes liberales* as a subject of education into the convents, presumably because it could not be considered essential since the nuns could not exercise pastoral duties. However, this did not diminish the sisters' self-confidence: there are many remarks in the convent chronicles which contrast the learning of the nuns and of the friars, and all come to the conclusion that the religious experiences of the sisters (which were seen as given by God himself) were superior to the monks' knowledge acquired from books,[117] an evaluation which echoes Gertrude's idea that 'she had deprived herself of the most delightful taste of true wisdom' while pursuing her studies.[118] It is in this context that the Dominican sisters developed their own mystical or mystically-influenced spirituality in the vernacular. They copied and collected in their libraries texts, mainly in the vernacular, which reflected their interests, and some of them became authors in order to write down their own experiences or those of fellow-sisters, while others wrote prayers or little tracts. Whatever the medium, the addressees were always, in the first place, their fellow sisters.

It can therefore be concluded that the Dominican sisters were not denied access to Latin culture because of their gender; after all, during the thirteenth and fourteenth centuries the nuns in convents of the older monastic tradition continued the use of the Latin language. From the foundation of their order, the Dominican sisters actively chose to use the vernacular wherever possible. They did this not only because of the conditions in which they lived but because of the potential which the vernacular had as an expression of a transformed spirituality. The Dominican approach to the religious life was much more direct and individual,[119] and therefore the vernacular served them well. In this they seem to have led the way, together with other religious women of the period like the beguines, for the following generations who demanded writings in the vernacular to satisfy their intellectual and spiritual needs.[120]

Notes

[1]   This essay examines the situation in the Dominican order's southern German province of Teutonia. Its findings do not necessarily extend to the other Dominican provinces because, to some extent, they had different traditions and habits. However, some similarities can be seen in the spiritual life of religious women in other parts of Europe, as the essays by Rosalyn Voaden and Susannah Mary Chewning reveal.

[2]   Denifle, 'Über die Anfänge der Predigtweise der deutschen Mystiker', 649: '[*constitutiones*] *publice legantur in refectorio per singulas ebdomadas in vulgari*'.

[3]   Cf. Hinnebusch, *History of the Dominican Order*, II, 3–18.

[4]   Cf. 'Constitutiones sororum', c. XIV, 343.

[5]   Denifle, 'Über die Anfänge der Predigtweise der deutschen Mystiker', 643. See also Wilms, *Das älteste Verzeichnis*.

[6]   Cf. Grundman, *Religiöse Bewegungen*, 312–13.

[7]   *Ibid.*, 187–8.

[8]   Hinnebusch, *History of the Dominican Order*, I, 387–93.

[9]   Freed, 'Urban development', 313, 322.

[10]   Grundmann, *Religiöse Bewegungen*, 315–17.

[11]   *Ibid.*, 315.

[12]   Zeller-Werdmüller and Bächtold, 'Ötenbach', 220; 227-9. The detailed remarks on food may be surprising at first, but as Bynum, *Holy Feast and Holy Fast*, has shown, attitudes towards food were an important aspect of women's spirituality.

[13]   Ancelet-Hustache, 'Unterlinden', 341.

[14]   Cf. e.g. Ancelet-Hustache, 'Unterlinden', 342.

[15]   Bihlmeyer, *Heinrich Seuse*, 107.

[16]   Cf. *Mittelalterliche Bibliothekskataloge*, III, 612 (sig. E LXVIII: sermons of Johannes Tauler; cf. Vetter, *Die Predigten Taulers*. The MS is to be found in the Stadtbibliothek Nürnberg, MS Cod. cent. VII, 74); 615 (sig. J II: Heinrich Seuse, *Leben Seuses; Büchlein der Ewigen Weisheit*; Seuse's letters; cf. Bihlmeyer, *Heinrich Seuse*, 7–195; 196–325; 360–401, *Briefbüchlein*; 405–494, *Großes Briefbuch*. This MS is lost); 633 (sigs. N XXII/N XXVII: the convent chronicles of Töss, St Katharinental, Ötenbach, Weiler. The MSS are to be found in the Stadtbibliothek Nürnberg, MS Cod. cent. V, 10a; MS Cod. cent. VI, 43b).

[17]   Leclercq, 'Feminine monasticism', 120–1.

[18]   Hinnebusch, *History of the Dominican Order*, I, 382.

[19] Cf. e.g. de Fontette, *Les religieuses*, 116.

[20] Walz, *Beati Iordani de Saxonia Epistulae*, XII, 15.4–6.

[21] *Ibid.*, XLVI, 51.20–24.

[22] Grundmann, *Religiöse Bewegungen*, 452–8.

[23] *Ibid.*, 463–4.

[24] *Ibid.*, 462.

[25] Ochsenbein, 'Latein und Deutsch', bases his results too exclusively on a survey of the prayer books which the sisters are recorded to have used, and most of which are now lost. A broader variety of sources discloses a rather different picture.

[26] The importance of liturgy in the context of Dominican convent life has been stressed on many occasions, most recently by Lewis in 'Music and dancing'.

[27] Latin was the language of the liturgy and as such had been fixed by canonical prescriptions since the early Middle Ages: cf. Janota, *Studien zu Funktion und Typus*, 64–71.

[28] Völker, 'Überlieferungsformen mittelalterlicher deutscher Predigten', 212–27.

[29] Ancelet-Hustache, 'Unterlinden', 429.14–31.

[30] Strauch, *Margarethe Ebner*, 44.9–16.

[31] Schröder, *Engelthal*, 2: '*Als sie ze tische sazzen, so saz die meisterin ze oberst. Als sie denne ein wenig gaz, so las sie in teutsche ze tisch.*' ('When they sat down to eat the mistress sat at the head of the table. After she had eaten a bit, she held table readings in German.') The fact that the language of the table reading is mentioned explicitly in a text concerning Engelthal's pre-Dominican practice indicates that this practice was later changed.

[32] Von Kern, 'Die Reformation des Katharinenklosters', 19.4–10. The admonition by Bartholomäus Texerius, written in German, prescribes table readings partly in Latin, partly in the vernacular.

[33] *Mittelalterliche Bibliothekskataloge*, III, 639–70.

[34] Kist, *Das Klarissenkloster in Nürnberg*, 157: '*Item sult ir auch wissen, daz man uns über jar alle tag latein zu tisch lißt und das ist uns gar ein unfüglich und unzimlich ding, besunder wan wir das nit versten*' ('You should also know that every day of the year we have Latin table readings, and this is unsuitable and incongruous because we do not understand them').

[35] There are no extant sources which discuss this matter. Johannes Meyer in his German translation of Humbert's *Liber de officiis*, takes into account circumstances in the convents and compares them to the brothers' habits. He still seems to take Latin table readings for granted, since he quotes the Latin Bible as possible matter for table readings (Johannes Meyer, *Ämterbuch*, Stadtarchiv Freiburg/Br., MS B 1 (H), no. 108, fo. 131v–132r).

[36] Cf. e.g. Vetter, *Töss*, 106.16–19; Strauch, *Margarethe Ebner*, 161–6 (Margarethe Ebner composed a prayer which she recited virtually every day); *Mittelalterliche Bibliothekskataloge*, III, 579–96 (a list of private prayer books the nuns of St Catharine's possessed); Ochsenbein, 'Privatgebetbücher', 379–98.

[37] Ochsenbein, 'Latein und Deutsch', 49.

[38] Cf. e.g. *Mittelalterliche Bibliothekskataloge*, III, 598–638.

[39] Cf. e.g. *Mittelalterliche Bibliothekskataloge*, III, 579–96, 598–638.

[40] Cf. e.g. Reichert, *Acta capitulorum generalium*, I, 47: '*Fratres sibi non faciant scribi psalteria vel alia scripta per moniales. vel alias mulieres.*' ('The brothers should not have nuns or other women write Psalters or other texts for them.') Ritzinger and Scheeben, 'Beiträge', no. 5, 37: '*Scriptrices sedeant cum aliis laborantibus in communi domo, sed hae non scribant aliis, donec conventus habeat libros necessarios.*' ('The copyist should sit in a common room with the other working sisters, but they should not write for outsiders until the convent itself has the necessary books.') Zeller-Werdmüller and Bächtold, 'Ötenbach', 231: '*Es kament (...) drei iunkfrawn, der kond eine schreiben und luminieren, die andre malen (...) Also schribent si und ander swester, daß von luminieren und von schreiben alle jar aus der schreibstuben gieng X mark.*' ('Three virgins arrived, of whom the first was able to write and illuminate, the second, to paint ... Thus they and other sisters copied [books] so that the scriptorium, through illuminating and copying, earned [the convent] ten marks every year.')

[41] Cf. e.g. the lives of the sisters of Adelhausen, Engelthal, St Katharinental, Kirchberg/Haigerloch, Kirchberg/Sulz, Ötenbach, Töss, Unterlinden, Weiler and the visions and revelations of Christine Ebner and Adelheid Langmann (Engelthal) and Margarethe Ebner (Medingen).

[42] Cf. e.g. Ruh, 'Mystische Spekulation in Reimversen', 184–211.

[43] Strauch, *Margarethe Ebner*, no. LVII, 270–1.

[44] Cf. e.g. Bihlmeyer, *Heinrich Seuse, Briefbüchlein*, 360–93.

[45] Cf. Finke, *Ungedruckte Dominikanerbriefe*, 27, n.1: '*Non moveat vos dilacio littere et retencio nuper misse, nam cum latine descripta sit, cuius periciam non habetis, idem vobis portitor et expositor forsitan esse volet.*' ('Do not be troubled by the delay and retention of the letter which I sent recently. As it is written in Latin, which you do not understand, the same man will act as your messenger and maybe your translator.')

[46] Hefele, *Freiburger Urkundenbuch*, II, LXIII–LXVIII.

[47] Bayerisches Hauptstaatsarchiv München, Pettendorfer Urkunden (documents of the former convent of Pettendorf), no. 1–251. The number of documents written in the vernacular gradually increased during the thirteenth to fifteenth centuries.

[48] Cf. e.g. the documents published in Löhr, *Teutonia im 15. Jahrhundert*, no. 41–181, addressed to different convents and priories; and Barthelmé, *La réforme Dominicaine au XVe siècle en Alsace*, 180–5.

[49] Whereas the constitutions only prescribe that very young girls should not be accepted ('*Nulla notabiliter iuvenis recipiatur in sororem*', 'Constitutiones sororum' c. XV, 342), later regulations were much more explicit, cf. Ritzinger and Scheeben, 'Beiträge', no. 5, 32. But even the constitutions prevented any girl younger than twelve from making her vows.

[50] The lives of the sisters often mention girls living in enclosure who are notably younger than twelve, cf. e.g. Vetter, *Töss*, 33.23, 48.10; Roth, 'Kirchberg bei Sulz', 105, 109, 118.

[51] Many girls were only admitted into a Dominican convent with the help of papal bulls; the usual description of such girls in the bulls is '*puellae litteratae*', cf. e.g. Rieder, *Monumenta Vaticana*, who enumerates ten girls from the Constance diocese who were admitted in this way during the fourteenth century (nos. 43, 48, 110, 749, 750, 767, 937, 1049, 1114, 1693). One of them was later rejected by the convent since she was, as it turned out, no '*puella litterata*' (*Urkundenbuch Zürich* XI, no. 4075, 58: '. . . *ipsa Elizabeth falso asseritur litterata*').

[52] Cf. e.g. Langer, *Mystische Erfahrung und spirituelle Theologie*, 109.

[53] [Humbert de Romanis], *Sermones beati Umberti Burgundi*, sermo 97, pp. 96–7.

[54] Christine Ebner, *Offenbarungen*, Württembergische Landesbibliothek, MS Cod. theol. 2° 282, fo. 107r.

[55] Cf. Ringler, *Viten- und Offenbarungsliteratur*, 176.

[56] Schröder, *Engelthal*, 49.

[57] Cf. Du Cange, *Glossarium*, V, 126, 127.

[58] Cf. e.g. Christine Ebner, *Offenbarungen*, Württembergische Landesbibliothek, MS Cod. theol. 2° 282, fo. 42r: '*buch der töhter von syon*' ('book of the daughters of Syon'); fo. 43r, 152v: '*daz buch daz da heisset ein uzzflizzen liht der gotheit*' ('the book which is called the emanating light of the Godhead' [of Mechtild of Magdeburg]).

[59] Cf. e.g. Christine Ebner, *Offenbarungen*, Württembergische Landesbibliothek, MS Cod. theol. 2° 282, fo. 113r, 132r.

[60] St Catharine's, St Gall, MS *Schwesternbuch*, fo. 245r.

[61] Cf. Du Cange, *Glossarium* V, 126, 127.

[62] Ancelet-Hustache, 'Unterlinden', 406.31.

[63] Cf. St Catharine's, St Gall, MS *Schwesternbuch*, fo. 255v.

[64] 'Constitutiones sororum' c. XV, 343.

[65] Creytens, 'Les constitutions primitives', 80: '*Sorores postquam officium ecclesiasticum didicerint diligenter, addiscere poterunt tantum ut quod legitur intelligant*'.

[66] Creytens, 'Les constitutions primitives', 60.

[67] Cf. e.g. Strauch, *Margarethe Ebner*, 44.14–16, 53.22–4.

[68] They used to read the translation of the mass texts and their explanation at least on Sundays, cf. the later catalogue of table readings (1455–1461), *Mittelalterliche Bibliothekskataloge*, III, 651–70.

[69] *Mittelalterliche Bibliothekskataloge*, III, 651.29–31.

[70] Sigs E XVII and EIII. Both MSS are lost.

[71] Sig. EII; Stadtbibliothek Nürnberg, MS Cod. cent. IV, 33: sermons of the Nuremberg preacher Albrecht Fleischmann, cf. Schneider, 'Fleischmann, Albrecht', 748–9.

[72] Sig. F II; Stadtbibliothek Nürnberg, MS Cod. cent. III, 85; cf. Buijssen, *Durandus' Rationale*, [12]–[15]; cf. Steer, 'Geistliche Prosa', 339–70.

[73] Sig. E. XXXVII; Stadtbibliothek Nürnberg, MS Cod. cent. VI, 431, fo. 1r–6v; cf. *Die Handschriften der Stadtbibliothek Nürnberg*, I, 108.

[74] Stadtbibliothek Nürnberg, MS Cod. cent. VI, 46a, fo. 68v: *'Daz ir aber latein nyt verstet daz schat euch nit zu ewiger sellikait wie woll es gar gut wer daz ir daz verstunt'*.

[75] Cf. Ancelet-Hustache, 'Unterlinden'. The inscriptions on the manuscript also indicate a widespread knowledge of Latin (317–18).

[76] *Ibid.*, 364–5.

[77] *Ibid.*, 365.

[78] *Ibid.*, 365.

[79] *Ibid.*, 430–1.

[80] *Ibid.*, 431.

[81] *Ibid.*, 505–6, 508.

[82] Johannes Meyer, *Chronica brevis O. P.*, 74.

[83] Ancelet-Hustache, 'Unterlinden', 506.6–9.

[84] Cf. e.g. König, 'Adelhausen', 167.

[85] Quoted according to: Hinnebusch, *History of the Dominican Order*, II, 4.

[86] Hinnebusch, *History of the Dominican Order*, II, 4.

[87] 'Constitutiones fratrum' c. XIII, 51: '*(ydonei fratres . . . recipiendos in moribus et scientia diligenter examinent.*' ('suitable brothers should carefully examine those who wish to be received [into the order] as to their morals and their knowledge.') Cf. the 'Constitutiones sororum' c. XIV, 342: '*Non recipiatur eciam aliqua. nisi cum diligenti examinacione. facta seorsum de moribus. et vita. et viribus corporalibus. et industria animi.*' ('Also, no girl should be admitted without a careful examination as to her morals, habits, physical strength, and diligence of mind.')

[88] 'Constitutiones fratrum', 162–81.

[89] 'Constitutiones fratrum', c. XIV, 172–3: '*In libris gentilium et phylosophorum non studeant . . . seculares scientias non addiscant: nec artes quas liberales vocant . . . sed tantum libros theologicos tam iuvenes quam alii legant.*' ('They should not study the writings of heathens and philosophers . . . [and] they should not learn the secular sciences: neither the young [monks] nor the others should read the arts called 'liberal', but only theological books.')

[90] Humbert de Romanis, *Expositio super constitutiones fratrum Praedicatorum*, 41: '*Notandum est autem quod studium non est finis ordinis, sed summe necessarium est ad fines . . ., scilicet ad praedicationes, et animarum salutem operandam, quia sine studio neutrum possemus.*' Translation by Hinnebusch, *History of the Dominican Order*, II, 4.

[91] Humbert de Romanis, *Expositio super constitutiones fratrum Praedicatorum*, 41.

[92] Metz, 'Le statut de la femme', 102–3.

[93] 'Constitutiones sororum' c. XXVIII/XXIX, 346–8.

[94] Cf. 'Constitutiones sororum' c. I–III, 339–40.

[95] Finnegan, *The Women of Helfta*, 6.

[96] Gertrude of Helfta, *Legatus*, 1:3.

[97] *Ibid.*, 1:1–3.

[98] *Ibid.*, 1:2.

[99] *Ibid.*, 1; written by a fellow sister: Finnegan, *The Women of Helfta*, 10.

[100] Finnegan, *The Women of Helfta*, 10; cf. also Rosalynn Voaden's essay in this volume.

[101] Finnegan, *The Women of Helfta*, 81. Unfortunately the convent library of Helfta is lost so that it is impossible to find out whether it contained complete works of these authors or combinations of parts of their texts; cf. Krämer, Handschriftenerbe, 343.

[102] Gertrude of Helfta, *The Herald*, 38; cf. Gertrude of Helfta, *Legatus* 1:3 '*tunc recognovit se longe fuisse a Deo in regione dissimilitudinis, dum studiis liberalibus nimis inhaerendo, neglexisset usque ad tempus illud mentis aciem lumini spirituali intelligentiae adaptare, atque humanae sapientiae delectationi avidius adhaerendo, verae sapientiae gustu suavissimo se privasset.*'

[103] Leclercq, *Love of Learning*, 239.

[104] *Ibid.*, 243.

[105] Cf. e.g. the writings of Margarethe Ebner (Strauch, *Margarethe Ebner*, passim) or Adelheid Langmann (Strauch, *Adelheid Langmann*, passim).

[106] Cf. e.g. *Mittelalterliche Bibliothekskataloge*, III, 599–601 (translations of biblical books); 601–2 (explanations of biblical texts, particularly the Ten Commandments); 603–4 (translation of New Testament books); 615–18 (lives of saints); cf. also 604.30–2, 609.5–10, 628.9–30.

[107] Burger, 'Theologie und Laienfrömmigkeit', 404.

[108] Cf. the studies of Köpf, 'Bernhard von Clairvaux' and 'Rezeptions- und Wirkungsgeschichte'.

[109] Köpf, 'Bernhard von Clairvaux', 67; cf. e.g. Strauch, *Margarethe Ebner*, 21.26–22.7.

[110] Köpf, 'Bernhard von Clairvaux', 61–3.

[111] Cf. e.g. *Mittelalterliche Bibliothekskataloge*, III, 627 (sigs. E XVIII, E XXV, E XXVI); 631 (sigs. N XII, N XIIII).

[112] Cf. e.g. *Mittelalterliche Bibliothekskataloge*, III, 601 (sigs. A XIIII).

[113] Cf. Steer, 'Geistliche Prosa', 339–70.

[114] Cf. e.g. Schneider, 'Fleischmann, Albrecht', 748–9.

[115] Cf. e.g. Langer's survey of the relations between Master Eckhart's theology and the spirituality of the Dominican sisters; Langer, *Mystische Erfahrung und spirituelle Theologie*, passim.

[116] Reichert, *Acta capitulorum generalium*, I, 47: '*Nec aliquis fratrum de cetero sermones vel collaciones vel alias sacras scripturas de latino transferat in vulgare.*' ('Besides, none of the brothers should translate sermons or collations or holy writings from the Latin into the vernacular.')

[117] Cf. e.g. Roth, 'Kirchberg bei Sulz', 124; König, 'Adelhausen', 159, 180; Bihlmeyer, 'Weiler', 76.
[118] Gertrude of Helfta, *The Herald*, 38.
[119] Cf. Bynum, *Jesus as Mother*, 87.
[120] Cf. Steer, 'Der Laie als Anreger und Adressat', 354–67.

Bibliography

1. Manuscripts

Bayerisches Hauptstaatsarchiv München, Pettendorfer Urkunden (documents of the former convent of Pettendorf, thirteenth–fifteenth centuries), nos. 1–251.
St Catharine's, Wil: MS *Schwesternbuch* of St Catharine's, St Gall (fifteenth century).
Stadtarchiv Freiburg/Breisgau, MS B 1 (H), no. 108: Johannes Meyer, *Ämterbuch*.
Stadtbibliothek Nürnberg, MS Cod. Cent. VI. 46 a.
Württembergische Landesbibliothek, MS Cod. theol. 2° 282: Christine Ebner, *Offenbarungen* (Revelations).

2. Printed Sources and Secondary Literature

Ancelet-Hustache, J. (ed.), 'Les "Vitae sororum" d'Unterlinden. Édition critique du manuscrit 508 de la Bibliothèque de Colmar', *Archives d'histoire doctrinale et littéraire du moyen âge* 5 (1930), 317–509.
Barthelmé, A., *La réforme Dominicaine au XVe siècle en Alsace et dans l'ensemble de la province de Teutonie* (Strasbourg, 1931).
Bihlmeyer, K. (ed.), 'Mystisches Leben in dem Dominikanerinnenkloster Weiler bei Esslingen im 13. und 14. Jahrhundert', *Württembergische Vierteljahreshefte für Landesgeschichte* n.s. 25 (1916), 61–93.
Bihlmeyer, K. (ed.), *Heinrich Seuse. Deutsche Schriften* (Stuttgart, 1907; reprint: Frankfurt-on-Main, 1961).
Birlinger, A. (ed.), 'Die Nonnen von Kirchberg bei Haigerloch', *Alemannia* 11 (1883), 1–20.
Birlinger, A. (ed.), 'Die Nonnen von St. Katarinental bei Dieszenhofen', *Alemannia* 15 (1887), 150–83.
Buijssen, G. H. (ed.), *Durandus' Rationale in spätmittelhochdeutscher Übersetzung. Die Bücher I–III nach der Hs. CVP 2765* (Assen, 1974).
Burger, C., 'Theologie und Laienfrömmigkeit. Transformationsversuche im Spätmittelalter', in H. Boockmann, B. Moeller and K. Stackmann (eds.), *Lebenslehren und Weltentwürfe im Übergang vom Mittelalter zur Neuzeit. Politik-Bildung-Naturkunde-Theologie. Bericht über Kolloquien der Kommission zur Erforschung der Kultur des Spätmittelalters 1983 bis 1987* (Göttingen, 1989), 400–20.

Bynum, C. W., *Jesus as Mother: Studies in the Spirituality of the High Middle Ages* (Berkeley, 1982).

Bynum, C. W., *Holy Feast and Holy Fast: The Religious Significance of Food to Medieval Women* (Berkeley, 1987).

Du Cange, C., *Glossarium mediae et infimae latinitatis* V, *conditum a Carolo du Fresne, Domino du Cange; auctum a monachis S. Benedicti, cum supplementis integris D. P. Carpenterii, Adelungii, aliorum, suisque digessit G. A. L. Henschel, editio nova aucta pluribus verbis aliorum scriptorum a L. Favre* (Niort, 1885).

'Constitutiones Sororum Ordinis Fratrum Praedicatorum', *Analecta Sacri Ordinis Praedicatorum* 3 (1897/98), 338–48.

Creytens, R., 'Les constitutions primitives des soeurs dominicaines de Montargis', *Archivum Fratrum Praedicatorum* 17 (1947), 41–84.

Denifle, H. S., 'Über die Anfänge der Predigtweise der deutschen Mystiker', *Archiv für Litteratur- und Kirchengeschichte des Mittelalters* 2 (1886), 641–52.

Doyère, P. (ed.), *Gertrud d'Helfta. Oeuvres spirituelles* II: *Le Hèraut (livres I et II)* (Paris, 1968).

Escher, J. and Schweizer, P. (eds.), *Urkundenbuch der Stadt und Landschaft Zürich*, IX: 1326–1336 (Zurich, 1920)

Finke, H. (ed.), *Ungedruckte Dominikanerbriefe des 13. Jahrhunderts* (Paderborn, 1891).

Finnegan, M. J., *The Women of Helfta: Scholars and Mystics* (Athens, Georgia, 1991).

Fontette, M. de., *Les religieuses a l'âge classique du droit canon. Recherches sur les structures juridiques des branches féminines des ordres* (Paris, 1967).

Freed, J. B., 'Urban development and the "Cura Monialium" in thirteenth-century Germany', *Viator* 3 (1972), 311–27.

Gertrude the Great, *Legatus divinae pietatis*, in *Revelationes Gertrudianae ac Mechtildianae*, I, ed. Dom L. Paquelin (Paris, 1875).

Gertrude the Great, *The Herald of God's Loving Kindness: Books One and Two*, trans. and ed. A. Barratt (Kalamazoo, 1991).

Grundmann, H., *Religiöse Bewegungen im Mittelalter. Untersuchungen über die geschichtlichen Zusammenhänge zwischen der Ketzerei, den Bettelorden und der religiösen Frauenbewegung im 12. und 13. Jahrhundert und über die geschichtlichen Grundlagen der deutschen Mystik. Anhang: Neue Beiträge zur Geschichte der der religiösen Bewegungen im Mittelalter* (2nd edn., Hildesheim, 1961).

Die Handschriften der Stadtbibliothek Nürnberg I: *Die deutschen mittelalterlichen Handschriften,* described by K. Schneider (Wiesbaden, 1965).

Hefele, F. (ed.), *Freiburger Urkundenbuch* II (Freiburg/Breisgau, 1951).

Hinnebusch, W. A., *The History of the Dominican Order* I: *Origins and Growth to 1500* (New York, 1966).

Hinnebusch, W. A., *The History of the Dominican Order* II: *Intellectual and Cultural Life to 1500* (New York, 1973).

[Humbert de Romanis], *Sermones beati Umberti Burgundi, Instituti Praedicatorum Generalis Magistri in ordine Quinti. In duabus partes divisi, Quibus habetur in promptu magna materia ad praedicandum, vel conferendum de Deo, sive ad omne genus hominum, sive in omni diversitate negotiorum sive secundum varietatem temporum, aut festorum. Concionatoribus Parochis, et quibusvis personis maxime utiles, cum sint summa doctrina, pietate, sacraeque scripturae sensibus referti* (Venice, 1603).

Humbert de Romanis, 'Instructiones de officiis ordinis' and 'Expositio super constitutiones fratrum Praedicatorum', in J. J. Berthier (ed.), *B. Humberti de Romanis Quinti Magistri Generalis Opera de vita regulari* II (Rome, 1889).

Janota, J., *Studien zu Funktion und Typus des deutschen geistlichen Liedes im Mittelalter* (Munich, 1968).

Kern, T. v. (ed.), 'Die Reformation des Katharinenklosters zu Nürnberg im Jahre 1428', *Jahresbericht des historischen Vereins in Mittelfranken* 31 (1863), 1–20.

Kist, J., *Das Klarissenkloster in Nürnberg bis zum Beginn des 16. Jahrhunderts* (Nuremberg, 1929).

König, J. (ed.), 'Die Chronik der Anna von Munzingen. Nach der ältesten Abschrift mit Einleitung und Beilagen', *Freiburger Diözesanarchiv* 13 (1880), 129–236 [='Adelhausen'].

Köpf, U., 'Bernhard von Clairvaux in der Frauenmystik', in P. Dinzelbacher and D. R. Bauer (eds.), *Frauenmystik im Mittelalter* (Ostfildern, 1985), 48–77.

Köpf, U., 'Die Rezeptions- und Wirkungsgeschichte Bernhard von Clairvaux. Forschungsstand und Forschungsaufgaben', in K. Elm (ed.), *Bernhard von Clairvaux. Rezeption und Wirkung im Mittelalter und der Neuzeit* (Wiesbaden, 1994), 5–65.

Krämer, S., *Handschriftenerbe des deutschen Mittelalters, Teil 1: Aachen–Kochel* (Munich, 1989)

Langer, O., *Mystische Erfahrung und spirituelle Theologie. Zu Meister Eckharts Auseinandersetzung mit der Frauenfrömmigkeit seiner Zeit* (Munich, 1987).

Leclercq, J., *The Love of Learning and the Desire for God. A Study of Monastic Culture* (2nd edn., New York, 1974).

Leclercq, J., 'Feminine monasticism in the twelfth and thirteenth centuries', in W. Skudlarek (ed.), *The Continuing Quest for God. Monastic Spirituality in Tradition and Transition* (Collegeville, 1982), 115–26.

Lewis, G., 'Music and dancing in the fourteenth-century Sister-Books', in A. Clark *et al.* (eds.), *Vox Mystica: Essays on Medieval Mysticism in Honour of Professor Valerie M. Lagorio* (Cambridge, 1995), 159–69.

'Liber Constitutionum Ordinis Fratrum Praedicatorum', *Analecta Sacri Ordinis Praedicatorum* 3 (1897/98), 26–60, 98–122, 162–81.

Löhr, G. M., *Die Teutonia im 15. Jahrhundert. Studien und Texte vornehmlich zur Geschichte ihrer Reform* (Leipzig, 1924).

Metz, R., 'Le statut de la femme en droit canonique médiéval', *La femme* 2 (Brussels, 1962), 59–113.

Ochsenbein, P., 'Deutschsprachige Privatgebetbücher vor 1400', in V. Honemann and N. F. Palmer (eds.), *Deutsche Handschriften 1100–1400. Oxforder Kolloquium 1985* (Tubingen, 1988), 379–98.

Ochsenbein, P., 'Latein und Deutsch im Alltag oberrheinischer Dominikanerinnenklöster des Spätmittelalters', in N. Henkel and N. F. Palmer (eds.), *Latein und Volkssprache im deutschen Mittelalter. Regensburger Kolloquium 1988* (Tübingen, 1992), 42–51.

Reichert, B. M. (ed.), *Acta capitulorum generalium Ordinis Praedicatorum* I: *Abanno 1220 usque ad annum 1303* (Rome, 1898).

Rieder, K. (ed.), *Monumenta Vaticana historiam episcopatus Constantiensis in Germania illustrantia. Römische Quellen zur Konstanzer Bistumsgeschichte zur Zeit der Päpste in Avignon 1305–1378* (Innsbruck, 1908).

Ringler, S., *Viten- und Offenbarungsliteratur in Frauenklöstern des Mittelalters. Quellen und Studien* (Munich, 1980).

Ritzinger, E. and Scheeben, H. C. (eds.), 'Beiträge zur Geschichte der Teutonia in der zweiten Hälfte des 13. Jahrhunderts', *Archiv der deutschen Dominikaner* 3 (1941), 11–95.

Roth, F. W. E. (ed.), 'Aufzeichnungen über das mystische Leben der Nonnen von Kirchberg bei Sulz im 14. und 15. Jahrhundert', *Alemannia* 21 (1893), 103–48.

Ruf, P. (ed.), *Mittelalterliche Bibliothekskataloge Deutschlands und der Schweiz* III: 'Nürnberg, Dominikanerinnenkloster St. Katharina' (Munich, 1932), 570–670.

Ruh, K., 'Mystische Spekulation in Reimversen des 14. Jahrhunderts', in V. Mertens (ed.), *Kurt Ruh, Kleine Schriften* II: *Scholastik und Mystik im pätmittelalter* (Berlin, 1984), 184–211.

Scheeben, H. C. (ed.), *Johannes Meyer O.P., Chronica brevis Ordinis Praedicatorum* (Leipzig/Vechta, 1933).

Schneider, K., 'Fleischmann, Albrecht', *Die deutsche Literatur des Mittelalters. Verfasserlexikon* II (2nd edn., Berlin, 1980), 748–9.

Schröder, K. (ed.), *Der Nonne von Engelthal Büchlein von der Genaden Uberlast* (Stuttgart, 1871).

Steer, G., 'Der Laie als Anreger und Adressat deutscher Prosaliteratur im 14. Jahrhundert', in W. Haug, T. R. Jackson and J. Janota (eds.), *Zur deutschen Literatur und Sprache des 14. Jahrhunderts. Dubliner Colloquium 1981* (Heidelberg, 1983), 354–67.

Steer, G., 'Geistliche Prosa', in I. Glier (ed.), *Die deutsche Literatur im späten Mittelalter, 1250–1370* II: *Reimpaargedichte, Drama, Prosa* (Munich, 1987), 306–70.

Strauch, P. (ed.), *Die Offenbarungen der Adelheid Langmann, Klosterfrau zu Engelthal* (Strasbourg, 1878).

Strauch, P. (ed.), *Margarethe Ebner und Heinrich von Nördlingen. Ein Beitrag zur Geschichte der deutschen Mystik* (Freiburg/Breisgau, 1882).

Vetter, F. (ed.), *Das Leben der Schwestern zu Töß* (Berlin, 1906).

Vetter, F. (ed.), *Die Predigten Taulers aus der Engelberger und der Freiburger Handschrift sowie aus Schmidts Abschriften der ehemaligen Straßburger Handschriften* (Berlin, 1910).

Völker, P.-G., 'Die Überlieferungsformen mittelalterlicher deutscher Predigten', *Zeitschrift für deutsches Altertum und deutsche Literatur* 92 (1963), 212–27.

Walz, A. (ed.), *Beati Iordani de Saxonia Epistulae* (Rome, 1951).

Wilms, H., *Das älteste Verzeichnis der deutschen Dominikanerinnenklöster* (Leipzig, 1924).

Zeller-Werdmüller, H. and Bächtold, J. (eds.), 'Die Stiftung des Klosters Ötenbach und das Leben der sel. Schwestern daselbst', *Zürcher Taschenbuch auf das Jahr 1888,* n.s. 12 (1889), 213–76.

3

All Girls Together: Community, Gender and Vision at Helfta[1]

ROSALYNN VOADEN

G ERTRUDE the Great of Helfta had a vision which began when
Christ told her:

> 'I have given to everyone a golden pipe of such power that she may draw
> whatever she desires from the infinite depths of my divine heart' . . . Then
> she perceived that the members of the community standing round the Lord
> were drawing draughts of divine grace for themselves . . . through the pipe
> which had been given them . . . And some appeared to be drawing directly
> from the interior of the divine heart.[2]

This graphic image offers an evocative representation of life in the
convent of Helfta in the closing decades of the thirteenth century: a
community of women, united in drawing spiritual nourishment from the
Sacred Heart, sharing a devotion directly inspired by the visions of three
of their number. The convent of Helfta, near Eisleben in Saxony, was
at this time a remarkable centre of women's piety and learning, and home
to three very influential visionaries – Mechtild of Magdeburg, Mechtild
of Hackeborn and Gertrude the Great, all of whom recorded their
revelations in some of the most vivid religious prose to survive from the
Middle Ages.[3] Mechtild of Hackeborn and Gertrude are also generally
credited with providing the impetus for the development of the cult of
the Sacred Heart, which achieved its most definitive medieval expression
in the visionary writings of these nuns of Helfta.[4]

The cult of the Sacred Heart as it evolved at Helfta gave spiritual
expression to the strong sense of female authority and ability which the
environment at the convent seems to have encouraged and supported.
Caroline Bynum speculates that women raised in convents, as were
Gertrude and Mechtild of Hackeborn, were less likely than their lay
contemporaries to be influenced by stereotyping of women as

intellectually and morally inferior.[5] I would like to expand this notion, and suggest that the sense of intellectual and moral authority which seems to have existed amongst the women at Helfta resulted in a mystical discourse incorporating two of the cardinal elements of their experience: membership in a community and biological femaleness. It is important to remember that although these nuns were dedicated to Christ and saw themselves as vessels for the divine word, they were also flesh and blood women living in a closed community. This awareness and experience provided them with evocative words and powerful images to communicate their visions. And out of this awareness and experience evolved the discourse which shaped the cult of the Sacred Heart at Helfta.

It is useful at this point in the essay to survey the evolution of the devotion to the Sacred Heart, and to consider briefly some of the principal characteristics of the cult as it developed at Helfta. The origin of the devotion to the Wounded Side and the Sacred Heart lies principally in exegetical interpretations of John 7: 38, 'Out of his belly shall flow rivers of living water', and of the *Song of Songs* 2: 14, 'My dove in the clefts of the rock, in the hollow places of the wall, shew me thy face . . .', and 4: 9, 'Thou hast wounded my heart, my sister, my spouse . . .'

It is a development of the veneration of the Five Wounds of Christ, which, by the second half of the twelfth century, was focused principally on the Wounded Side as the source of the sacraments and as the entrance to the Sacred Heart.[6] The Venerable Bede, Aelred of Rievaulx, Guerric of Igny, Adam of Perseigne, and Bernard of Clairvaux, among others, commented on the Wounds of Christ and the Sacred Heart. Bernard in particular, in his Sermons on the *Song of Songs*, helped to popularize the cult of the Sacred Heart. In 'Sermon 61', for example, he wrote:

> The secret of his heart is laid open through the clefts of his body; that mighty mystery of loving is laid open . . . God . . . has even led us by the open clefts into the holy place.[7]

The cult of the Sacred Heart found its most ardent medieval devotees in German and Belgian convents in the twelfth and thirteenth centuries. Mechtild of Hackeborn and Gertrude the Great at Helfta were probably its most active proponents.[8] In the development of the cult at Helfta those features of the original veneration which were focused on and expanded were those which reflected the consciousness of a community of women. One of the features which became a nucleus for devotional expression was the image of the Sacred Heart as a place of shelter, a home for the community of the faithful, a sanctuary where they could be comforted and restored. One night Mechtild of Hackeborn, suffering from a severe headache, asked Christ for solace.

> Our Lord then showed her the wound in his heart and said, 'Go in here, so that you may rest'. And she entered with great gladness and joy into the heart of God which was like a most beautiful house . . . Then it seemed to her that there were as many silken pillows there as she had previously had painful throbbings in her head.[9]

Another way in which the cult reflected the environment at Helfta is that the Sacred Heart became a site of female biological characteristics: it bleeds, it flows, it opens, it encloses. Sometimes it is quite overwhelmingly fleshly. Medieval illustrations of the Sacred Heart resemble nothing so much as a vagina. The wound was graphically represented as a slit between two gaping edges; sometimes, but not always, drops of blood were shown emerging. One of Gertrude's revelations offered a particularly vivid description of the wound in the Heart, a description replete with female imagery.

> And immediately I saw you opening with both hands the wound of your deified heart, the Tabernacle of divine faithfulness and infallible truth, and commanding me to stretch forth my right hand. Then, contracting the aperture of the wound in which my hand was enclosed, you said 'See, I promise to keep intact the gifts which I have given you.'[10]

The strong sense of female community which evidently existed at Helfta enabled the visionaries of Helfta to appropriate traditional discourses reducing women to corporeal, impure essences, and to transform those discourses by inscribing the female on to the divine. The discourse of the Sacred Heart as it appears in the writings of the visionaries of Helfta, employs images drawn from biological *female* characteristics – blood, flowing, opening and enclosure – rather than culturally determined *feminine* characteristics such as compassion and nurturing. These latter characteristics were almost a commonplace in later medieval devotional works designed to stimulate affective piety, works which encouraged identification with the humanity of Christ, and movement towards a loving God. Such works presented Christ as gentle, non-threatening, nourishing, and compassionate, and specifically related these qualities to motherhood.[11] While some of these works used images drawn from physical aspects of maternity – lactating, pain in labour, and weaning were the most common – it was their association with motherhood which justified their use in this context, not their association with a woman's body. In other words, the feminization of Christ was largely achieved by separating the cultural concept of motherhood from the biological reality of female corporeality. Jesus as Mother did not have a great deal to do with women; it did have a lot to do with how men thought a woman would be if only she were 'more like a man'.

At Helfta, Mechtild of Hackeborn and Gertrude the Great subverted this traditional separation of feminine from female in their representations of the Sacred Heart. As befits a group of women dedicated to virginity, that is, rejecting the possibility of motherhood, maternal images are not highly privileged in their meditations. Such images are certainly used, but no more frequently than images of paternity or nobility, for example, and much less than nuptial and bridal imagery. The visionary writings of the nuns of Helfta reflect a positive sense of self which perhaps diminished the impact of misogynistic perceptions of their female corporeality and gave them confidence in their spiritual authority.

In this essay I first offer evidence that the community at Helfta was, in fact, a place of mutual support, spiritual reassurance and practical assistance. It was an environment which encouraged as well as facilitated the cult of the Sacred Heart, a devotion celebrating the community of the faithful, focusing on massed gatherings, on inclusivity, on interconnection, on the many rather than on the one. Although some of this evidence is taken from historical records, the bulk of it is drawn from the writings of the three visionaries: Mechtild of Hackeborn, Mechtild of Magdeburg and Gertrude the Great. In the second part of the essay I explore, in the writings of the Helfta visionaries, a phenomenon which I consider was fostered by their experience in this close community of spiritual women: the attribution to Christ of physical female characteristics which are not primarily maternal; that is to say, the inscription of the female on to the divine in the cult of the Sacred Heart at Helfta.

The convent of Helfta was founded at Mansfeld in Germany in 1229. There is a lukewarm dispute among modern historians over whether its affiliation was Benedictine or Cistercian, but current consensus is that this is a relatively meaningless issue, and that, while the nuns were not officially incorporated into the Cistercian order, they did follow Cistercian practices and were strongly influenced by the spirituality of

Citeaux.[12] By the late thirteenth century, the period this essay is concerned with, the spiritual advisors to the nuns were Dominicans from the nearby town of Halle.[13] Helfta was chiefly notable for two things in the closing decades of the thirteenth century: the high level of learning and culture there, and the presence of three noted visionaries – Mechtild of Magdeburg, Mechtild of Hackeborn, and Gertrude, later to be given the soubriquet 'the Great'.

It was under the supervision of the abbess Gertrude of Hackeborn that Helfta flourished and established itself as a centre of both women's learning and spirituality.[14] Gertrude of Hackeborn was elected abbess in 1251 at the age of nineteen, and ruled the community – which numbered close to one hundred by the end of her rule – for forty years. She was obviously a gifted abbess, and earned great praise. It was her expressed intention that the nuns of Helfta should be educated and cultured: she stated that should the study of letters be neglected, soon the Scriptures would no longer be understood and monastic life would decay.[15] Novices were instructed in the subjects of the *trivium* (grammar, rhetoric and logic) and some advanced to the *quadrivium* (arithmetic, geometry, astronomy, music). The writings from Helfta demonstrate familiarity with the Church fathers, and with theologians such as Bernard of Clairvaux, Aquinas and the Victorines. In addition, the nuns of Helfta copied and illuminated manuscripts, produced exquisite embroidery and significant music. All the records and representations of Helfta agree in portraying a harmonious community which stimulated both intellectual and spiritual growth, a community where women were encouraged and empowered. This was all the more remarkable in that it occurred at a time of civil and religious unrest, when the convent was several times menaced by the proximity of armies or of marauding barons.

From 1270 to the close of the century, Helfta was a centre of visionary activity which seems to have permeated the community and resulted in what Caroline Bynum describes as 'a conscious effort to establish and hand on to a next generation of sisters, and to readers outside the cloister a spiritual teaching and a collective reputation'.[16] A brief chronology will help to trace the evolution of this complex and intertwined communal transcendentalism.

In 1270, Mechtild of Magdeburg sought refuge at Helfta after spending most of her life as a beguine at Magdeburg. She probably acted as the catalyst for the visionary activity at Helfta. She had experienced visions from the age of twelve, but it was not until 1250, when she was in her early forties, that she felt compelled to make a record of her experiences. In this she was encouraged by her confessor, Heinrich of Halle. The result was the first six books of *Das fliessende Licht der Gottheit* (*The Flowing Light of the Godhead*), an account of the revelations made to Mechtild, an account that is a lyrical, often erotic, celebration of the love of God for the soul. This work was written in Middle Low German, edited by her spiritual director, the Dominican Heinrich of Halle, and circulated fairly widely. It excited considerable controversy, to the extent that, on the advice of her spiritual director, she sought shelter at Helfta in 1270, in her early sixties.[17] Presumably, he felt that enclosure would afford the visionary both protection and the respectability which her status as a beguine failed to provide. Her works were undoubtedly already known to the nuns of Helfta, and during her time there she composed a seventh book of *Das fliessende Licht* which, because of the blindness which struck soon after her arrival, was dictated to another nun.

At the time of Mechtild's arrival at Helfta, Mechtild of Hackeborn was about thirty, and Gertrude was fourteen. Both had entered the convent as small children – Gertrude at five, and Mechtild at seven. Their upbringing within the secure, enlightened atmosphere of Helfta convent had a positive influence on their sense of self as women and spiritual beings. Subsequent to Mechtild of Magdeburg's arrival both Mechtild of Hackeborn and Gertrude experienced visions. Gertrude's began at age twenty-five, when she had a conversion experience.[18] Previously, as she herself tells us, she had been a lukewarm nun, deriving her greatest pleasure from the study of classical literature.[19] Following her conversion experience, she abandoned her classical studies, and gave all her intelligence to spiritual works. She also continued to have revelations and in 1289 she felt compelled to write them down. This work became Book Two of the *Legatus divinae pietatis* (*The Herald of God's Loving-Kindness*). The remainder of the *Legatus*, which functions in part as a spiritual biography of Gertrude and in part as a record of further revelations, was written by another nun.

This same nun – who will be called the Third Nun – also assisted in recording the revelations of Mechtild of Hackeborn, which were entitled the *Liber specialis gratiae* (*The Book of Special Grace*).[20] We do not know exactly when Mechtild started having visions, except that it was a number of years before they were written down in 1291. They were written by Gertrude and the Third Nun, at first without Mechtild's knowledge, and then, following a vision in which Christ told her of his desire that they be committed to writing, with her assistance.[21]

The interconnectedness of the three visionaries is evident in their work. All three mention the others; they consult the others about their visions, they give each other spiritual testimonials, they enquire of God on each other's behalf. There are similar images, echoes of language, reflections of each other's visions. This is particularly evident in the works of Mechtild of Hackeborn, Gertrude and the Third Nun. Because Mechtild of Magdeburg had written the bulk of her revelations before coming to Helfta, only Book Seven of *Das fliessende Licht*, written at Helfta with the aid of another nun, reflects the influence of the communal life on the elderly visionary.

It is clear that the nuns valued the ties of affection and shared devotion as a means of intensifying their spiritual experiences and deepening their understanding. After Gertrude had been internally imprinted with the stigmata, she wrote of sitting in the refectory at supper beside 'a certain person' – probably Mechtild of Hackeborn – to whom she had revealed her secret.[22]

> I often felt the fervour of my devotion increased by such an interchange. Whether it was your spirit, Lord, that prompted this, or human affection, is not clear to me. I have, however, heard from someone skilled in such matters that such a secret may be more profitably revealed to someone who is not only a close friend by reason of her faithful goodness but also a superior by reason of the respect due to greater age.[23]

It seems that Gertrude was unconcerned about distinguishing between the effect of the spirit of God and the effect of the spirit of friendship; in her view, both worked in harmony to lead her to heightened spiritual awareness.

The nuns were also accustomed to guide each other in their devotions and share the benefits of their divine communion. Gertrude recounts seeking advice as to how she should respond to Christ's imprinting of his wound in her own heart. She went to a sister – again, probably Mechtild of Hackeborn – whom she describes as having 'attuned her inner ear more reliably and sensitively than I have, I am afraid, to catch the continual flow of [Christ's] loving whispers'.[24] On another occasion, Gertrude had a vision in which Christ offered her remission of future sins in exchange for any act offered in memory of his mercy; she asked if the same benefit could be extended to other sisters, and Christ agreed.[25]

Mechtild of Hackeborn was described by Gertrude and the Third Nun as sharing the spiritual consolation she had received from God with all those who asked for her guidance. They wrote:

> Let God be blessed, who has given us such a mediator with himself, who shows herself the tender mother of the unfortunate by her continual prayers, her zealous instruction and her consolation.[26]

Although this passage could be read as a conventional enumeration of Mechtild's virtues, the countless examples in her revelations of her practical concern for her fellow nuns, and accounts of her deeds on their behalf defy such an interpretation. For example, on one occasion Mechtild asked Christ, at the request of another nun, whether she was receiving communion too often, and whether there was any danger in this.[27] Her caring for her fellow nuns went beyond concern for their spiritual welfare alone, and reveals an understanding of the importance of harmony in the community. She spoke with Christ about a sister who was troubled by ill-feeling from another nun;[28] another time Mechtild asked Him to comfort a sister who was sad and troubled.[29] On the latter occasion it is interesting that Christ's response stressed the importance of family relationships.

> I am to her a father in creation; I am to her a mother in redemption, I am to her a brother in the dividing of my kingdom; and I am to her a sister in sweet fellowship.[30]

The community of Helfta offered its members the support of a family, and the sisterhood of nuns provided 'sweet fellowship'.

Inevitably, all was not entirely sweetness and light, and occasional glimpses of the inevitable tensions which arise in any community lend an entirely human credibility to the depiction of Helfta in the writings. For instance, there are accounts which reveal despair, anger, and competitiveness among the sisters. There are even occasional gentle rebukes. In one such case, the Third Nun wrote of a vision of Mechtild of Hackeborn, in which she saw Gertrude walking back and forth before the throne of God, who praised her extravagantly, concluding 'her whole life yields praise and glory to me'. Mechtild, somewhat tartly, then said, 'My Lord, if her life is like this, why then is she able to judge rather severely on occasion the aberrations and faults of others?'[31]

Although this last example perhaps reveals a slight strain between Gertrude and Mechtild, more important is the fact that it shows Gertrude as the subject of one of Mechtild's visions. In addition to documenting the entwined devotional lives of the visionaries of Helfta, their writing offers striking evidence that they discussed their visionary experiences with each other, and, as above, figured in each other's visions. Such evidence is to be found not only in the descriptions of the experiences themselves, but also in the language which the nuns employed in those descriptions.

One of the most vivid examples of this mystical mutuality occurs when Gertrude, and Mechtild, separately, experienced mystical union. Mechtild described a vision where she was swept up into a house which she knew to be the heart of Christ.

> And she fell prostrate onto the earth, and on the pavement where she fell was a great cross . . . And from the middle of that cross came a sharp golden dart and pierced her through the heart.[32]

Gertrude achieved mystical union when she had just received the sacrament, and was returning to her place in the choir. She described it thus:

> It seemed to me as if something like a ray of sun came out from the right hand side of the crucified Christ . . . that is from the wound in the side. It had a sharp point like an arrow, and, astonishingly, it stretched forward, and, lingering thus for a while, it gently elicited my love.[33]

Common images and allegories also occur; of course, these are understandable and inevitable given the collective authorship of the *Legatus* and the *Liber*. However, these commonalties do emphasize the shared experience of the visionaries and the sense that these experiences are rooted in the community. Even the physical features of the convent are captured in the visions. Gertrude described herself sitting, in physical reality, in the courtyard at Helfta.

> I had gone into the courtyard before Prime, and was sitting beside the fish-pond absorbed by the pleasantness of the place. The crystalline water flowing through, the fresh green trees standing around, the freedom of the birds, especially of the doves, wheeling in flight, all gave me pleasure . . .[34]

This earthly experience is reflected in some of Mechtild of Hackeborn's revelations. In the *Liber* she described a vision of crystal waters in which swam 'a great multitude of fish with scales all of gold'.[35] In another vision, she saw a well of pure water, with trees all around at the base of a hill where there is 'a great multitude of angels, flying like birds, with bells of gold giving a wonderfully sweet sound'.[36]

All three of the visionaries had visions of other members of the community, both individually and together. Gertrude saw both Mechtild of Magdeburg and Mechtild of Hackeborn after their deaths; Mechtild of Hackeborn saw her sister, the Abbess Gertrude, surrounded by the choirs of heaven; Mechtild of Magdeburg had a vision of the entire community being chosen by God to be 'shining mirrors on earth and sparkling mirrors in Heaven'.[37] All these images suggest that the community was spiritually united, and that the prayers and revelations of one were believed to profit the whole. The effect of a lack of companionship is correspondingly reflected in the works of Mechtild of Magdeburg, who spent the greater part of her life in some isolation as a beguine, and therefore did not enjoy the benefits of community living until her old age. This lack is manifested in her writing in frequent images of loneliness and marginality. However, in the revelations written after her arrival at Helfta she frequently extolled the merits of the community. One particularly telling example is a lovely allegory entitled 'Concerning a Spiritual Convent', in which each of the officers of the convent – abbess, cellarmistress, stewardess, and so on – personify various virtues. The verse concludes:

> Whoever wants to enter the convent
> Must live in divine joy,
> Here and in eternal life.
> Happy are they
> Who remain therein.[38]

Similarly, Gertrude wrote that those sisters who move toward God holding each other's hands approach most closely the divine radiance.[39] And Mechtild of Hackeborn described a joyful vision in which she saw the entire community dancing around the Abbess Gertrude on the anniversary of her death. The song that they sang, *O Mater nostra*, entered into Christ's heart and emerged as a divine melody. Thus, in Mechtild's vision, the many were united through the Sacred Heart into a single harmony, just as in the convent the community was united in devotion.

It was this supportive and harmonious environment which enabled Gertrude the Great and Mechtild of Hackeborn to develop their sense of spiritual authority and to appropriate a wide range of activities which were traditionally gendered masculine. For example, both advised their fellow nuns on such matters as confession, absolution and taking communion. In their visions, both Mechtild and Gertrude participated in administering the sacrament. Neither Mechtild of Hackeborn, Gertrude, nor the Third Nun used *topoi* of weak women or frail females. In this they differed from the majority of women visionaries; Hildegard of Bingen, for example, characterized herself as *paupercula femina*, a poor little female creature, even though she advised popes and emperors. The Helfta visionaries did not present themselves as women – their gender was not an issue, just as it was not an issue for their male contemporaries. If they are weak it is only in the sense that all sinners are weak. They do not apologize for their writing or for their visions on the grounds of their sex. It is highly significant that neither the *Legatus* nor the *Liber* mentions consultation with spiritual directors. In this these works are unusual, since most women's visionary writing integrates reference to approval by ecclesiastical authorities with the text of the revelations.[40] It is also worth noting that both the *Liber* and the *Legatus* were written by women of the community, in Latin.[41] No male scribes or translators seem to have been involved.[42]

Indeed, members of the clergy are hardly mentioned in either the *Legatus* or the *Liber*, and certainly not in any advisory capacity. Instead, both Gertrude and Mechtild of Hackeborn at times took on, either in their visions or in life, quasi-clerical roles. For example, Mechtild, in a vision, administered the chalice to the court of Heaven; Gertrude, when no priest was available to hear their confession, was encouraged by God to absolve her sisters of their sins, so that they could take communion.

In this light it is instructive to consider Mechtild of Magdeburg, most of whose life was spent outside the convent; she serves as a striking contrast to her younger sisters. Although, like all visionaries, she felt compelled to communicate her visions, she often identifies herself as weak, or frail, or unfit to write because she is a woman. In her visions she is often the outsider, the Poor Soul at the Court of Heaven, dazzled by the glory. She mentions her spiritual director, and records his encouragement of her writing. Her spiritual director, Heinrich of Halle, almost certainly arranged and edited her visions; they were later translated into Latin by Dominican friars. Additionally, Mechtild of Magdeburg had a more traditional approach to the devotion of the Sacred Heart, and images of the heart and the wounded side do not feature prominently in her work. When such images do appear, they are often concrete and graphic rather than symbolic, and serve to provoke identification with Christ's pain and suffering. For example, she had a vision in which Christ showed her his wounds.

God revealed Himself to my soul and showed me the wounds in His heart, saying: 'Behold how they have wounded Me!' My soul replied: 'Alas, Lord, why did you suffer such great pain?'. . . Our Lord replied:

'My body was humanly dead
At the moment that My heart's blood
Flowed from My sides with the rays of the
Divinity'.[43]

Mechtild of Magdeburg's visions of the Sacred Heart, even those she recorded after coming to Helfta, reveal little of the female imagery which is so much a part of the revelations of Gertrude and Mechtild of Hackeborn.

In contrast, the visions and images of the Sacred Heart of both Gertrude and Mechtild of Hackeborn are extraordinarily rich and varied – and numerous. I intend to concentrate on those which reflect female biology: images of enclosure, of blood, of flowing, of the vagina.

Women were – and usually still are – far more likely than men to be confined to the house, to be kept inside by domestic chores, maternal responsibilities, and patriarchal restrictions. As nuns they were cloistered, not permitted the wandering life of the friar or the public exposure of the preacher. In general women are culturally enclosed to a far greater extent than men.[44] They are also biologically enclosing; there is a space within women which can be entered, a space where children are conceived, sheltered and nourished. The Helfta visionaries, especially Mechtild of Hackeborn, frequently depicted the Sacred Heart as a house. There is something particularly female in their use of this image, in their focus on that space within, their sense of love being enclosed within, of union and creation occurring inside. Mechtild of Hackeborn had a vision which is so labyrinthine in its portrayal of mutual enclosure that it almost defies comprehension. She saw a great house, wonderfully built, and within that great house was a little house made of cedar, and covered with plates of silver. Christ sat in the middle of the little house. She understood the great house to be Christ's heart, and the little house to be her own heart, which enclosed Christ. So the Sacred Heart enclosed Mechtild, whose heart in turn enclosed Christ. This complex mutual indwelling is reminiscent of those Russian dolls which nest inside each other.[45]

Gertrude characterized the Sacred Heart as 'eternal solstice, safe dwelling place . . . heavenly garden of eternal delights'.[46] In one vision Christ not only invited her into his heart, but also told her: 'now look among the other parts of my body and choose for yourself other places in which you can lead the monastic life, because from now on my body will be your cloister.' She chose his feet for a hall, his hands for a workshop, his mouth for a parlour, his eyes for a library and his ears for a confessional.[47]

Gertrude also had visions in which she took Christ into the shelter of her own heart.

> You granted me the grace of understanding that, abused and harassed by all and sundry, you were asking me . . . for a dwelling place to rest in. For the next three days, whenever I returned to my heart I saw you in the likeness of a sick man reclining on my breast.[48]

There is one vision in the *Liber specialis gratiae* which some might claim dramatically reflects a (pre-feminist) woman's sensibility. In this vision, entitled *De coquina Domini*, Christ, speaking to Mechtild of Hackeborn, likened his heart to a kitchen.

> My kitchen is my divine heart; as a kitchen in a home is shared and open to all, to slaves as well as to the free, so my heart stands open to all, ready to fulfil their desires.[49]

Although it may be true that women are aware of the kitchen in a way which most men are not, and that kitchens, like women, are the source of nourishment, this vision also incorporates those images of enclosure which are so much a part of the visions of the Helfta nuns. Here the kitchen is clearly located within the house, the room surrounded by the building just as the Sacred Heart or a woman's womb is surrounded by the body.

Whereas Mechtild of Hackeborn tended to have visions in which she, or others, entered into the Sacred Heart, Gertrude's visions principally celebrated the union of her heart with Christ's within their bodies. Frequently this was accompanied by an exchange of fluid. Christ told her:

> From her [Gertrude's] childhood I have borne and carried her in my embrace, keeping her unspotted for myself, until the moment when she joined herself to me with her whole will; and then in turn I gave myself completely, with all the strength that is mine as God, to her embrace. For this reason her heart's burning love for me ceaselessly caused my inmost being to melt into her, so much so that as fat melts in the fire, so the sweetness of my divine Heart melted by the heat of her heart, is distilled continuously in to her soul.[50]

But the most important fluid featuring in the visions of the nuns of Helfta is blood. The blood which flows from the Sacred Heart is cleansing and healing. Mechtild described the blood 'of his fresh red wound' as 'the very medicine for healing man's soul'.[51] It is often combined with water, or turns into water. Both flow with great plenitude to wash the souls of sinners.

> He opened the gate of his divine heart . . . and there she saw a flood of running water from the East into the West . . . This soul [Mechtild] entered into this water, and there she was washed clean of all filth and spots of sin.[52]

Gertrude told of being washed in 'the fountain of love', that is, the blood and water issuing from Christ's heart.[53] She also commented that 'although blood is in itself an unpleasant thing, it is praised in Scripture because it is shed for Christ'.[54] This acceptance of blood could well be founded not only on the distinction between sacred and profane blood, but also on the familiarity with blood which is part of a woman's experience.[55] Medical opinion during the Middle Ages generally held that menstruation was necessary and healthful for women, because it eliminated potentially harmful fluids.[56] The flow of blood posed no danger to women – in fact, quite the opposite. Contact with it was, however, usually deemed harmful to others.[57] A community of women, isolated from male company and perceptions, could be assumed to find a flow of blood much less threatening than their male contemporaries; images of blood and flowing would excite quite a different resonance.[58] Like the blood from the Sacred Heart in the visions of the nuns of Helfta, the flow of menstrual blood is cleansing and healing.

One of the most striking of the female images is the union of the soul, or of the visionary, with the Sacred Heart.[59] I have already mentioned that the wound in the heart resembles the vagina in shape; it also resembles it in function in that it allows for entrance into the body. Both Gertrude and Mechtild of Hackeborn experienced a number of visions in which they were joined to the Wounded Side, and then entered into the Sacred Heart. In one such vision Mechtild was lying on a bed, when Christ lay beside her, embraced her with his naked arm against His Wounded Side, and joined their hearts together.[60] In an even more graphic occurrence, Gertrude was embraced by Christ against his Wounded Side.

> After a little while, raising herself, she perceived that through the contact with the wound of love in the Lord's most sacred side, her left side had been drawn into a kind of ruddy scar. Then, as she was going to receive the body of

Christ, the Lord himself seemed to receive the consecrated host in his divine mouth. It passed through his body and proceeded to issue from the wound in the most sacred side of Christ, and to fix itself almost like a dressing over the life-giving wound. And the Lord said to her: 'Behold, this host will unite you to me in such a way that on one side it touches your scar and on the other my wound, like a dressing for both of us.'[61]

I stated above that the cult of the Sacred Heart inscribed the female on the divine; in this vision the divine is then reinscribed on the female, in that same complex mutual reflection which occurred with Mechtild of Hackeborn's image of the heart as a house described earlier.

The supportive, empowering environment at Helfta encouraged the women of the community to develop a strong sense of spiritual authority and to appropriate, expand, and give uniquely female expression to the cult of the Sacred Heart. I began this essay with Gertrude's description of all the members of the community drawing nourishment from the Sacred Heart. I end it with the vision, replete with vivid images of flowing sweetness, experienced by the Third Nun before she recorded Mechtild of Hackeborn's revelations in the *Liber specialis gratiae*. She dreamt that Mechtild offered to all the sisters in the choir pieces of honeycomb from a vessel which she held. When she came to the narrator, Mechtild gave her a piece of bread soaked in the honey.

> And while she held that bread in her hands, miraculously that morsel of bread together with the honey both began to grow into a loaf, so that the morsel of bread grew into a whole loaf, and the honeycomb permeated the loaf within and without, and dripped through her hands. While she held the loaf it dripped in such plenty and abundance that it wet all her lap and then ran over and moistened all the earth around.[62]

In her book on women's writing Patricia Yaeger writes:

> The honey-mad woman . . . gives us a map for defining a countertradition within women's writing, a tradition in which the woman writer appropriates the language 'racked up' in her own body and starts to sing. A blissful consumer and purveyor of language, the honey-mad writer is a symbol of verbal plenitude, of woman's capacity to rewrite her culture.[63]

Honey-mad. Were the nuns of Helfta honey-mad? I think they were: the writing women of Helfta did indeed appropriate the language 'racked up' in their own bodies. Mechtild of Magdeburg, Gertrude, and Mechtild of Hackeborn articulated their visions in words and images drawn from their physical experiences as women and from the companionship of the cloister. They rewrote their culture by inscribing the female on the divine.

In so doing they created a mystical discourse centred on the Sacred Heart, developing a devotional cult which reflected their shared female biology and gave spiritual expression to their sense of community.

Notes

1. In this essay, all quotations from the works of the three visionaries are given in modern English. In the notes I first give references to the book and chapter of the Latin editions of Gertrude (*Legatus*) and Mechtild of Hackeborn (*Liber*), and to the German edition of Mechtild of Magdeburg (*Licht*). Details of these editions are found in the bibliography. I then give the reference for the translation I have used. All translations of Mechtild of Hackeborn are my own, since there is no modern English translation of the *Liber specialis gratiae*.

2. *Legatus* 3: 30; *Herald*, Winkworth, 192. Winkworth uses the masculine pronoun in her translation of this passage; however, since this is the 'generic masculine' and given that the vision refers specifically to the female community of Helfta, I have substituted the feminine pronoun.

3. Mechtild of Magdeburg wrote *Das fliessende Licht der Gottheit*, Gertrude wrote *Legatus divinae pietatis*, and Mechtild of Hackeborn was responsible for *Liber spiritualis gratiae*. Editions and translations of these works are given in the bibliography.

4. The cult of the Sacred Heart as it existed during the Middle Ages differed significantly from the devotion to the Sacred Heart which evolved in the late seventeenth century as a result of the visions of Margaret Mary Alacoque (1647–90) and on which the modern devotion to the Sacred Heart is based. Two useful explorations of the medieval cult of the Sacred Heart are Leclercq, 'Le Sacré-coeur dans la tradition Bénédictine au moyen âge', and Vagaggini, 'La devotion au Sacré-coeur chez Sainte Mechtilde et Sainte Gertrude'.

5. Bynum, *Jesus as Mother*, 252.

6. Leclercq, 'Sacré-coeur', 13.

7. Bernard of Clairvaux, 'Sermon 61', 4–5; *On the Song of Songs* III: 144–5.

8. McDonnell, *Beguines*, 318.

9. *Liber* 2: 23.

10. *Legatus* 2: 20; *Herald*, Winkworth, 125.

11. The most useful and comprehensive study of maternal representations of Christ is Bynum, *Jesus as Mother*, 110–69.

12. See, for example, Bynum, *Jesus as Mother*, 175 n.13, and Vagaggini, 'La dévotion', 31 n.1.

13. McDonnell, *Beguines*, 403.

14. It is probably useful at this point to clarify names and identities: there were two Gertrudes and two Mechtilds at Helfta at the same time, leading to some

understandable confusion among future generations of editors and historians. Gertrude of Hackeborn was abbess of the community from 1251–91; her younger sister, Mechtild of Hackeborn (d.1298) was a visionary, as was the other Gertrude (d.1302). The other Mechtild, Mechtild of Magdeburg (d.1282), was also a visionary who entered Helfta around 1270 as an elderly woman, after a life spent as a beguine. Mechtild of Magdeburg was born around 1207–10, and there are suggestions that she died as late as 1297; see, for example, Bynum, *Jesus as Mother*, 177, where she gives both dates. However, Hans Neumann has analysed all available data and argues persuasively for the earlier date of 1282 (Neumann, 'Beiträge', 70).

15 Finnegan, *Women of Helfta*, 11–12.

16 Bynum, *Jesus as Mother*, 180.

17 Meumann, 'Beiträge', 58–9.

18 Gertrude, *Legatus* 2: 1; *Herald*, Barratt, 100–1.

19 *Legatus* 2: 1; *Herald*, Barratt, 100–1.

20 This title was frequently corrupted to *Liber spiritualis gratiae (Book of Spiritual Grace)*; this is the form which the fifteenth-century Middle English translation, *The Booke of Gostlye Grace*, adopted.

21 *Liber* 5: 22.

22 *Herald*, Barratt, 110 n.2.

23 *Legatus* 2: 4; *Herald*, Barratt, 110.

24 *Legatus* 2: 5; *Herald*, Barratt, 113.

25 *Legatus* 4: 7; see Bynum, *Jesus as Mother*, 204.

26 *Liber* 4: 39; see Bynum, *Jesus as Mother*, 221.

27 *Liber* 3: 26.

28 *Liber* 4: 51.

29 *Liber* 4: 50.

30 *Liber* 4: 50.

31 *Legatus* 1: 11; *Herald*, Barratt, 74.

32 *Liber* 2: 25.

33 *Legatus* 2: 5; *Herald*, Barratt, 113. Of course, these remarkably phallic images of mystical union are not unique to Mechtild and Gertrude. Other examples include Beatrice of Nazareth, who also had her heart pierced by a flaming arrow, and, of course, Teresa of Avila, who writhed in ecstasy on the tip of an angel's spear, and was immortalized thus by Bernini.

34 *Legatus* 2: 3; *Herald*, Barratt, 105.

35 *Liber* 2: 2.

36 *Liber* 1: 13.

37 *Licht*, 7: 14; *Flowing Light*, Galvani and Clark, 220.

38 *Licht* 7: 36; *Flowing Light*, Galvani and Clark, 241.

39 *Legatus*, 4: 1; Bynum, *Jesus as Mother*. 201.

40 It should be noted that Julian of Norwich is also unusual in this regard, at least as far as we can tell from the extant manuscripts. For a close examination of

topoi of authorization in the writing of women visionaries, see my essay 'God's Almighty Hand'. My D.Phil. dissertation considers the issue of ecclesiastical authorization and control of women visionaries in considerable detail.

[41] The use of Latin in the texts enabled Gertrude and the Third Nun effectively to disguise their gender. They habitually referred to themselves as narrators as *illa persona* (that person) which is grammatically feminine in Latin, whether it refers to a man or a woman. Readers could therefore easily assume that the narrator/scribe was male. This assumption was certainly made by the Middle English translator, who consistently refers to the scribe as 'hym'. For several examples see *Booke* 5: 14, 16. Whether Gertrude and the Third Nun intended this 'misapprehension' is impossible to determine.

[42] Marie-Luise Ehrenschwendtner, in her essay in this volume, considers the use of the vernacular and of Latin in the writings of women in Dominican convents in southern Germany. In the course of the essay she examines the factors which led Helfta to be a centre of Latin literacy while contemporary Dominican nuns tended to use the vernacular almost exclusively.

[43] *Licht* 6: 24; *Flowing Light*, Galvani and Clark, 193.

[44] A valuable study of the way in which the architecture of medieval convents reflected the cultural enclosure of women is Gilchrist, *Women and Material Culture*, especially 150–69.

[45] *Liber*, 1: 19.

[46] *Legatus,* 2: 8; *Herald*, Barratt, 123.

[47] *Legatus,* 3: 28; *Herald*, Winkworth, 191.

[48] *Legatus,* 2: 14; *Herald*, Barratt, 136.

[49] *Liber*, 2: 23.

[50] *Legatus,* 1: 3; *Herald*, Barratt, 48.

[51] *Liber*, 1: 19.

[52] *Liber*, 2: 2.

[53] *Legatus,* 2: 4; *Herald,* Barratt, 111.

[54] *Legatus*, 3: 30; *Herald*, Winkworth, 196. Interestingly, Gertrude's insight about the ambiguity of blood continues: 'similarly, the neglect of religious duties, for motives of obedience or fraternal charity, pleases God so much that it too might well be termed glorious'. Both blood and neglect of religious duties would seem matters subject to a single – negative – interpretation. Gertrude's sophisticated understanding recognized the possibility of other perceptions.

[55] Caroline Bynum notes that unusual bleeding, such as nosebleeds, was perceived as a sign of holiness in many beguines in the Low Countries during this period (*Holy Feast and Holy Fast*, 123, 214).

[56] Cadden, *Sex Difference*, 268.

[57] Hildegard of Bingen, however, used menstrual blood as an ingredient in a cure for leprosy (Cadden, *Sex Difference*, 72). It is significant that a woman should be able to separate menstrual blood from the taboos surrounding it, and consider it solely for its natural properties.

58 Consider also the copious amounts of blood in the revelations of Julian of
   Norwich (*Revelation*, 8, 14).
59 I make this distinction between soul and visionary because at times it is quite
   clear that there is a *corporeal* union taking place, between Christ in his humanity and the human visionary. At other times, it is specified that it is the
   soul which unites with the Sacred Heart. The latter is more common in the
   revelations of Mechtild of Magdeburg; Gertrude and Mechtild of Hackeborn
   described bodily union more frequently.
60 *Liber*, 2: 32.
61 *Legatus*, 3: 18; *Herald*, Winkworth, 184.
62 *Liber*, 5: 24.
63 Yaeger, *Honey-Mad Women*, 28–9.

Bibliography

Bernard of Clairvaux, *On the Song of Songs*, I–IV, trans. K. Walsh and I.
   Edmonds (Kalamazoo, 1979–83).
Bynum, C. W., *Jesus as Mother: Studies in the Spirituality of the High
   Middle Ages* (Berkeley, 1982).
Bynum, C. W., *Holy Feast and Holy Fast: The Religious Significance of Food
   to Medieval Women* (Berkeley, 1987).
Cadden, J., *Meanings of Sex Difference in the Middle Ages* (Cambridge, 1993).
Chopp, R. S., *The Power to Speak: Feminism, Language, God* (New York, 1991).
Finnegan, M. J., *The Women of Helfta: Scholars and Mystics* (Athens, Georgia,
   1991).
Gertrude the Great, *Legatus divinae pietatis*, in *Revelationes Gertrudianae ac
   Mechtildianae*, I, ed. Dom L. Paquelin (Paris, 1875).
Gertrude the Great, *The Herald of God's Loving Kindness: Books One and Two*,
   trans. and ed. A. Barratt (Kalamazoo, 1991).
Gertrude the Great, *Gertrude of Helfta: the Herald of Divine Love*, trans. and
   ed. M. Winkworth (New York, 1993).
Gilchrist, R., *Women and Material Culture: the Archaeology of Religious Women*
   (London, 1994).
Gilligan, C., *In a Different Voice: Psychological Theory and Women's Devel-
   opment* (Cambridge, Mass., 1982).
Hamburger, J., 'The visual and the visionary: the image in late medieval mo-
   nastic devotions', *Viator* 20 (1989), 161–82.
Howard, J., 'The German mystic: Mechtild of Magdeburg', in K. Wilson (ed.),
   Medieval Women Writers (Athens, Georgia, 1984), 153–85.
Julian of Norwich, *A Revelation of Love*, ed. M. Glasscoe (Exeter, 1976).
Leclercq, J., 'Le Sacré-coeur dans la tradition Bénédictine au moyen âge', in A.

Bea *et al.* (eds.), *Cor Jesu: Commentationes in litteras encyclicas PII PP. XII 'Haurietis Aquas'* (Rome, 1959), I, 3–28.

McDonnell, E. W., *The Beguines and Beghards in Medieval Culture, with special emphasis on the Belgian scene* (New Brunswick, 1954).

Mechtild of Hackeborn, *Liber specialis gratiae* in *Revelationes Gertrudianae ac Mechtildianae*, vol. II, by Gertrude the Great, ed. Dom L. Paquelin (Paris, 1875).

Mechtild of Hackeborn, *The Booke of Gostlye Grace of Mechtild of Hackeborn*, ed. T. A. Halligan (Toronto, 1979).

Mechtild of Magdeburg, *Das fliessende Licht der Gottheit*, I–II, eds. H. Neumann and G. Vollman-Profe (Munich, 1990–3).

Mechthild of Magdeburg, *Flowing Light of the Divinity*, trans. C. M. Galvani and ed. S. Clark (New York, 1991).

Neumann, H., 'Beiträge zur textgeschichte des "Fliessenden Lichts der Gottheit" und zur lebensgeschichte Mechtilds von Magdeburg', *Nachrichten der Akademie der Wissenschaften in Göttingen* (1954), 27–80.

Petroff, E. A. (ed.), *Medieval Women's Visionary Literature* (Oxford, 1986).

Stierli, J., *Heart of the Saviour: A Symposium on Devotion to the Sacred Heart* (New York, 1958).

Vagaggini, C., 'La devotion au sacré-coeur chez Sainte Mechtilde et Sainte Gertrude' in A. Bea *et al.* (eds.), *Cor Jesu: Commentationes in litteras encyclicas PII PP. XII 'Haurietis Aquas'* (Rome, 1959), I: 31–48.

Voaden, R., 'God's Words, Women's Voices: *Discretio Spirituum* in the Writing of Late-Medieval Women Visionaries' (University of York D.Phil. thesis, 1994).

Voaden, R., 'God's almighty hand: women co-writing the book', in L. Smith and J. Taylor (eds.), *Women, the Book and the Godly* (Cambridge, 1995), 55–66.

Wood, C. T., 'The doctor's dilemma: sin, salvation and the menstrual cycle in medieval thought', *Speculum* 56 (1981), 710–27.

Yaeger, P., *Honey-Mad Women: Emancipatory Strategies in Women's Writing* (New York, 1988).

4

'Discreet and Devout Maidens': Women's Involvement in Beguine Communities in Northern France, 1200–1500

PENELOPE GALLOWAY

Since discreet and devout maidens do not find it suitable to remain in their parents' homes among secular minded and shameless persons without grave danger, they take refuge nowadays in monasteries . . . but those who are unable to find monasteries which will receive them live together in a single house . . . Under the discipline of one who excels the others in integrity and foresight, they are instructed in manners and letters, in vigils and prayers, in fasts and various torments, in manual work and poverty, in self-effacement and humility. For we see many who, scorning the riches of their parents and rejecting the noble and wealthy husbands offered them, live in profound poverty, having naught else but what they can acquire by spinning and working with their hands, content with shabby clothes and modest food.[1]

THIS quotation from a sermon by Jacques de Vitry represents his definition of the motivation, functions and responsibilities of a particular group of religious women known as beguines, topics which have concerned writers since the beguine movement emerged in the thirteenth century. Involvement in beguine life is not necessarily synonymous with membership of a specific beguine community and the focus of this study lies with the women who provided financial and material support to beguine houses: their patrons. Those who played a substantial role include not only members of the ruling families of Flanders, without whose patronage the history of the beguine movement would have been brief and inglorious, but the large numbers of women who were connected at a local level with both the organization and funding of individual houses. This includes women from the surrounding urban community and the beguines themselves who played an active part in the sustenance of their own houses. It is important to consider the roles of these various groups, to assess what they hoped to gain from investing in beguine communities and to examine the limitations on their power. The essentially female nature of the beguine movement enhances the potential significance of women's association with beguine communities while the lack of formal connections between beguine houses renders the beguine movement particularly suited to consideration at a local level.

The historiography of the beguine movement is still dominated by Ernest McDonnell's seminal work *The Beguines and Beghards in Medieval Culture with Special Emphasis on the Belgian Scene* which was published in 1954. The two most influential modern scholars working on the beguines – Walter Simons and Joanna Ziegler – agree that McDonnell's book has had a paralysing effect on scholarship, utilizing as it does almost every document concerning beguines in Belgium. As the title of McDonnell's work suggests, the history of the beguine movement in the Low Countries and, in other works, in Germany, has been considered at length.[2] In contrast to this the numerous beguine communities in what is now northern France have been seriously neglected by historians. Bernard Delmaire has concluded that more than twenty towns in the area contained beguine houses.[3] This study focuses on the neighbouring towns of Douai and Lille which, with Saint-Omer, constituted the territory known as *la Flandre gallicante*.[4]

Emerging from the extraordinary spirit of religious fervour which gripped Europe at the start of the thirteenth century, beguines differed substantially from all earlier groups within the western church in a number of important respects. Theirs was above all a women's movement, a reversal of tradition. Beguines did have male counterparts, referred to variously as beguins in southern France and beghards in the Germanic lands. However, as a group they never achieved the same measure of permanence as the beguines nor did they spread widely in northern Europe. This is due in part to the fact that beghard communities never received patronage on the same scale as did beguine houses. Beghard convents always contained fewer inhabitants than those of the beguines, and beghards, whether living alone by begging or in a convent, were always more vulnerable to accusations of illegal preaching and heresy.

The beguine movement was also unique in that it had no definite Rule, single leader, mother house or organizational structure. Previously the hallmark of a successful religious organization such as the Cistercians had been its ability to subordinate local conditions to the requirements of a universal system. In the strictest sense beguines were not part of a single movement at all, simply communities of women reacting to the conditions of urban and commercial life. Individual beguine houses appear to have had little or no connection with one another and donations give no sign that contemporaries saw links between beguine houses, which are discussed separately, often in different sections of a document. Each beguine community regulated its own order of existence and defined the way in which members of the house were to behave. It is no coincidence that the beguine movement developed in northern France, Rhineland Germany and Flanders, which were among the most populous and highly industrialized areas of Europe in the later Middle Ages. In her essay 'The Desire to Corrupt: Convent and Community in Medieval Wales', Jane Cartwright concludes that while England had its share of extra-regular religious groups, which often centred on hospitals, Welsh women appear to have lacked a religious vocation. Certainly, in comparison with Cartwright's putative figure of thirty-five women living in religious communities in medieval Wales, the smallest beguine houses begin to look populous. However, the cities of the Low Countries and Rhineland Germany, in which the vast bulk of beguine communities existed, attracted many more women than did the Welsh countryside.[5] Unlike nuns, beguines took no irrevocable vows. Initiation was simple. Aspirants appeared before the parish priest or bishop's officer, promised to observe celibacy while living in the community and to cultivate a humble and frugal lifestyle. At the initiation ceremony each beguine was presented with her 'habit', which appears to have consisted of the attire of townswomen, devoid of ornamentation and bright colour. As in so much else concerning beguines, practicality appears to have been the over-riding consideration. They were free to leave the beguinage at any time to marry or enter an established order. John Malderus, bishop of Antwerp from 1563 to 1633, stated:

> It was a common capacity of many pious women in Belgium to rejoice in excellence rather than to promise it. They preferred to remain chaste perpetually than to vow perpetual chastity. Likewise they were more eager to obey than to vow obedience, to cultivate poverty by frugal use of their fortunes than to abandon everything at once; they might be kinder to the poor if something were left.[6]

The problem of who these women were and what motivated them to become beguines has intrigued several generations of historians without providing any finite solution. Some writers saw the beguine movement as an expression of protest by the urban poor.[7] Yet, research has shown that, far from constituting a refuge for society's impoverished underclass, the first beguines tended to be drawn from the newly affluent bourgeoisie.[8]

The voluntary poverty which loomed so large in the lives of the *mulieres sanctae* apparently held little appeal for those who were poor by necessity rather than choice. Other historians considered the women to be part of a demographic surplus.[9] Local feuds, wars, crusades and the large numbers of celibate secular and regular clergy may have removed a substantial proportion of the male population, resulting in a surplus of marriageable women. However, Ludo Milis suggests that such a surplus had always existed but only became prominent after the disruption of protective agrarian society. There does appear to be considerable evidence that many of the women who entered beguinages were from a rural background. However, actual figures are scarce until the seventeenth century. It has also been postulated that the beguine movement offered a socio-economic solution to urban women who found the range of their employment options curtailed. Particularly from 1300 on, beguine communities provided a means for women to circumvent the stranglehold of craft guilds. Following successive economic crises in the fourteenth century, precipitated by famines and plague, guilds became increasingly exclusive, narrowing labour opportunities for women in towns. The presence of beguines on lists of taxpayers in thirteenth-century Paris[10] demonstrates the success of beguine communities in providing women with economic opportunities, through weaving, spinning, sewing and laundering,[11] and caring for the sick and teaching.[12]

In his writings Jacques de Vitry postulates the significance of spiritual motives in the rise of beguine communities. The hypothesis that beguine communities were formed because more conventional religious orders found the deluge of women too much, particularly after Premonstratensian nunneries were disbanded and the Dominicans renounced responsibility for their convents, appears less certain in the wake of John Freed's discovery that the statutes of the Cistercians from 1228 forbidding the foundation of Cistercian convents and renouncing the order's role in the care of nuns were largely ignored.[13] Flemish nunneries were, however, few and somewhat exclusive: recruiting primarily from the nobility. Some women may have been attracted to the beguine movement specifically *because* they considered nunneries to be too affluent and comfortable. In many respects the same factors which influence the motivations of patrons of beguine communities apply to the women who sought to join beguine houses. These factors are the subject of consideration below.

The structure of the beguine movement, as befits such a spontaneous group, which recognized no single founder or legislator, manifested itself in a range of forms, each of which attracted different types of patronage and support. Single women, living at home with their own families or scattered throughout the city, represent one type of beguine life. They acted as patrons themselves, identifying with monasteries, either by handing over parts of their property or engaging in works of charity.

Other women, frequently under the guidance of local clergy, formed settlements known as beguine convents, often clustered around established religious communities or in the vicinity of a hospital. Such convents tended to attract considerable support from members of the local community, male and female. The women submitted to a grand mistress and in organization and daily practices often emulated nunneries. In some cases beguine convents constituted separate enclaves within the cities of northern Europe. Curtis beguinages, as these townships were called, contained streets, gardens, churches, cemeteries, hospitals and collegiate buildings, separated from the surrounding city by a high, encircling wall. In certain towns curtis beguinages came to constitute entire parishes. These largest of the beguine communities attracted the most support from members of the ruling families. Jeanne and Marguerite, sisters and successive countesses of Flanders in the thirteenth century, founded all but two of the beguinages in Flanders and Hainault.

The importance of patronage to beguine communities is clear from the history of beguines living isolated in the world, who were without such support. Successive ecclesiastical legislation rendered them increasingly vulnerable to harassment and persecution, including the forfeiture of beguinal privileges. In 1273 Bruno, bishop of Olmütz, wrote to the pope demanding '. . . have them married or thrust into an approved order'.[14] The General Council of Lyons in 1274 began official repression of fringe communities like the beguines, a process which culminated in the decree of the Council of Vienne in 1312. The latter Council stated

> . . . these women promise obedience to nobody and they neither renounce their property nor profess any approved Rule . . . [their] way of life is to be permanently forbidden and altogether excluded from the Church of God.[15]

Beguines living in common were to be tolerated as long as they stayed in their convents and accepted clerical supervision. Their critics within the church, however, took this opportunity to persecute them. In Cologne, for instance, under archiepiscopal edict all beguine associations were dissolved and integrated into orders approved by the pope. The women were accused of crimes ranging from illegal preaching and doctrinal errors to vagrancy, prostitution and lesbianism. These last allegations of moral laxity are reminiscent of descriptions of the religious communities of medieval Wales considered by Jane Cartwright elsewhere in this volume. Beguines were most frequently accused of harbouring a sect of heretical mystics, known as the Followers of the Free Spirit. [16] These people were thought to repudiate the Church and its sacraments, believing themselves to be so at one with God that the moral laws and normal means of grace no longer applied to them. Marguerite Porete, a beguine from Hainault, was burned at the stake in Paris in 1310, under the charge of heretical mysticism. A century before, Ida of Nivelles had been accused of quietism – the complete and passive abandonment of self and will to God – but her life as a Cistercian nun protected her. Porete's position as a beguine, however, made her vulnerable.

The strategic importance of French Flanders was such that the region was disputed over by the king of France and his vassal the count of Flanders throughout the high Middle Ages with Edward III of England also claiming sovereignty on occasion. From 1305–69 Lille, Douai, Orchies and their respective castellanies actually passed to the French crown but otherwise they remained part of Flanders, although the French royal presence, usually in the form of troops and military action, was frequently felt.

In the thirteenth century Douai was prominent as one of the wealthiest and most powerful centres of the Flemish cloth trade, producing some of the finest and most expensive cloth in Europe.[17] Such success brought political eminence. In 1289 representatives of the commune of Douai were advising the count of Flanders on a range of matters.[18] This economic and political authority was significant in the development of the town which was dominated by a wealthy bourgeoisie.

Unlike Douai, Lille was a medieval new town which developed near the castle built around 1054 by Baldwin V, count of Flanders. Lille had a market by 1066 and from 1127 at the latest it was the site of a fair. After 1191 Lille picked up some of Arras' trade in cloth but it was never as dependent on textiles as Douai. Fertile soil in the area made it, like Douai, a grain exporter but its development and prominence was due more to the frequent presence of the count's government than to economic factors. When the county of Flanders passed to Philip the Bold, duke of Burgundy, on his marriage to Margaret of Male in 1369, Lille continued to play an important role as an administrative centre. This position was further enhanced in 1386 when Philip reorganized the administration of his duchy into two main territories. A single combined council and accounting office at Lille was responsible for the government of Flanders, Artois, Rethel and the other northern lands. In 1463 a new palace was completed for Philip the Good at Lille.

Douai was the site of no great abbey or cathedral. The vigorous religious life of the town was dominated by two chapters of Augustinian canons, those of St Ame and of St Pierre. The mendicant orders arrived in both Douai and Lille in the mid-thirteenth century. The Dominican convent in Lille, founded around 1224, was the first to be established in the county of Flanders and preachers from Lille played a significant role in attracting the patronage of the countesses Jeanne and Marguerite towards the Dominican order. The Dominicans arrived in Douai later, benefiting from the support of Marguerite, countess of Flanders, who provided them with the land to build a male convent in 1271. As at Valenciennes and Lille the Franciscans established themselves outside the walls of Douai, ensuring that they had more immediate contact with the inhabitants of the surrounding countryside.

The geographical proximity of the towns of Douai and Lille does not preclude tremendous differences in terms of the development of their respective religious houses. In the variety of its beguine communities Douai is extraordinary: records have been found from fifteen institutions.[19] In addition to small convents the town sustained a beghard convent and two beguinages. The beguinage of Wetz, which was primarily referred to as a hospital, was founded in 1245 by a local merchant, Gervais de la Ville while the beguinage of Champfleury was, by 1273, home to at least one hundred beguines.[20] It is difficult to find traces of beguines who lived alone or in pairs outside these communities. Often the only references to their existence are found in testamentary evidence. The convent of Fressain, for example, is mentioned for the first time in December 1337 in the will of Marie Blokiele.[21] The convent founded by Bernard Pilates which appears in the sources under a range of names and was intended to contain ten 'poor women beguines' is mentioned most often.[22] In 1362 the number of women in Pilates' house was reduced to six due to the diminution of the convent's revenue.[23]

Many wills refer in general terms to 'poor beguines of Douai'[24] or to the beguines of a specific parish. We know of an Agnes le Cuveliere who lived with a fellow beguine, Bietris.[25] There are also references to rural beguine communities at Hornaing, which is situated between Douai and

Valenciennes and at Sin (now known as Sin-le-Noble), a village close to Douai.[26] This simply did not occur elsewhere in Flanders where the beguines remained an urban phenomenon and it was extremely unusual even in the Rhineland.

The figure of fifteen beguine communities does not, however, include the convent of St Thomas, founded as a hospital in 1378 by Gauthier de Bellain.[27] This institution also appears to have acted as a leper house. In 1415 Alexandre du Pont, master of the foundation, offered places for deserving beguines. They worked in the hospital and lived independently in the convent. The extent to which beguine communities formed independently of one another and developed in an indeterminate manner is typified by institutions, such as the hospital of St Thomas, which are not invariably described in sources as beguine communities. Similarly, although the founders of the Cistercian abbey of Près are described as beguines in two poems – one written in Latin, the other French *c*.1218 – recounting the establishment of a Cistercian abbey near Douai, foundation documents refer to them simply as women.[28] This fluid terminology makes the basic task of identification of beguine communities rather difficult. The simplest strategy appears to be that used by Walter Simons and Michel Lauwers in their short survey of beguine communities in Tournai. Simons and Lauwers discuss communities of semi-religious women mentioned in sources as *les Soeurs Noires* and *les Soeurs Grises* as part of the beguine movement, if not by name, then clearly in terms of their way of life.[29]

By contrast, sources from Lille, which was similar in population to Douai throughout the later Middle Ages, indicate that the town contained only one beguine house: the hospital of St Elisabeth, situated at the gate of St Peter. Although the exact date of its foundation is unknown, the beguinage is mentioned in texts from 1245 on and appears to have been one of the largest beguine communities in Europe, incorporating substantial grounds including a herb garden and individual houses and employing a chaplain. However, despite its size the beguinage in Lille did not constitute an independent parish. It survived not only the medieval period but also the French Revolution. The last four beguines resident in the beguinage at Lille did not leave until 1855.

The beguine communities of Douai and Lille benefited from the enthusiasm that the countesses of Flanders felt towards the beguine movement. Shortly before her death Jeanne purchased land and houses in the parish of Saint-Albin to establish a community of beguines in Douai.[30] Marguerite continued the project, establishing a parish church at Champfleury in 1245, and, in 1276, exempting the beguines from all taxes imposed on them.[31] Similarly, sources from 1276 attest that Marguerite founded the beguinage of St Elisabeth's at Lille.[32] The beguinage of Wetz in Douai, although founded by Gervais de la Ville, was placed under the protection of the countess of Flanders.[33]

Lacking the power base of an international order, beguines were dependent on the support of influential patrons. The patronage of successive countesses and counts of Flanders and close supervision of beguine communities by the bishops of Arras/Cambrai and of Tournai was decisive in the survival of beguines in French Flanders following the Council of Vienne's decision to exclude them from the established Church. The powerful position enjoyed by influential patrons of beguines ensured that they maintained a significant measure of control over the women. Marguerite of Flanders placed the beguine parish of Champfleury and the beguinage of St Elisabeth's under her jurisdiction, withdrawing the women in one respect from the local community by ensuring that the *échevins* (town aldermen) and magistrate of Douai and Lille had no control over the beguines.[34] In 1260 she gave permission for individual beguines to build houses within the confines of Champfleury as long as they agreed to obey the *souveraine* who, if she proved unsuitable, was to leave the house and be replaced by another mistress.[35] Subsequent letters from the countess detail further the structure of authority in the beguinage. The *souveraine* had to be a member of the house and would be aided in her task by the seven most capable beguines.[36]

Jeanne and Marguerite were by no means the only rulers in Europe to support the beguine movement. Louis IX of France founded various beguine houses, including the beguinage of Paris. Louis' brother Robert, count of Artois, was exceptional in France and the Low Countries, in that he did not endow beguine communities. Nor were all female rulers equally supportive. Marie of Burgundy, daughter and successor of Charles the Bold, ordered the beguines to leave Champfleury in 1477 to provide a retreat for the nuns of the Cistercian abbey of Près, whose home had been destroyed. In 1479 the duchess also replaced the beguines serving the leper hospital of St Thomas with religious of the Third Order of Saint Francis. Jeanne and Marguerite of Flanders may have been influenced to support the beguine movement by their gender but their actions were also driven by more pragmatic concerns.

The Ghent Memorial, drawn up at the instance of the bishop of Tournai in 1328, noted that

> Jeanne and her sister Marguerite . . . had observed that these counties teemed with women who were denied suitable marriage . . . and that daughters of respectable men of noble and ignoble birth, desired to live in chastity but on account of numbers or the poverty of their parents were unable to do so easily.[37]

The writer of the Ghent Memorial was one of many contemporaries who attributed the phenomenal popularity of the beguine way of life to the considerable number of women who were unable to find a suitable marriage partner.

Other writers, such as Jacques de Vitry in the sermon cited above, believed that aspiring beguines actively chose the religious life over marriage. Less enthusiastic accounts of female religious life criticized beguines on the grounds that the women rejected all prospective husbands and were attempting to escape from the duties of matrimony. Clearly, not all medieval writers believed that women entered beguine communities only after failing to snare a husband. Whether the number of marriageable women significantly exceeded that of available men or not, the Ghent Memorial and Jacques de Vitry clearly attest to the fact that people *believed* there were a tremendous number of unmarried women in thirteenth-century Flanders. Regardless of whether or not women joined beguine communities in preference to marriage, this supposed surge in the female population was perceived as the reason why a large number of laywomen sought to live in religious communities. However, the wording of the Ghent Memorial suggests that the initiative for many of the numerous beguine communities founded in the early thirteenth century rests with the countesses, Jeanne and Marguerite, as much as with aspiring beguines. Whether they were created as the result of tremendous demand from the populace or not, the plethora of beguine houses which emerged in the thirteenth century certainly helped the countesses to direct the extraordinary surge in popularity of the religious life among laywomen in Flanders.

Ostensibly, beguinages were established to shield the women within from external influence in their quest for a more religious life. Founders were acting from purely spiritual motives: creating an atmosphere suited to contemplation and meditation. The erection of high walls, even moats, around beguinages were measures intended to protect the all-female community from robbery, sexual harassment, and even abduction and forced marriage. One case of abduction is known from Bruges in 1345.[38] In 1242 Countess Jeanne issued a specific order to all her bailiffs and magistrates, protecting all women who were or wished to be beguines from such abuse.[39]

However, these caring measures may have belied suspicion of female religious aspirations, especially those of such an apparently extensive number of women, requiring not only support but also confinement in order that they might be closely observed. In the thirteenth century a few of the clergy voiced explicit distrust. Gilbert of Tournai asserted that beguines had unauthorized vernacular translations of the Scriptures, none of which he was prepared to specify.[40] Even supporters of beguines, such as Jacques de Vitry, worried about the possibility of the women living on the streets as itinerant beggars.[41] Jacques de Vitry and Siger of Lille actively discouraged the beguines Marie of Oignies and Margaret of Ypres, their respective spiritual charges, from begging.[42] This concern is also voiced in the royal confirmation of the customs of the beguinage at Lille. This document states that the beguinage was established 'to prevent the beguines from wandering about town'.[43] One of the key notions behind the creation of beguine communities, from the point of view of the ruling families who sought to maintain civic obedience, was that within a beguinage the large numbers of women who desired to live a religious life were easy to control and to shield from undesirable influences. Similarly the Rule of the beguinage of Lille was written not by a member of the community or by the spiritual director of the beguines but at the court of Philip the Bold, duke of Burgundy.[44] Even before this rule was promulgated in 1401 the beguines had been living in accordance with rules provided by Marguerite's son, count Guy of Flanders, and confirmed in 1299 by Philip, king of France.[45] Nor was Lille unique in this respect. The regulations of the beguinage of Ghent were written by officials of Louis of Mâle.[46] The price of royal patronage of individual communities often appears to have been the loss of some autonomy and the compulsory withdrawal from the traditional authority of the local community, which may have distanced beguinages from the surrounding urban milieu.

The spiritual directors of beguine communities, often friars from the local Dominican house, acted as a co-ordinating force in the development of the beguine movement, not least because the leading spiritual guides and confessors of the countesses were Dominicans such as Hugues de Saint-Cher and Jacques de Halle. Siger of Lille, the spiritual director of Marguerite of Ypres, was a private councillor to Marguerite of Flanders. From the documentary evidence available it is difficult to prove that these men had a direct influence on the countesses' attitudes to beguines but some connection between their appointment as advisors and the growth of the beguine movement may be surmised.

Founding and supporting beguine communities undoubtedly provided the countesses of Flanders and their successors with considerable spiritual benefits and satisfaction. The desire to aid religious houses and poor women is hardly unusual in the nobility of the medieval period. Elsewhere in this volume Jennifer Ward stresses the role of the noblewoman as benefactor in medieval England, both in terms of her local parish and of other religious communities. Patricia Skinner also discusses the importance rulers and their biographers placed on charitable giving as a quality of kingship. However, the active role played by countesses Jeanne and Marguerite in the promotion of the beguine movement as opposed to supporting Dominican nuns, for example, is noteworthy. The absence of a single Rule, mother house and centralized organization offered founders, especially members of the ruling family, considerable authority over individual communities. Nevertheless, without the substantial financial support offered by royal patrons the beguine movement would never have been so widespread in Flanders. The example set by the countesses ensured the popularity of beguine houses among lay patrons for much of the thirteenth century.

Although their role was significant, the countesses of Flanders were not responsible for the foundation of every beguine house in their lands. A significant number of the smaller beguine houses in Douai were founded by female members of the local community. In 1265 the will of Agnes de Corbie made provision for the foundation of a beguinage in her home for 'poor beguines, women and the elderly'.[47] In this context it is important to remember that beguines were members of more than one community, not only that of the beguinage but also of the wider urban milieu. The relationship between individual women and the families they withdrew from in order to enter beguine houses may be discerned using wills and other documents concerning donations. Beguines were not distanced from the local community by monastic vows or devotion to a centralized order. This helped to ensure the maintenance of a link between the religious women and their families, the existence of which is evident from the fact that many smaller beguine communities were founded and patronized by members of a single family, from whose ranks the majority of recruits often came. Family members resided together in a number of houses in the town of Mons: Alice de Plankes and her niece Marguerite,[48] Catherine de Baufe and her sisters,[49] and Marguerite de Blarignes and her daughter

Marie to name but a few.[50] In other cases it can be very difficult to distinguish between the founder and the occupant of a beguine house. The convent of Harnes, mentioned for the first time in a will of 1314, was founded by Marie de Harnes, a beguine who lived there.[51] Such houses lacked revenue and often returned to the family concerned when occupants ceased to be beguines. Sometimes founders of both sexes would retire to the community they had created. Gervais de la Ville, the founder of the hospital of Wetz in Douai, gave the new community all the property he owned in Douai on the understanding that he and his wife could stay there for the rest of their lives.

The majority of local patrons of beguine communities preferred to give after their death. The town of Douai offers excellent testamentary evidence, as its archive contains more than two thousand wills dating from the thirteenth to the sixteenth centuries. These provide a significant amount of information not only concerning the beguine houses involved but also revealing the motivations of donors. The extent of the beguines' success in attracting donations from laymen and laywomen may be discerned from a sample of sixty-five wills written in Douai between 1249 and 1299.[52] Twenty-eight contain no references to beguine communities. Of these twenty-eight testators some, such as Jehan Iouskart, make no bequests to religious houses at all. These documents constitute the briefest wills found in the series. Those bequests which are included are concerned exclusively with small amounts of money, often given to other members of the deceased's family. It is possible to state categorically that during the second part of the thirteenth century the people of Douai who had a substantial amount of property and wealth to distribute in their wills made some form of donation to a beguine community. However, this does not imply extraordinary commitment to the beguine way of life on the part of the men and women of Douai. Cases such as Ysabiel de Saint-Aubin, who gave her entire fortune to the hospital of Wetz, are unusual.[53] This donation was made during her lifetime, the rest of which was spent as a resident of the beguinage. The majority of references to beguines are inconspicuously situated in an inventory of religious institutions, indicating that little distinction was made between communities of laywomen and members of religious orders. The will of Margherite Mulet makes forty-four references to religious communities as far afield as the Franciscans and Dominicans of Paris. Towards the end of the list we find 'to the hospital of St John in front of St Peter's and to the hospital of Wetz . . . I marche.'[54] In this context it would have been more remarkable to find no reference to beguines in some form.

Beguine houses differed to such a great extent in terms of size, function and social origins of inhabitants that it is extremely difficult to establish particular features common to every beguine community which would attract patrons. The most popular beguine houses in terms of bequests are the beguinages of Champfleury and Wetz. In view of their size in comparison to the other beguine communities in Douai this is hardly surprising. However, the terminology of the testaments is revealing. In all wills written by men and some of those written by women, both communities are described as hospitals, often with no reference to the inhabitants and are situated in association with the crusading orders of St John and St Samson. The will of Lambelet le Boulenger may stand as an example: 'to the hospital of Seigneur Gervais, to St Samsons and to the hospital of Champfleury to each of these houses 3 shillings'.[55] The charitable role of these beguine houses and their involvement in the care of the sick and elderly may have been more attractive to patrons than the spirituality of the women who lived there. Such references demonstrate that beguines may be added to Skinner's list of widows and orphans as the natural recipients of charity. The allusion to Gervais de la Ville is also relatively common in testamentary evidence and the often cursory mention of the hospitals in most wills prompts speculation as to the extent to which money was given out of devotion to beguine life as opposed to expected practice or association with the name of the founder: Gervais or the *échevin* Bernard Pilates or even the countess of Flanders.

Unfortunately, due to the absence of evidence it is possible only to speculate on the extent to which beguines who were known to members of the surrounding community acted as visual examples of pious devotion to their fellow citizens. This is certainly the role Jacques de Vitry desired for Marie of Oignies, whose *vita* he wrote following her death in 1213, in order to spread information concerning her exemplary behaviour. The intense piety of individuals such as Marie of Oignies, whose hagiographers were swift to note that she had received the stigmata several years before St Francis of Assisi, may also have contributed to the enthusiasm with which male and female lay patrons donated to beguine communities in the thirteenth century. The ritual language of wills refers to donations given for the sake of the donor's soul and the souls of his (or her) ancestors. To this end those who donated money or property to the community at Wetz in the later thirteenth century were remembered in masses in the Dominican church, located in the immediate vicinity of the beguinage. Thus, although the prayers of the beguines, who were laywomen, may have been considered less efficacious for the souls of the dead, they were able to call on the support of the friars who could celebrate obituary masses. In terms of attracting patronage, the beguines of Wetz also benefited from the relics of the cult of the eleven thousand virgins and nineteen martyrs which were held in a chapel within their house. By such traditional means the new religious communities sought to compete against the established orders for a finite number of sources of patronage.

References to individual beguines are less numerous. There are, however, a number of bequests made by women to beguines living elsewhere, such as Mons and Valenciennes. This implies personal support for the beguine movement as a specific form of religious life. Certain individuals, in this sample all female, devote a considerable amount of money and space in their wills to beguine communities. The most striking example of financial benevolence is the will of Marien, daughter of William le Caucheteur, written in November 1282. She makes bequests to the beguines of Lille and Arras as well as to various beguine houses in Douai and individual beguines.[56] A number of women refer to particular beguines by name, implying a more personal relationship. The testament of Marie de Lens mentions 'Marien the begine and Catheline, her sister'.[57] Marie of Oignies, mistress of one of the earliest beguine houses, persuaded a wealthy cousin to patronize her small community.[58] In many cases *souveraines* were from wealthy families and relatives remained an excellent source of revenue for beguine houses.

The majority of gifts appear to have been in the form of relatively small amounts of money, although there are cases of beguine communities being given land and property, even books. Beguines in Tournai received a bequest of Augustine's *Soliloquies* and *Meditations* and a sermon on the Passion by Jean Gerson.[59] The art historian Judith Oliver has suggested that beguines may have been involved in the production of Psalters and devotional books for patrons, but, unfortunately, has little evidence to support her claim.[60]

The example of Marguerite sans Pegniet demonstrates the limitations of the power of local patrons. She left instructions in her will for her house on the Rue d'Infroy to become a beguine community. However, in November 1352 her executors on instruction from the *échevins* gave her property to the beguinage of Wetz.[61] With the exception of beguine communities under the control of the countess of Flanders, municipal authorities retained considerable power over beguine houses. The magistrate of Douai controlled the number of women in the communities of Wetz and Pilates. The latter was restricted to thirteen in September 1490 due to lack of funds. In Strasbourg municipal authorities could even force beguines to work in hospitals in times of plague. Therefore women in beguine communities and their lay supporters found themselves dependent not only on priests to celebrate mass and hear confessions but on the approval of the secular authorities to enable communities to develop.

The final group of patrons of beguine communities are the women themselves. Paradoxically, beguines in Douai were responsible for the foundation of a Cistercian nunnery. Three sisters, Sainte, Rosselle and Foukeut de la Hale and their companion Marie, sought the support of the bishop of Arras and Pope Honorius III to construct the nunnery of Près in 1218. Their foundation predates the first beguinages of Douai by thirty years (the beguine houses of Champfleury and Wetz were founded in 1245) and illustrates the efforts of women to find a place in religious life, whether as beguines or Cistercians. Bernard Delmaire is convinced that had the women lived in the 1240s when it would have been possible for them to live in an established beguine community they would have remained beguines.[62]

Due to the unique nature of the beguine movement, women were not forced to give up all their worldly goods on entering a beguine house. Individuals were able to retain property and those who could afford to were positively encouraged to build private houses within the beguinage, which they would share with one or two others. Evain de l'Euwe, described in 1306 as a shopkeeper and draper, bought several houses, vineyards, gardens and tenements on the rue des Wetz when she entered the beguinage of Wetz in Douai in 1311.[63] An inquiry carried out by the Burgundian *Chambre des Comptes* in 1400 established that the beguines in the hospital of St Elisabeth in Lille lived in groups of two and three in houses within the courtyard.[64] On the owner's death the house became the property of the beguinage. Clearly not all beguines sought a refuge from poverty. However, this relative prosperity is in contrast to the established presentation of beguines as emerging from the lower classes. Catherine Dhérent has worked on demarcation of class boundaries in medieval Douai and notes, almost as an aside, that no woman from Douai's patrician families, a term she uses to indicate political significance in addition to wealth, became beguines. Dhérent's work is entirely in keeping with the prevalent conception that after the first generation of affluent women rejected the wealth of their parents by joining beguine communities, beguinages recruited primarily from the urban poor.[65] This is implicit in the work of McDonnell, from whence it has been widely disseminated, seemingly supported by documentary evidence. Examination of wills, donations and royal grants from Douai and Lille reveals that beguines are routinely described as poor, sick and pitiable. In 1337 Marien Graniele of Douai gave all her clothing to poor beguines.[66] Nor is her terminology unusual: in 1245 Gervais de la Ville founded the beguinage at Wetz in Douai for 'poor, sick and disabled beguine women who are in good repute . . . and beguines to serve and take care of the sick women'.[67] Margaret of Flanders' letter of support for this foundation also refers to 'poor women, known commonly as beguines'.[68] These examples are corroborated by statistical analysis of donations to beguine communities in Douai and Lille. To give only one example, from a total sample of thirty-seven wills which mention beguine communities in Douai from 1249 to 1299, twenty-one refer to the women as poor and sick.[69] Such references to beguines as poor and sick – and, by implication, weak, pitiable and unable to pose a significant threat to anyone – are not uncommon in the surviving documents.

I would attest that a closer examination of these documents reveals that this terminology is misleading and that beguines were not necessarily impoverished. Both Countess Marguerite of Flanders and John the Fearless, duke of Burgundy, placed daughters in the beguinage of St Elisabeth's in Lille. In 1439 Isabella of Portugal, duchess of Burgundy, requested that the beguines of Lille accept Jeanneton, the illegitimate child of her predecessor, John the Fearless, into their community.[70] Such an action may have encouraged other noble families to place some of their daughters in beguine houses. These women could hardly be described as poor and pitiable. On a less elevated level, in June 1285 Catherine dou Mariskiel, a beguine of Lille, gave 80 pounds to the abbey of Clairmarais to ensure that alms were given to the poor and masses said for her soul on the anniversary of her death. The donation was guaranteed by three houses which she owned in Lille, near the parish church of Saint Andrew which was itself near to the beguinage.[71] In the early fourteenth century the total population of the beguinage of Wetz was restricted to eighteen women. Of these, at least seven beguines owned land and a significant amount of property in Douai and elsewhere in Flanders. The evident prosperity of so many beguines is somewhat at odds with accepted historical opinion. Even beguines who did not have property to sell or pass on in their wills cannot be dismissed as poverty stricken. In her will Marien d'Annoeulin, a beguine of Douai, disposed of what she described as several good pieces of furniture and a little more than 3 pounds in cash.[72] Nor is there any evidence that the majority of beguines in Douai and Lille were chronic invalids. These examples serve to demonstrate that descriptions of beguines as poor, weak and pitiable are to a great extent merely rhetorical devices, used to encourage support for beguine houses and that it is dangerous to generalize concerning the motivations and social origins of beguines.

Women who could depend on such resources were encouraged to share their good fortune with their less affluent sisters. In some cases the statutes of beguine communities insisted that individual members supported their poorer colleagues. Those who were able to work outside the beguine community did so. In this way they sustained weaker members of the community and created a unique system of female solidarity which practically ensured the self-sufficiency of the beguinage. The lives of these women are in contrast to those studied by Patricia Skinner in her essay. The sources she examines depict women as unlikely to be able to support themselves or their dependents, regardless of whether or not they were able to work. The beguines of Flanders certainly benefited from more positive legislation than their southern Italian counterparts in terms of property ownership. However, the successes enjoyed by beguines in maintaining their communities financially appear to lend weight to Skinner's argument that lone women may well have managed their finances with greater skill and success than has hitherto been assumed. In 1526 a census report from Zoutleeuw noted, 'the beguinage consists of three members, these are the beguinage itself, the beguine hospital and the Holy Ghost Table; all contribute mutually to give alms to the needy in the beguinage.'[73] Thus beguines not only devoted their lives to their respective communities, they also acted as benefactors to needy members in terms of financial, physical and – by their prayers – spiritual help.

This paper has examined the range and influence of women's involvement in beguine communities in northern France in the later Middle Ages. Although the role of countesses Jeanne and Marguerite was crucial to the development of the beguine movement in Flanders and Hainault their contribution to beguine communities should not be viewed in purely altruistic terms. In the absence of a central governing body individual patrons could gain considerable influence over a particular house. Beguine communities offered a means to direct the large numbers of laywomen who sought a religious life. As such they were supported by a number of thirteenth-century rulers of both sexes. The motives of members of the local community in founding or supporting beguine houses are more varied and difficult to discern. In many cases local women do appear to have associated themselves more closely with beguine houses than did male patrons. The unique nature of the beguine movement was such that the beguines themselves were encouraged, even forced by statute, to act as patrons of their individual communities. Patronage of beguine houses was by no means gender-specific, but the beguine movement did offer women patrons of all classes considerable freedom to contribute to the development of a particularly female form of religious life.

Notes

1. Vitry, 'Second sermon to virgins', 46.
2. Schmitt, *Mort d'une hérésie*, Asen, 'Die Beginen in Köln', and Neumann, *Rheinischen Beginen und Begardenwesen*, concentrate on the development of the beguine movement in Germany. Schmitt contains further bibliographical details.
3. Delmaire, 'Les béguines dans le Nord de la France', 121. Delamaire invites other historians to augment this brief article with more archive work in northern France.
4. A general survey of the history of this area is provided by Nicholas in *Medieval Flanders*. Political developments in the region are examined by Vaughan in his volumes on successive Burgundian dukes: *Philip the Bold; Philip the Good; John the Fearless; Charles the Bold.*
5. See Simons, 'The beguine movement' and Nicholas, *The Domestic Life of a Medieval City*, for a detailed examination of this phenomenon.
6. Ryckel, *Vita S. Beggae*, 73.
7. Troeltsch, *Grundlagen*, 362.
8. Grundmann, *Religiöse Bewegungen im Mittelalter*, 167.
9. *Ibid.*, passim.
10. Michäelsson, *La taille de Paris, 1296*, 158; *La taille de Paris, 1297*, 5.
11. Espinas and Pirenne, *Documents à l'industrie drapière*, I, 42, 307, II, 401.
12. The beguine mystic Beatrice of Nazareth was educated in a beguine school. See Bowie, *Beguine Spirituality*, 86.
13. Freed, 'Urban development and the *curia monialium*', 341.
14. Höfler, *Analecten*, 27.
15. Hefele and Leclerq, *Histoire des Conciles*, 681.
16. This assertion is found in Lambert, *Medieval Heresy*. The Heresy of the Free Spirit is explored in greater depth in Lerner, *The Heresy of the Free Spirit* and Schmitt, *Mort d'une heresie.*
17. Chorley, 'The cloth exports of Flanders and northern France' explores Douai's role in the economy of northern Europe in greater depth.

[18] Nicholas, *Medieval Flanders*, especially 150–89.

[19] These are detailed in Delmaire, 'Les béguines dans le Nord de la France', 156–7.

[20] Testament of Jean de Vi, Archives Municipales de Douai (AMD) FF861.

[21] AMD FF862.

[22] AMD GG layette 191, Pilate 290.

[23] AMD GG layette 191, Pilate 524.

[24] Amongst others the will of Marien, daughter of William le Caucheteur, November 1282. AMD FF862.

[25] AMD FF661. Printed in Espinas, *La vie urbaine de Douai au moyen âge* III, no. 528, October 1269, 396.

[26] Sources concerning the beguine house of Sin are now inaccessible but are transcribed in Brassart, 'L'ancien béguinage de Sin-lez-Douai', 136–7. The only source concerning the beguines of Hornaing is printed in Dhérent, 'Le commerce de Douai', 390.

[27] Duthilloeul, *Histoire ecclésiastique*, 121 includes a brief reference to this community. Brassart, *Notes historiques* prints the available sources, 176–83.

[28] Delmaire, 'Deux récits versifiés', 331–51.

[29] Lauwers and Simons, *Béguins et Béguines*, 19–28.

[30] Brassart, *Notes historiques*, 106.

[31] *Ibid.*, 124.

[32] Denis du Péage, *Documents sur le béguinage de Lille*, 27.

[33] Brassart, *Notes historiques*, 303.

[34] *Ibid.*, 303.

[35] *Ibid.*, 147.

[36] *Ibid.*, 147.

[37] Ghent Memorial in Paul Fredericq, *Corpus documentorum Inquisitionis haereticae pravitatis Neerlandicae*, 1, 176. This passage is repeated in the Rule of the beguinage of Ghent ratified by Louis de Mâle in 1354, a French copy of which was in the possession of the beguinage of Lille where it continues *'entre aultres ils ont fondées une court de béghuines dans nostre porte à Gand que l'on appelle la court de Saint Élisabeth, lequel est entouré de fossets et de murs et au millieu une église et y proche une chimentière et une hospital pour les béghuines mallades de ladicte court que lesdictes dames de flandres ont donnée'*, Archives Hospitalières de Lille (AHL), 3 Series E/3 and Archives département du Nord (ADN), B 20040, no 19915.

[38] Simons, 'The beguine movement', 89.

[39] This document is printed in Miraeus and Foppens, *Opera diplomatica*, III, 592.

[40] De Tournai, *Collectio Scandalis*, 197.

[41] Vitry notes with relief that 'not one among this great multitude of holy women was found in the whole diocese of Liège who was forced . . . to beg publicly.' Vitry, *Vitae Mariae Oigniacensis*, 20.

[42] *Ibid.*, 61 and De Cantimpré, *Vita Margareta de Ypres*, 117.

[43] ADN, B 1528, document 4211.

[44] ADN, 162H1, document 4.

[45] ADN, B 1528, document 4211.

[46] Béthune, *Cartulaire du béguinage*, document 130, 89–92.

[47] AMD GG 191, 27 May 1265.

[48] Archives de l'État à Mons (AEM), Trésorerie des chartes des comtes de Hainaut, rec. 48, piece 178 and rec. 20, piece 19.

[49] Archives de la Ville à Mons (AVM), documents 1339–1341.

[50] AEM, Trésorerie des chartes des comtes de Hainaut, rec. 48, piece 178.

[51] AMD FF 862.

[52] AMD FF 861.

[53] AMD GG 191, April 1289.

[54] AMD FF 862 1320.

[55] AMD FF 861, May 1271.

[56] AMD FF 861.

[57] AMD FF 861, August 1270.

[58] Vitry, *Vitae Mariae Oigniacensis*, 76.

[59] Grange, 'Choix des testaments', documents 738 and 801.

[60] Oliver, *Gothic Manuscript*, especially 118, 206. Simons, 'Beguines and Psalters', reviews this work, noting the problems concerning evidence.

[61] Brassart, *Notes historiques*, 109.

[62] Delmaire, 'Deux récits versifiés de la fondation de l'abbaye des Près á Douai', 241.

[63] AMD FF 669.

[64] Denis du Péage, *Documents sur le béguinage de Lille*, 80–1.

[65] Dhérent, *Les familles patriciennes de Douai*, 33.

[66] AMD FF 862.

[67] Brassart, *Notes Historiques*, 156.

[68] *Ibid.*, 303.

[69] AMD FF 861.

[70] ADN, H Cumulus, document 11943.

[71] Archives Municipales de Metz, collection Salis, II 233/5.

[72] AMD FF 862.

[73] Simons, 'The beguine movement', 93.

Bibliography

Asen, J., 'Die Beginen in Köln', *Annalen des historischen Vereins für den Niederrhein* 111 (1927), 81–180.

Baker, D. (ed.), *Medieval Women* (Oxford, 1978).

Béthune, J. (ed.), *Cartulaire du béguinage de sainte Elisabeth à Gand* (Bruges, 1883).

Bowie, F., *Beguine Spirituality* (London, 1989).

Brassart, F., 'Note sur l'ancien béguinage de Sin-lez-Douai', *Souvenirs de la Flandre Wallonne* 7 (1867), 135–42.

Brassart, M., *Inventaire générale des chartes, titres et papiers appartenant aux hospices et au bureau de bienfaisance de la ville de Douai* (Douai, 1840).

Brassart, M., *Notes historiques sur les Hôpitaux de Douai* (Douai, 1842).

Cantimpré, T. de, 'Vita Margareta de Ypres', ed. G Meerseman, *Archivum Fratrum Praedicatorum* 19 (1948), 106–29.

Chorley, P., 'The cloth exports of Flanders and northern France during the thirteenth century: a luxury trade?', *Economic History Review* 40, 2nd ser. (1987), 349–79.

Dancoisne, M. l'abbé, 'Mémoire sur les établissements religieux du clergé séculier et du clergé régulier qui ont existé à Douai avant la révolution', *Mémoires de la société d'agriculture, de sciences et d'arts séant à Douai avant la révolution* 9, 2nd ser. (1866–7), 1–278.

Delmaire, B., 'Deux récits versifiés de la fondation de l'abbaye des Près à Douai', *Revue du Nord* 241 (1979), 331–51.

Delmaire, B., 'Les béguines dans le Nord de la France au premier siècle de leur histoire (vers 1230 – vers 1350)', in Michel Parisse (ed.), *Les Religieuses en France au XIIIe siècle* (Nancy, 1989), 121–62 .

Denis du Péage, Paul, *Documents sur le béguinage de Lille, 1245–1841* (Lille, 1942).

Dhérent, C., *Les Familles patriciennes de Douai de 1280 à 1350* (Paris, 1979).

Dhérent, C., 'L'assise sur le commerce des draps à Douai en 1304', *Revue du Nord* 65 (1983), 367–97.

Duthilloeul, H., *Histoire écclesiastique et monastique de Douai et de sa contrée* (Douai, 1861).

Espinas, G., *La Vie urbaine de Douai au moyen âge*, I–IV (Douai, 1913).

Espinas, G. and H. Pirenne (eds.), *Recueil de documents relatif à l'histoire drapière en Flandre*, I–IV (Brussels, 1906–24).

Fredericq, P. (ed.), *Corpus documentorum Inquisitionis haereticae pravitatis Neerlandicae* (Ghent, 1889–1900).

Freed, J., 'Urban development and the *curia monialium* in thirteenth-century Germany', *Viator* 3 (1972), 311–27.

Gold, P. Schine, *The Lady and the Virgin: Image, Attitude and Experience in Twelfth-Century France* (Chicago, 1985).

Goody, J., Thompson, E. P. and Thirsk, J., *Family and Inheritance: Rural Society in Western Europe, 1200–1800* (London, 1976).

Grange, A. de la, 'Choix de testaments tournaisiens antérieurs au XVIe siècle', *Annales de la Société historique et archéologique de Tournai* 2 (1897), 1–238.

Grundmann, H., *Religiöse Bewegungen im Mittelalter* (Berlin, 1935).

Hachez, F., 'Le béguinage de Mons', *Messager des Sciences et des Arts* (Ghent, 1849), 277–302.

Hanawalt, B., *Women and Work in Preindustrial Europe* (Indiana, 1986).

Hefele, Ch-J. and Leclerq, H., *Histoire des conciles*, V–VI (Paris, 1912–1915).

Höfler, C., *Analecten zur Geschichte Deutschlands und Italiens* (Munich, 1946).

Howell, M., *Women's Work, the Structure of Market Production and Patriarchy in Late Medieval Cities of Northern Europe* (Chicago, 1986).

Johnson, P. D., *Equal in Monastic Profession: Religious Women in Medieval France* (Chicago, 1991).

Kelly, J., *Women, History and Theory* (Chicago, 1984).

Keyser, W. de, 'Aspects de la vie béguinale à Mons aux XIIIe et XIVe siècles', *Études et documents du Cercle royal d'histoire urbaine et d'archéologie d'Ath et de la région et musées athois* 7 (1986), 204–26.

Koch, G., *Frauenfrage und Ketzertum im Mittelalter* (Berlin, 1962).

Lambert, M., *Medieval Heresy. Popular Movements from the Gregorian Reform to the Reformation* (2nd edn., London, 1992).

Lauwers, M. and Simons, W., *Béguins et Béguines à Tournai au bas moyen âge* (Tournai, 1989).

Lawrence, C. H., *Medieval Monasticism* (London, 1984).

Lerner, R., *The Heresy of the Free Spirit in the Later Middle Ages* (Los Angeles, 1972).

Little, L. K., *Religious Poverty and the Profit Economy in Medieval Europe* (London, 1978).

McDonnell, E., *The Beguines and Beghards in Medieval Culture* (Rutgers, 1954).

Meersemann, G., 'Les débuts de l'ordre des frères prêcheurs dans le comté de Flandre (1228–1280)', *Archivum Fratrum Praedicatorum* 17 (1947), 57–98.

Meersemann, G., 'Les Frères Prêcheurs et le mouvement dévot en Flandre au XIIIe siècle', *Archivum Fratrum Praedicatorum* 19 (1948), 69–130.

Meersemann, G., 'Jeanne de Constantinople et les Frères Prêcheurs', *Archivum Fratrum Praedicatorum* 20 (1949), 122–68.

Michäelsson, K. (ed.), *Le Livre de la taille de Paris de l'an 1296* (Göteborg, 1958).

Michäelsson, K. (ed.), *Le Livre de la taille de Paris de l'an 1297* (Göteborg, 1962).

Miraeus, A. and Foppens, J., *Opera diplomatica et historica*, II (Louvain, 1723).

Neumann, E., *Rheinischen Beginen und Begardenwesen* (Meisenheim, 1960).

Nicholas, D., *The Domestic Life of a Medieval City: Women, Children and the Family in Fourteenth Century Ghent* (Lincoln, 1985).

Nicholas, D., *Medieval Flanders* (London, 1992).

Nichols, J. A. and Shanks, L. T., *Medieval Religious Women* 1: *Distant Echoes* (Kalamazoo, 1984).

Oliver, J., *Gothic Manuscript Illumination in the Diocese of Liège c. 1250–1330* (Leuven, 1988).

Paris, M., *Chronica Majora*, in H. R. Luard (ed.), *Chronicles and Memorials of Great Britain and Ireland during the Middle Ages* (Rolls Series, 1874), II, 559–64.

Parisse, M., *Les Religeuses en France au XIIIe siècle* (Nancy, 1989).

Plouvain, M., *Souvenirs à l'usage des habitans de Douai* (Douai, 1822).

Rouche, M. (ed.), *Histoire de Douai* (Lille, 1985).

Ryckel, J., *Vita S Beggae, ducissae Brabantiae andetennensium, Begginarum et Beggardorum fundatricis* (Leuven, 1631).

Schmitt, J. C. , *Mort d'une hérésie. L'église et les clercs face aux béguines et aux beghards du Rhin supérieur du xive et xve siècle* (Paris, 1978).

Shahar, S., *The Fourth Estate: A History of Women in the Middle Ages* (London, 1983).

Simons, W., 'The beguine movement in the southern Low Countries: a reassessment', *Bulletin de l'Institut Historique Belge de Rome* 59 (1989), 63–105.

Simons, W., 'Beguines and Psalters', *Ons Geestelijk Erf* 65 (1991), 23–30.

Southern, R., *Western Society and the Church in the Middle Ages* (Harmondsworth, 1970).

Thompson, S., 'The problem of the Cistercian nuns in the twelfth and thirteenth centuries,' in Baker (ed.), *Medieval Women*, 227–53.

Tournai, G. de, *Collectio de scandalis Ecclesiae*, ed. I. Döllinger (Vienne, 1882).

Troeltsch, E., *Grundlagen der christlichen Kirchen und Gruppen* (Tübingen, 1923).

Vaughan, R., *Philip the Bold. The Formation of the Burgundian State* (Cambridge, Mass., 1962).

Vaughan, R., *John the Fearless. The Growth of Burgundian Power* (London, 1966).

Vaughan, R., *Philip the Good. The Apogee of Burgundy* (London, 1970).

Vaughan, R., *Charles the Bold. The Last Valois Duke of Burgundy* (London, 1973).

Vitry, J. de, 'Second Sermon to Virgins', *Die Exempla aus den Sermones feriales et communes*, ed. J. Greven (Heidelberg, 1914), 32–54.

Vitry, J. de, *Historia Occidentalis*, ed. J. Hinnebusch (Fribourg, 1972).

Vitry, J. de, *Vitae Mariae Oigniacensis*, ed. and trans. M. King (Saskatchewan, 1986).

Ziegler, J., 'The *Curtis* Beguinages in the southern low countries: interpretation and historiography,' *Bulletin de l'Institut Historique Belge de Rome* 57 (1987), 31–70.

Ziegler, J., *Sculpture of Compassion. The Pietà and the Beguines in the Southern Low Countries, c. 1300–1600* (Rome, 1992).

Ziegler, J., 'Secular canonesses as antecedent of the Beguines in the Low Countries: an introduction to some older views', *Studies in Medieval and Renaissance History* 13 (1992), 117–35.

5

Mysticism and the Anchoritic Community: 'A Time . . . of Veiled Infinity'[1]

SUSANNAH MARY CHEWNING

The time of abjection is double: a time of oblivion and thunder, of veiled infinity and the moment when revelation bursts forth . . . Jouissance, in short . . . It follows that jouissance alone causes the abject to exist as such. One does not know it, one does not desire it, one joys in it [on en jouit]. Violently and painfully. A passion.[2]

1

WHILE many texts written by men in the Middle Ages were made accessible to women, as well as to men, few were written specifically for a female audience. A list of such works would include *Sawles Warde*, the *Ancrene Wisse*, several female hagiographic works, and a text which has intimate connections to anchoritic mysticism, *þe Wohunge of Ure Lauerd*. All of these works were produced for communities of women who were instructed by men and who shared spiritual experiences in early thirteenth-century England.

Medieval mysticism is, as I will define it, primarily concerned with written texts, and it is most frequently written in the language of the feminine. It occupies a unique position within literary history, however, because, while mysticism is embodied in the written Word, it is conceived in the soul of the mystic, and must be translated from the ecstatic, extra-linguistic realm of experience to the material and confined realm of language. In this way, mysticism is closely related to what the French philosopher Julia Kristeva has referred to as the *chora*: the pre-linguistic, pre-nominal location of a child who has not yet learned to differentiate itself from its mother's body. Judith Butler has argued that there is a 'cultural configuration of language' which 'generates the trope of pre-discursive libidinal multiplicity'.[3] The *chora* is the location where

The title page of *þe Wohunge of Ure Lauerd*.
Reproduced by permission of the British Library
(MS Cotton. Titus. D.xviii, f. 127r.)

such a generation takes place, and to which we all wish to return. Within the *chora* one exists but has not yet developed a sense of self. This is similar to mysticism in that the hope of the mystic is to lose her sense of self in the *non*-discursive libidinal multiplicity found in the presence of the Divine. The mystic's desired loss of subjectivity is well articulated in the anonymous fourteenth-century treatise, *The Cloud of Unknowing* (now thought to be by a Carthusian monk).

> For he may make sorow ernestly þat wote & feliþ not only what he is, bot þat he is . . . þis sorow, when it is had, clensiþ þe soule, not only of synne, bot also of peyne þat he hav deseruid for synne . . . & ȝit in al þis sorow he desireþ not be vnbe . . . hym listiþ riȝt wel be . . . þof al þat he desire vnsesingly for to lakke þe wetyng þe felyng of his beying.[4]

> [When he knows and feels not only what he is but that he is, a man can experience sorrow authentically . . . This sorrow, when it is experienced, cleanses the soul not only of sin but also of the pain that derives from sin . . . And yet, in all this sorrow, he does not desire to cease to exist . . . He wishes very much to be . . . But he does [also] desire unceasingly to be rid of the awareness of feeling of his being.][5]

It is the desire of all humans, according to Kristeva, to return to the memory of the *chora* in the same way that the mystic desires to be made one within the extra-linguistic embrace of the Divine.

While the mystic's experience itself, reflected in her written text, is one that is wordless, it can only be brought out of the realm of the spirit and into the realm of human communication if it is spoken and written down. Through contemplation of God, the mystic moves beyond her body into a realm of direct communication with the Divine – a communication not expressible through human speech, but always articulated by the mystic in writing.[6] This paradox of the wordlessness of mysticism is at the heart of a definition of the genre, and has been a part of most definitions since the nineteenth century. One such traditional definition was written by Jacques de Marquette in the late 1940s:

> Both because of the unusual nature of their processes, and of the fact that their objects are transcendent to those of the usual perceptions which originated our ordinary psychological activity and our languages . . . mystics find it impossible to convey their experiences to their sense-bound contemporaries. At best their descriptions can have but a symbolic or allegorical value.[7]

Yet some mystics have been able to convey their experiences to an audience, through their texts. The mystic, as we know her from medieval

Christian mystical work, is a writer who attempts to write in human language about an experience which cannot be expressed in any language, but which can, none the less, be comprehended somehow.

2

My primary focus in this study will be on *þe Wohunge of Ure Lauerd*. This text, written in a north-west Midlands dialect, was copied before 1250, and is found only in British Library MS Cotton Titus D.xviii.[8] Because some of the texts within the 'Katherine Group' appear in the Titus manuscript, *þe Wohunge* has been incorrectly identified as part of it, but is more accurately identified with the 'Wooing Group', which also includes *On God Urieson of Ure Lefdi*, *On Wel Swuðe God Urieson of God Almighti*, and two pieces entitled by a modern editor *On Lofsong of Ure Louerde* and *On Lofsong of Ure Lefdi*.

The medieval context of the *Wohunge* places it among the earliest works of English mysticism. It is likely to have been influenced (either directly, through textual influence, or indirectly through the influence of a twelfth-century 'zeitgeist')[9] by earlier works of Christian mysticism such as Pseudo-Dionysius's *Mystical Theology*, Bernard's Sermons on the *Song of Songs*, Anselm's *Meditations*, and Hildegard of Bingen's *Scivias*. As Peter Dinzelbacher has pointed out:

> Whereas the new trends in intellectual history, the 'Renaissance of the twelfth century', and those in the history of aesthetics . . . have already an unshakeable place in our concept of the middle ages, it is not so recognized that there is also a history of emotions, the turning point of which must be located in this very century. The nearly synchronous discovery of divine and human love as expressed in experienced mysticism on the one hand and courtly love on the other is as important an indicator of the rise of a new *mentality* . . . as is the creation of a new intellectual climate.[10]

The *Wohunge* is roughly contemporary with Mechtild of Magdeburg and the other mystics of Helfta, discussed in Rosalynn Voaden's essay in this volume; rather than arguing for these German texts' later influence upon English mystics such as Richard Rolle and Julian of Norwich, it can be argued that the English texts and the German texts of the thirteenth century share similar sources and influence, and develop according to similar needs and beliefs within their respective communities. As Dinzelbacher argues, *pace* the exceptional position the British Isles may have had in many respects during the central middle ages, in the field of mystical spirituality the English undoubtedly did participate in the mainstream of European history without showing much substantial difference from what one can observe on the continent, with which of course close contact existed, especially on the ecclesiastical level.[11]

The text of the *Wohunge* is a meditation on the crucifixion and on the mystic's involvement with Christ's passion and resurrection. The author uses many sensual and erotic terms and images to describe Christ. The word *lefman* (lover) is used several times, and the speaker describes herself alternatively as a whore (because of the temptations of the flesh) and a bride of Christ, an image which is also frequently used in the German texts I have referred to above.

We can make certain assumptions about the provenance of the *Wohunge* based on our knowledge of the *Ancrene Wisse* and the existence of communities of anchoresses and anchorites in England in the twelfth and thirteenth centuries. The *Ancrene Wisse* was composed no earlier than 1200.[12] Its most likely source is Aelred of Rievaulx's *De Institutione Inclusarum*, written in the last half of the twelfth century. One important difference between the *Ancrene Wisse* and its source is obvious: Aelred wrote in Latin. The author of *Ancrene Wisse* (though he made references to Latin) wrote in vernacular English. He meant to be understood by the actual women for whom he was writing, as opposed to Aelred, who probably expected the women's religious orders to follow a Latin rule, like their masculine counterparts. Thus the existence of the English texts in the 'Katherine Group' and the 'Wooing Group' is not surprising. If there was an audience for a Rule in English, then there must also have been enough female recluses or hermits in England to read devotional treatises, prayers, and poems, like the *Wohunge*.

The best portrait that can be made of the author of the *Wohunge* is that he was possibly a religious (there are many historical examples which can all serve as models) who was responsible for the education and training of one or more anchoresses. The best portrait of the audience of the text can be made by looking at the assumptions made by the author. Because the text is not in Latin, we can conclude that his audience was not Latinate and may not have been familiar with classical devotional works. On the other hand, his audience was probably familiar with vernacular literature, particularly saints' lives (the imagery of which is clearly used in the composition of the *Wohunge*). It is also likely that the audience of the *Wohunge* was familiar with the language and imagery of *fin amour*. Christ is seen, traditionally, as the Bridegroom (which follows a direct source of the *Wohunge*, Bernard's Sermons on the *Song of Songs*), but the fullest description of Him describes him as a courtly lover. He possesses all the virtues of a knight – beauty, generosity, wisdom, power, nobility, even courtesy. About half-way through the poem, Christ is described with the following characteristics:

> þenne
> þu wið þi fairnesse . þu wið ri
> chesce . þu wið . . . larges-
> ce . þu wið wit & wisdom . þu wið
> maht & strengðe . þu wið nobles
> ce & handeleic . þu wið meknes
> se & mildeschipe & mikel debo
> nairte . sibnesse . þu wið
> alle þe þinges þat man mai lu-
> ue wið bugge . haues mi luue
> chepet[13]

[(So you with your beauty, / you with your riches), / you with generosity, / you with wit and wisdom . you with power and strength, / you with nobility and courtesy, / you with meekness and mildness and great gentleness, / you with kinship, / you with all the things one can buy love with, / have bought my love.][14]

For its audience to understand fully what all of these characteristics represent, it must have been exposed to other literary works in which similar descriptions are found. Thus our image of the audience of the text is one of educated, possibly aristocratic, women who chose (or were coerced into) the convent rather than marriage. What is exceptional about these women is that they were literate in English, obviously articulate and learned enough to read such a powerful text as the *Wohunge*, understanding its allusions to Scripture and to devotional literature. As Nicholas Watson writes, 'the anchoritic works suggest a spirituality which demanded considerable self-knowledge and subtlety on the part of those who attempted it; the brilliance and humanity of the works should be seen as reflecting their audience as much as on their authors.'[15]

In summary, what we know about the author and audience of this text (as with many medieval works) is limited by the lack of information recorded about them during their own lifetimes. But there is enough textual and contextual evidence to argue that women were this poem's assumed audience. It is intriguing to think about the implications for the author of this work – could it have been a woman? In fact many critics have already argued that this poem was created by a female author, but with very little evidence to go on. The theory that the author of the *Wohunge* is female goes back to W. Meredith Thompson's Early English Text Society edition. Thompson agrees with E. Einenkel's comment in 1882 that, 'the preponderance of enthusiasm over thought, and the "innigkeit" [of the text] bespoke feminine (and spontaneous) composition.'[16] Thompson speculates that one of the three anchoresses referred to in the *Ancrene Wisse* is the author of the *Wohunge*, and he suggests

> that she was a woman of privileged birth . . . who had some sharp reversal, was deserted by kith and kin, had constantly to struggle against world, flesh and devil because of a passionate nature – whose authorship would also indicate a cultivated religious milieu.[17]

Thompson's romanticized views have been challenged by E. J. Dobson[18] and, more recently, by Watson, who writes that Thompson's assumptions concerning the gender of the poem's author 'imply condescension toward both the anchoresses and the works, and create an unreal barrier between the "Wooing group" and the other [male-authored] anchoritic works'.[19] Bella Millett has argued that the author of the *Wohunge* was probably male, though the persona created by the author may well be feminine, since it was most likely written for a female audience.[20] And yet the biological sex of the author is really not at issue here at all. *þe Wohunge of Ure Lauerd* is a poem in which the persona or speaker is certainly female, or at the very least she describes herself using feminine pronouns. If the speaker is feminine, then it might be argued that the voice is disruptive of established codes of masculine power. The authorship of the poem may well be masculine, but the message and the power behind what is said are most clearly other than masculine, that which, based on a binary definition of gender, may be characterized as feminine.[21]

þe Wohunge of Ure Lauerd is a very useful text to discuss any definition of mysticism for a number of reasons. It was written in England, yet it exhibits many of the stylistic and literary techniques which generally characterize 'German' mysticism. It was written for a female audience, indeed a female community, presumably made up of several kinds of religious women, from laywomen to anchoresses to nuns. This community, much like that of the audience of the *Ancrene Wisse*, would have read this text (hence its vernacular language) and would have seen it as a guidebook. *þe Wohunge of Ure Lauerd* also had an exemplary function, describing the possible reward to be expected by a woman who followed the Rule, and who took literally her designation of Bride of Christ. The existence of this text as a male-authored source of wisdom for women would not in itself be unusual; the use of a feminine persona within such a text would be more so. The uncertainty surrounding the sex of the author is important to my argument, because I do not seek to prove that a woman authored the poem; instead, I would argue that the persona identified in the text is culturally feminized and that the act of writing the mystical text itself is an act of feminine writing, whether the text is actually written by a man or a woman.

3

The relevance of the *Wohunge* to a study of women's communities is clear. Devotional literature written by and for medieval women seems to have been generated most frequently within communities: the cloister, the beguinage, the anchorhold. Such communities were not always officially governed or established by an Order. They existed, and yet they were not (it would appear) significant enough to the Church to require an external system of governance or authority. The women who lived in unofficial or semi-official communities were simultaneously orthodox and transgressive by their very existence. They were orthodox in their devotion and desire to seek Christian perfection; they were transgressive by their mere presence in the communities, and by the means by which they recorded their mystical experiences.

The anchoritic life was distinct from the lives of other medieval religious in several ways. They were seen, by some, as 'spiritual aristocrats'. Within the manuscripts of works like *Sawles Warde* and the *Wohunge* are also included the lives of female martyrs such as Margaret and Katherine. As Watson points out, 'there is a persistent implication in the [works] that anchoresses are the latter-day equivalents of the martyrs.'[22] Like the communities of nuns and beguines, there was no actual order that determined the rules for life within the anchorhold. In the case of anchoresses, however, a rule of sorts did exist in the *Ancrene Wisse*. This work instructed the anchoresses in matters of dress, food, prayers, and contact with the outside world. The life of the anchoress was more confined than that of any other religious of the period. She was, in effect, a hermit. Leaving the anchorhold was strictly forbidden. In this respect, her situation was different from communities of nuns and beguines, for example, for whom much of their time was spent in ministering to the community. Ideally, the anchoress would have no commerce with the outside world except through her maidservant (whom she rarely saw and who would deliver letters and messages for her), her confessor, and any traveller who wished to speak to her. This kind of conversation (like the one documented between Julian of Norwich and Margery Kempe) would have taken place through a black curtain.

Each anchoress would participate in her own funeral mass in order to be considered dead to her past life and material concerns. Sharon Elkins describes the ritual of enclosure, recorded 'near Canterbury in the mid- to late-twelfth century':

> the ritual of enclosure took place during a mass, over which a bishop normally officiated. The recluse lay prostrate during the office of readings in the western part of the church, 'where it is customary for women to stay' . . . After the recluse was sprinkled with holy water and censed with the thurible, she stood to receive two lit candles . . . after the gospel reading, the recluse made her petition . . . [after a homily of further readings] the choir intoned the funeral antiphon . . . and the rites for the dying were begun . . . with holy water and incense, the celebrant prepared the recluse's cell, called a 'sepulcher' in the liturgy. She would then enter her 'sepulcher' singing the antiphon, 'Here I will stay forever, this is the home I have chosen.'[23]

The bishop would then sprinkle dust over the recluse and the service would end with the 'prayers traditionally said over the body of the deceased in the bier'.[24] The recluse or anchoress would then be left alone in her cell.[25] This initiation ceremony was not too far removed from that of the enclosure of the nun within the cloister (in some cases), and the degree of personal commitment expected of the woman was also similar. An anchoress relinquished all her goods, all personal relationships, and was not expected to leave the anchorhold until her death; if a nun wished to leave the cloister and rescind her vows, contact would have to be made with the Pope for permission to be given. Indeed in twelfth-century England, many nuns seem to have lived very much like communities of anchoresses and it was only later that they were organized into convents. As Brian Golding explains, in his account of the Gilbertines, 'The girls are segregated from the world, pledged to eternal virginity, and reserved for the heavenly bridegroom. They are said to be enclosed as *ancillae Christi*; they are exiles from their land, family, and father's house, "imprisoned" from the world.'[26] However the other alternative for religious life, the beguinage, was quite distinct.

Galloway writes: 'Each beguine community regulated its own order of existence and defined the way in which members of the house were to behave . . . beguines took no irrevocable vows . . . aspirants appeared before the parish priest or bishop's officer, promised to observe celibacy while living in the community and to cultivate a humble and frugal lifestyle.'[27] It would be much easier for a beguine to leave her community. As Galloway writes, 'They were free to leave the beguinage at any time to marry or enter an established order.'[28] The idea of the beguinage never caught on in England as it did on the continent; however, the mystical tradition was expressed in all three levels of female religious life. There were beguine mystics (such as Mechtild of Magdeburg and Marguerite Porete), mystics who lived as nuns (such as Gertrude of Helfta and Hildegard), and of course, anchoritic mystics, such as Julian of Norwich and the anonymous speaker of the *Wohunge*.

History tells stories of many women, some abbesses, others simply members of communities whose devotion was recorded in song and often in Latin *vitae*. Etheldreda of Ely, for example, was beatified and worshipped as a saint, beginning in the seventh century, largely due to the record of her *Life* in Bede, and his subsequent *Hymn to Virginity* in her honour. A fourteenth-century translation of Bede, found in *The South English Legendary*, says of Etheldreda that 'heo was euere clene mayde. wiþ oute sunne of folye';[29] she maintained her chastity throughout two marriages and was given the position of abbess at Ely by the bishop Wilfrid, her closest friend. Christina of Markyate is another early female product of a religious community whose life was recorded as an example of piety and virtue. Like Etheldreda's Wilfrid, Christina has a male friend and supporter, in this case Geoffrey, abbot of St Albans. For many years Christina had lived platonically with Roger the hermit, who taught her about the religious and ascetic life but who, according to tradition, so feared contact with the opposite sex that he 'never consented to see her face'.[30] After Roger's death, Christina moved to St Albans, where Geoffrey looked after her 'material and spiritual welfare'.[31] According to her medieval biographer, 'Christina always called the abbot "her beloved", whilst he on his side referred to her as his *puella*.'[32] He writes, 'The virgin Christina . . . cherished [Geoffrey] with great affection and loved him with a wonderful but pure love . . . Their affection was mutual, but different according to their standards of holiness.'[33] Christina and Geoffrey frequently reported dreams and visions involving one another, some with very ambiguous imagery.[34]

Even in their own time their friendship was questioned, and often slandered as 'worldly'.[35] As Elkins writes,

> Christina's *vita* compared her accusers to those who had 'despised the disciples of Christ because they took women about with them ... Christine [lit] ..., a special candle each Sunday ... to enlighten the abbot and put an end to the shamelessness of her detractors, whom she pitied.[36]

If the author of her *Vita* is to be trusted, then we have in Christina and Geoffrey a relationship between medieval ascetics which was deeply emotional, certainly edged with the sensual, and completely accepted and affirmed by their community and Church.

However, perhaps at the same time as more women began to enter the cloister and the anchorhold (and certainly before the thirteenth century), the Church determined that such relationships between men and women were inappropriate. After the tenth century, 'the moral equality of women with men in the ascetic community threatened [male] ambitions ... [female ascetics] were relegated to a hidden 'private' sphere within monasticism as within the laity.'[37] Aelred of Rievaulx, for example, in the mid-twelfth century, insists that female recluses avoid all human contact, even that of other women. This is particularly interesting when one considers Aelred's earlier arguments in favour of friendship between men.[38] Aelred's insistence that anchoresses remain in solitude sets the stage for the mystical transcendence experienced by so many of them, for in place of the love of human beings, Aelred argues for an intense and focused meditation upon God, divine love, and the recluse's symbolic marriage to Christ, prefigures the imagery of the *Wohunge* and other mystical texts produced by women. Aelred instructs his sister to 'picture herself as being at the crucifixion and watching as the soldier opened Jesus' side.'[39] Compare this to the *Wohunge's*,

> A. iesus swa swet hit is wið þe
> to henge. forhwen þat iseo o þe
> þat henges me biside. þe mu-
> chele swetnesse of þe. rea
> ues me fele of pine.[40]

[Ah Jesus, so sweet it is to hang with you. For when I took on you who hang beside me, your great sweetness snatches me strongly from pain.][41]

In the *Wohunge,* and similarly in contemporary works such as *Sawles Warde* and *Ancrene Wisse*, the narrator finds herself on the cross with

Christ, not only watching the action and kissing his abject body as Aelred describes, but being pierced and beaten *with* him, celebrating her physical death with his in order to find even more glory in a mutual resurrection.

The main problem with reading the feminine persona of this text is, as I have already suggested, the possibility that the author (though unidentified) may be male. If he is, then we find in the *Wohunge* a paradox of gender and subjectivity focused on the distinctiveness of feminine experience. The nature of mysticism – a loss of identity and selfhood through immersion in the power of the Divine – requires that which, it might be argued, is culturally denied to women: subjectivity. Patriarchal culture has systematically deprived women of subjectivity through what Foucault has called the juridico-discursive power of language and law. Desire has always already been masculine desire; the desire of women has been consistently repressed. Yet desire is at the heart of the mystic's experience: she desires a union with God. Since her subjectivity has been denied her by her very culture, she must develop one artificially in order for it to be dissolved in God's presence. For male mystics, who are not culturally denied subjectivity, its loss is expressed through a process of feminization, as is revealed when Bernard of Clairvaux, in his Sermons on the *Song of Songs*, likens the contemplative to 'the woman who does good',[42] and when the thirteenth-century Carthusian, Guigo de Ponte, describes mystical union in the language of female eroticism, or (as Dennis Martin has put it) as 'a loving, yearning longing clinging to God for dear life, an opening up of oneself in order to be penetrated by the Spirit.'[43]

The female mystic, in contrast, must become what has been referred to as a 'virile woman', denying her feminine qualities and pursuing a masculine perfection. In a sense, a system of masculinization was in place for the female ascetic when she entered the cloister: her rule of governance and her order were both determined by (and originally written for) men. Her dress would be similar to the habits of her male contemporaries; her food, her style and order of prayer, the schedule of her daily activities – all of these aspects of the female ascetic's life would have been patterned after those of male ascetics. Two characteristics would be quite different, however. Not only would female communities have much stricter regulations about friendships with both men and women, but also, as women, they would be denied the education afforded to their brethren and would therefore be denied access to the language of the Church: Latin. To use Lacanian terminology, these women were thus, quite literally, denied access to the Symbolic as it existed within their culture.

It is not surprising, then, that we find in *Ancrene Wisse* and the *Wohunge*, as well as in female-authored texts, a move on the part of the speaker to identify with the body of Christ – a male body – and to speak and write in a language to which women had access (the vernacular). A subjectivity could be appropriated through an identification with the dying Christ which could then be freely surrendered by the woman in her self-abjection before the Divine. Access to the symbolic could (and would) be appropriated later, *after* the experience, through the written text often produced by these women – and there are many women whose texts have survived: Hildegard of Bingen, Mechtild of Magdeburg, Gertrude of Helfta, Mechtild of Hackeborn, Elizabeth of Schonau, Marguerite Porete, Catherine of Siena, Hadewijch of Brabant, Beatrice of Nazareth, Marguerite of Oingt, Angela of Foligno, Catherine of Genoa, Bridget of Sweden, Julian of Norwich, and Margery Kempe.

The central metaphor of these anchoritic poems (indeed of mysticism itself) is the surrender of one's subjectivity (however it has been appropriated) and contemplation of the body of Christ. In the *Wohunge of Ure Lauerd* and in other texts within the 'Wooing Group', this abjection of self is clear: 'þre / fan fihten aʒaines me . . . þe werld / mi flesch. þe deouel. þe world / to make me þewe. Mi fles to / make me hore. þe deuel þurh / ut þise twa to drahe me to / helle'[44] [Three foes fight against me . . . the world, my flesh, and the devil; the world, which fights to make me a slave, my flesh to make me a whore, the devil through these two to drag me to hell].[45] She goes on to say, 'Bote þer þurh / understonde i þat tu wult hauei / mei to lefmon & to spuse'[46] [But therefore I understand that you will have me as your lover and your spouse]; Christ will make her his bride in spite of her fallen state; he will love her even though she is subject to sin. Christ is both desired and imitated by the speaker of the *Wohunge* and he is seen by her as a model for behaviour and devotion.

The images of abjection, both the speakers' and Christ's, which run throughout the 'Wooing Group' make explicit the means by which the feminine is defined in the texts: the feminine is submissive, fallen, biologically-centred and driven by desire. However, because Christ, too, is described in all of these ways, the feminine is ultimately empowered and given a sense of authority. The process of immasculation has brought the mystic to a moment of transcendence. There is, in a sense, an exchange of gender between the female mystic and Christ. Both Mary and Christ are seen as desired feminine Others. The mystic, once she has appropriated a sense of masculinity from her participation in the text and in the mystical experience itself, becomes the wooer and is endowed with masculine characteristics. However, once the experience of mysticism actually takes place, the genders shift again from masculine wooer of feminine Divine to masculine, knightly Divine and submissive, feminized mystic. The wooer and the wooed both undergo abjection of body and self, and the outcome is one of transformed selfhood in the face of a mystical experience.

Thus it seems that at the heart of any definition of mysticism must be a discussion of gender. The nature of the mystical experience – a loss of subjectivity and self through a union with a divine Other – requires what might be called a feminization of the mystic, whether the mystic is male or female. This relationship is a simple metaphor of power: during the experience of mysticism, the mystic becomes silent, wordless, de-humanized, completely obliterated in the presence of God in much the same way that women have often been culturally or socially obliterated by patriarchal power. Before her abjection can take place, however, a woman must first construct or appropriate a subjectivity, which she can then surrender – this surrender is thus typical of both the masculine and feminine experiences. If the aim of a mystic, male or female, is to be 'feminized' by the experience, then mystical writing itself may be seen as feminine.

4

Derrida argues that the act of writing has a feminine quality which enables the writer (as the Other) to 'deconstruct', or internally subvert, the established code of order of patriarchal language. In this sense, any language which serves to deconstruct tradition and patriarchal power can be seen as a feminine language.[47] From this deconstructive argument, the French feminists have developed the theory of *l'écriture féminine*. The term originates with Hélène Cixous, who argues that writing is an embodied activity, and that a writer's attempt to deny the physiological nature of writing, and its influence upon her body, is 'both a falsification of the nature of the writing process, and an attempt to control meaning in compliance with the dictates of masculine law'.[48] Thus the claim by French feminists, to 'write the body', relates not only to opening up one's writing to one's gender, but also to freeing one's

creative impulse by involving the body in the writing process. Kristeva
goes further with this notion in her discussion of the semiotic. As I
suggested earlier, for Kristeva the root of human identity is in the
chora. She argues that in order for a writer to 'write the body', she
must identify and recall the semiotic pre-linguistic moment, and that
this is most often achieved in the language of poetry. She writes that
the poetic is 'the "territory of the mother" ... [and] suggests that it
provides an opportunity for alternative forms of meaning, identity and
pleasure to those laid down by the power relations implicit' in
patriarchal language.[49] Thus Kristeva's semiotic and poetic expression
of the *chora* can be seen as a feminist interpretation of what Derrida
described when he wrote about the feminine qualities of subversive
writing. An important parallel can be drawn here between my definition
of mysticism and the opposition between experience and verbal
transmission within it and the opposition of the symbolic (linguistic)
and the semiotic (pre-linguistic) as defined by Kristeva. Just as the poet,
in Kristevan terms, exists outside of the symbolic and within the pre-
linguistic and orderless realm of the semiotic, so does the mystical
experience (and the mystic herself) exist outside of language and
signification (and thus the symbolic order).

Kristeva also describes the notion of the *abject*, in which the subject
or ego is threatened with extinction, whether it is by death, infection,
or as in the case of the mystic, spiritual annihilation. For Kristeva, the
abject can be experienced only through complete obliteration of the self
(the subject) in another object. The abject, which has traditionally been
understood as that which is low or debased, is interpreted by Kristeva
as the human experience of (and fear of) debasement through biological
waste and death. We are confronted with death in our own bodies through
waste and excrement, and we fear the power of such decay to absorb
us.[50] She further argues, however, that there is an 'abjection of self' in
which a subject, completely debased and corrupted by the presence of
some Other subject (whether it is produced by emotional, spiritual, or
environmental influences), can find expression in its lack of its own
presence and its subjugation to the presence of the Other. Kristeva argues
that all humans desire a connection with 'something outside', whether
that something is represented by another human being or by the presence
of the Divine. When one's ego collapses through a union with that Other,
that moment is one's connection with the abject, which is desirable in
some ways because it is 'edged with the sublime';[51] we desire it, and
yet we fear its power to engulf us.

The relationship between the experience of the mystic, in which one's identity and ego are submerged in the power of the Divine Other, is explored only briefly by Kristeva in *Powers of Horror*, but somewhat more at length by Luce Irigaray in her chapter, 'La Mystérique'. Irigaray's term *la mystérique* is a combination of the French words *mystic* and *hystérique*, creating an image of a hysterical, mad feminine subject who has experienced a moment of mystical vision. She writes that this experience of mysticism is feminine, that it is

> the only place in the history of the West in which woman speaks and acts so publicly ... [it] is the place where 'she' – and in some cases he, if he follows 'her' lead – speaks about the dazzling glare which comes from the source of light that has been logically repressed, about 'subject' and 'Other' flowing out into an embrace of fire that mingles one term into another.[52]

When the speaker in the *Wohunge* makes such statements as 'Iesu swete iesu / þus tu faht for me aȝenes / mine sawle fan. þu me deren/nedes wið like. & makedes of me / wrecche þi leofman & spuse' [Jesus, sweet Jesus, in this way you fought for me against the enemies of my soul. You vindicated me with your body, and made of me, a wretch, your lover and spouse],[53] one hears in her voice this understanding that, having been gloriously won from her foes, her own body, and even her soul, now exist only in Christ. In other words, she has experienced the abjection of self, and 'joyed in it', as Kristeva describes. The abject appears even more forcefully throughout the text. Close to the end of the poem, the speaker describes Christ as 'humiliated ... brought low for my love'.[54] Images of penetration fill the final passages of the poem, as the passion, death and resurrection of Christ are played out.

> hu ha þe bunden swa
> hetelifaste þat te blod wrang ut at
> tine finger neiles as halhes
> bileuen & bunden ledden rewli &
> dintede unrideli o rug & o schul
> dres. & bifore þe princes buffeted &
> beten. Siðen bifore pilat hu þu
> was naket bunden faste to þe pi
> ler. þat tu ne mihtes nowhider
> wrenche fra þa duntes.[55]

[how they bound you so cruelly tight that the blood was wrung out at your finger-nails, as the saints believe; and, bound, led you wretchedly, and, struck you harshly on your back and shoulders, and buffeted and beat you before the princes – then, before Pilate, how you were stripped, bound fast to the pillar, so that you could in no way flinch from the blows.][56]

The combination of feminine and masculine images here – flowing blood and the pillar – underscores the dualistic nature of the gendered body of Christ in this poem.

Anchoritic mysticism, then, examined through the theories of French feminism, can be seen as inherently feminine in its poetic nature and in its power to subvert traditional discourse. Medieval mysticism, especially that found in anchoritic texts such as *þe Wohunge of Ure Lauerd*, represents a medieval expression of *l'écriture féminine* which exists as a means of transgressing and disrupting convention and tradition. This disruption is accomplished through its use of the erotic and sensual imagery which is characteristic of most mystical writing after 1200, and through its non-conventional language (in that it is, after 1200, written almost exclusively in the vernacular), and finally through its connection to the abject, something systematically marginalized by patriarchal society because of its relationship to the semiotic/pre-symbolic, and thus 'feminine' expression of the *chora*. Mysticism is first and most importantly a transgressive means of expression. It is non-traditional, non-mainstream; the mystic is always one who is different.

According to Monique Wittig, heterosexual gender is culturally and socially determined, while that which is not heterosexual is not part of that culture or society, though perhaps affected by it; the homosexual exists outside of the heterosexual. Her concern is with the lesbian, and she suggests that lesbianism functions outside of traditional gender because it has no meaning outside of 'heterosexual systems of thought and heterosexual economic systems'.[57] She argues that a lesbian is not a woman because a lesbian is not defined, as a 'woman' always must be, in relation to men.[58] This idea might also be applied to the mystic, who is non-traditional, unorthodox, and cannot be understood in the conventional sense of human experience; thus she cannot be completely defined by the standards of orthodox tradition, whether it is a tradition of theology or literature. Wittig gives to the lesbian the power to be within 'a free cultural space – free of violence, free of control, even free of social determination'.[59] This might also be said of the mystic who, by defying tradition and convention, provides for herself a similarly free cultural, political, literary, and theological space. Thus, just as the lesbian is, for Wittig, 'beyond the categories of sex (woman and man)', so, too can the mystical writer be seen as beyond the categories of traditional definitions of Christian expression and, thus, like the lesbian, beyond traditional categories of gender. The entire nature of gender and its relationship to mysticism must thus be called into question and re-examined. Rather than dividing mysticism into that which is female-authored or male-authored, a new definition can be presented in which the genre is determined as culturally feminine, possibly even lesbian (according to Wittig's definition), whether the mystical text itself is written by a man or a woman.

My argument is that the genre of mysticism represents some expression of a culturally feminine theological and perhaps literary impulse, one expressed by both men and women in the Middle Ages. Thus, if it can be argued that the voice or at least the persona of the mystic is feminine, then the sex of the author herself is not important; it is the genre which is gendered, not simply the texts within it. Thompson had a sense of this notion of mysticism, at least as it was represented in the text of *þe Wohunge of Ure Lauerd*, as a feminine means of expression. In his introduction, he wrote that

> Whoever wrote the *Wohunge* has left it strongly marked with individuality, immediacy, and an almost complete independence of conventional surroundings, earthly intercessors, and hierarchical orders; [and] marked with a passionate elevation which has much less of the sense of sin than most of the related writings, and a self-absorption of will and heart leading to the all but entire self-forgetfulness which marks the true mystic.[60]

I would go one step further with this characterization and give this author credit with moving both into and beyond entire self-forgetfulness. If we are to consider Kristeva's notion that the mystic's complete lack of self leads to an ultimate affirmation of self in the abject, then what we see in the *Wohunge* is a mystic who has at least started to understand that transition. In this text, we find a voice giving words to what can surely not be fully grasped in human language. And yet the text is there, and the mystic, resisting, perhaps, the struggle that has taken place for her soul, affirms her own presence in the presence of God, using language to express the extra-linguistic, using physical images to describe her liminal experience, and reminding us that, as Kristeva would argue, the ultimate experience of self may only occur when the self (however it has been constructed) has been completely lost in the Other.

Notes

1 This essay is based on a paper presented at the Southeast Medieval Association, September 1994, Marymount University, Arlington, VA.
2 Kristeva, *Powers of Horror,* 9.
3 Butler, *Gender Trouble*, 91.
4 *The Cloud of Unknowing*, ed. Hodgson, 46–7.
5 *The Cloud of Unknowing*, trans. Progoff, 162–3.
6 Unless I am referring specifically to men, I will refer to the medieval mystic throughout this text with the feminine pronoun. I think this makes sense for the sake of specificity and clarity, as well as further dramatizing what I think must be seen as the feminization of the mystic through the mystical experience.
7 Marquette, *Comparative Mysticism*, 22.
8 Watson, 'Methods and objectives', n.10.
9 See also Dinzelbacher, 'Beginnings of mysticism', 126.
10 *Ibid.*, 127.
11 *Ibid.*, 127.
12 Elkins, *Holy Women*, 156.
13 *þe Wohunge*, ed. Thompson, lines 253–62.
14 Savage and Watson, *Anchoritic Spirituality*, 251.
15 Watson, 'Methods and objectives,' 146
16 *þe Wohunge,* ed. Thompson, xviii.
17 *Ibid.*, xviii.
18 Dobson, *Origins*, 154.
19 Savage and Watson, *Anchoritic Spirituality*, 418–19.
20 Millett, 'Women in No-Man's Land', 98–9.
21 By *Other* here I mean that which is the negation of the dominant paradigm, yet by which the dominant paradigm defines itself. In the case of the Christian Middle Ages, the dominant paradigm is patriarchy, phallogocentrism. Thus the Other is that which is the negation of the patriarchal. This includes, but is not limited to, the feminine.
22 Savage and Watson, *Anchoritic Spirituality*, 20.
23 Elkins, *Holy Women,* 151.
24 *Ibid.*, 152.
25 Evidence exists that some recluses lived in communities, within the same anchorholds (Elkins, *Holy Women*, 159). Because of this, both Aelred's *Rule for a Recluse* and the *Ancrene Wisse* make comments about friendships between women. Elkins writes, '[Aelred] discouraged visits from nuns and other women ... the recluse was to "sit alone then, in silence, listening to Christ and speaking with him ... For then she is with Christ, and he would not care to be with her in a crowd"', *Holy Women*, 154. Elkins goes on to argue that by the time of the 'Katherine Group' (the period in which the *Wohunge*

was probably first written), a fear of close relationships between celibates – heterosexual relationships as well as homosexual – was growing, so that by the late thirteenth century recluses were even further restricted: 'virginity was protected and the friendships abandoned', *Holy Women*, 160.

[26] Golding, *Gilbert of Sempringham*, 20; cf. Thompson, *Women Religious*, 16–37.

[27] See article, this volume, by Galloway above, 94.

[28] *Ibid.*

[29] From my unpublished edition of the Life of St Etheldreda, transcribed from Bodl. 779 (Vernon), line 14.

[30] Elkins, *Holy Women*, 22.

[31] *The Life of Christina of Markyate*, ed. and trans. Talbot, 9.

[32] It is difficult not to think here of the narrator of the *Wohunge* as she refers to Christ as her beloved (*lemman*). Throughout the text (and those of the other anchoritic works of the period) use of romantic language is encouraged and a very fine line is drawn between the explicitly sexual metaphors used by the authors and the reality of cloistered virginity that faced their audiences.

[33] *The Life of Christina of Markyate*, ed. and trans. Talbot, 138.

[34] In one of her visions, Christine 'while "rapt in ecstasy", saw herself in the presence of Christ. There she saw Geoffrey, "encircled with her arms and held closely to her breast",' Elkins, *Holy Women*, 36.

[35] *Ibid.*, 37.

[36] *Ibid.*. 37

[37] McNamara, 'The Herrenfrage', 7.

[38] Elkins, *Holy Women*, 153.

[39] *Ibid.*, 155.

[40] *þe Wohunge*, ed. Thompson, ll. 598–602.

[41] Savage and Watson, *Anchoritic Spirituality*, 256.

[42] Martin, *Fifteenth-Century Carthusian Reform*, 215.

[43] *Ibid.*, 219.

[44] *þe Wohunge*, ed. Thompson, ll. 270–9.

[45] Savage and Watson, *Anchoritic Spirituality*, 251–2.

[46] *þe Wohunge*, ed. Thompson, ll. 290–3.

[47] Derrida, *Of Grammatology*.

[48] Cixous, 'The Laugh of the Medusa', 251.

[49] Quoted by Sellers, *Language and Sexual Difference*, 103.

[50] Kristeva, *Powers of Horror*, 5.

[51] *Ibid.*, 11.

[52] Irigaray, *Speculum of the Other Woman*, 191.

[53] *þe Wohunge*, ed. Thompson, ll. 568–79; translation is from Savage and Watson, *Anchoritic Spirituality*, 256.

[54] Savage and Watson, *Anchoritic Spirituality*, 253.

[55] *þe Wohunge*, ed. Thompson, lines 467–76.

[56] Savage and Watson, *Anchoritic Spirituality*, 254.

[57] Wittig, *The Straight Mind*, 32.

[58] Kristevan semiotics is, according to Terry Eagleton, 'opposed to all fixed, transcendental significations . . . [it] throws into confusion all tight divisions between masculine and feminine – it is a "bisexual" form of writing – and offers to deconstruct all the scrupulous binary oppositions . . . by which societies such as ours survive', *Literary Theory*, 189. The similarity between this bisexual sense of the semiotic and Wittig's idea of the lesbian work well together in understanding feminine mysticism.

[59] Fuss, *Essentially Speaking*, 43.

[60] þe Wohunge, ed. Thompson, xxiv.

Bibliography

Aelred of Rievaulx, *The Works of Aelred of Rievaulx*, I, ed. M. P. Macpherson (Spenser, MA, 1971).

Aelred of Rievaulx, *De Institutione Inclusarum: Two Versions*, eds. J. Ayto and A. Barratt (London, 1984).

Bede, *Historical Works*, trans. J. E. King (Cambridge, MA, 1930).

Burns, E. J., *Bodytalk: When Women Speak in Old French Literature* (Philadelphia, 1993).

Butler, J., *Gender Trouble: Feminism and the Subversion of Identity* (London, 1990).

Chodorow, N., *Feminism and Psychoanalytic Theory* (New Haven, 1989).

Cixous, H., 'The Laugh of the Medusa', trans. K. Cohen and P. Cohen in E. Marks and I. de Courtivron (eds.), *New French Feminisms: An Anthology* (New York, 1980), 245–64.

The Cloud of Unknowing, trans. I. Progoff (New York, 1957).

The Cloud of Unknowing, ed. P. Hodgson (Salzburg, 1982).

Derrida, J., *Of Grammatology*, trans. G. Spivak (Baltimore, 1977).

Dinzelbacher, P., 'The beginnings of mysticism experienced in twelfth-century England' in M. Glasscoe (ed.), *The Medieval Mystical Tradition in England* (Cambridge, 1978), 111–31.

Dobson, E. J., *The Origins of Ancrene Wisse* (Oxford, 1976).

Eagleton, T., *Literary Theory: An Introduction* (Minneapolis, 1983).

Edwards, A. S. G. (ed.), *Middle English Prose: A Critical Guide to Major Authors and Genres* (New Brunswick, 1986).

Elkins, S., *Holy Women in Twelfth Century England* (Chapel Hill, 1988).

Fisher, S. and Halley, J. E (eds.), *Seeking the Woman in Late Medieval and Renaissance Writings: Essays in Feminist Contextual Criticism* (Knoxville, 1989).

Foucault, M., *The History of Sexuality*, I–III (New York, 1978–80).

Fuss, D., *Essentially Speaking: Feminism, Nature, and Difference* (New York, 1989).

Golding, B., *Gilbert of Sempringham and the Gilbertine Order, c.1130–c.1300* (Oxford, 1995).

Irigaray, L., *Speculum of the Other Woman*, trans. G. C. Gill (Ithaca, 1985).

Jones, A. R., 'Julia Kristeva on femininity: the limits of semiotic politics', *Feminist Review* 18 (1984), 56–73.

Kristeva, J., *Powers of Horror: An Essay in Abjection* (New York, 1982).

Kristeva, J., *The Kristeva Reader*, trans. T. Moi (New York, 1986).

Lacan, J., *Écrits: A Selection*, trans. A. Sheridan (New York, 1977).

The Life of Christina of Markyate: A Twelfth-Century Recluse, ed. and trans. C. H. Talbot (Oxford, 1959).

Lomparis, L. and Stanbury, S. (eds.), *Feminist Approaches to the Body in Medieval Literature* (Philadelphia, 1993).

McNamara, J., 'The Herrenfrage: the restructuring of the gender system, 1050–1150', in C. Lees (ed.), *Medieval Masculinities: Regarding Men in the Middle Ages* (Minneapolis, 1994), 3–30.

Marquette, J. de, *An Introduction to Comparative Mysticism* (New York, 1949).

Martin, D., *Fifteenth-Century Carthusian Reform: The World of Nicholas Kempf* (New York, 1992).

Mechtild von Magdeburg, *The Flowing Light of the Divinity*, ed. S. L. Clark, trans. C. M. Galvanti (New York, 1991).

Millett, B., 'Women in No-Man's Land: English recluses and the development of vernacular literature in the twelfth and thirteenth centuries', in C. Meale (ed.), *Women and Literature in Britain, 1150–1500* (Cambridge, 1993), 86–103.

Newman, B., *From Virile Woman to WomanChrist: Studies in Medieval Religion and Literature* (Philadelphia, 1995).

Savage, A. and Watson, N. (eds.), *Anchoritic Spirituality: Ancrene Wisse and Associated Works* (New York, 1991).

Schulenburg, J. T., 'The heroics of virginity: Brides of Christ and sacrificial mutilation', in M .B. Rose (ed.), *Women in the Middle Ages and the Renaissance: Literary and Historical Perspectives* (Syracuse, 1986), 29–72.

Sellers, S., *Language and Sexual Difference* (New York, 1991).

Thompson, S., *Women Religious: The Founding of English Nunneries after the Norman Conquest* (Oxford, 1991).

Watson, N., 'The methods and objectives of thirteenth-century Anchoritic devotion', in M. Glasscoe (ed.), *The Medieval Mystical Tradition in England* (Cambridge, 1987), 132–53.

Wittig, M., *The Straight Mind and Other Essays* (London, 1992).

þe Wohunge of Ure Lauerd, ed. W. M. Thompson (London, 1958).

6

Communities of Otherness in Chaucer's
Merchant's Tale

CYNTHIA KRAMAN

THERE are many types of communities, including communities of the marginalized, one might say, communities of othernesses comprised of representations, texts, concepts, cultural groups who are appropriated as other in any cultural moment. Chaucer's *Merchant's Tale*, characterized by Charles Muscatine as 'mixed',[1] is mixed not only in terms of genres and highly various source material, but is also an admixture of such communities. This paper proposes to investigate the tale and its others: the body of woman, the sexual body, landscape, and Jewish text and its understandings.

While there have been critical discussions of Chaucer's *Merchant's Tale* and landscape, most notably D. W. Robertson's 'The Doctrine of Charity in Medieval Literary Gardens' as well as an ongoing gender discussion of the tale as part of the 'marriage group', this discussion sees the *Tale* as an exploration, even a valorization, of the ability, even the necessity, of the human imagination restlessly to project its desires on to a series of 'that which it is not' in order to define and discuss what it is or may be. It remains as well an investigation of sexuality. In Chaucer's hands this develops into an ironic review of contemporary *idées reçues* on the female body. However, the *Tale* does yet more. Because the *Tale*'s primary landscape originates in the *Song of Songs*, a text used by both the central Christian culture and the marginal community of Jewish scholars to define itself and each other,[2] their discussions attach to those already delineated. This layering of othernesses suggests the ambiguous nature of the other as something feared and desired in one and the same moment.

The concept of otherness incites the scrutiny of absence and presence, since the designated other is so often erased or fetishized[3] as an expression of cultural anxieties. This magic is linked in much current thought[4] to the female body, which as fetish is a provocative and disturbing presence, as erasure a longed-for and tantalizing absence. This body, a vexed subject in any culture, becomes particularly desirable and dangerous as an object of Christian taboo – its physicality, location and even its existence become problematic. Within the tradition of landscape *descriptio* a solution emerges – that of handling the female body and rendering it less hot to handle in language by linking it through description to landscape. The body, absorbed into the language of flowers and trees, is effectively disembodied.

A figure often used in this process in medieval literature is the *hortus conclusus* or enclosed garden. The figure of the *hortus conclusus* becomes, by the late Middle Ages, a well-known piece of landscape *descriptio*.[5] It bifurcates into two seemingly oppositional *loci*, both involving the body of woman. On the one hand it is the delicious garden of love and metonymically, the body of the beloved; closed, exclusive, difficult to secure, but ultimately approachable and even penetrable by the bold lover. On the other hand it is Ecclesia, the unconquerable Holy Church, embodied on earth as Mary, forever virginal and intact.[6] These two understandings are exploited in the *Merchant's Tale* for sheer humour, a strategy already used by madcap goliardic wits for two centuries, as well as Welsh bards, whose *Cywyddwyr* poetry, in the many examples Cartwright provides in her essay in this volume, are full of blasphemous love lyrics. But in Chaucer's hands the absurdity of the situation becomes an opportunity for a more serious sort of play, one which amounts to a thorough review and commentary upon contemporary representations and receptions of the body of woman in literature.

This technique of attaching the body to landscape is shared with the text which provides the originary moment for the walled garden, the short biblical poem known as the *Song of Songs* and specifically verse 4:12 'My sister, my spouse, is a garden enclosed, a garden enclosed, a fountain sealed up.' The poem is a love song. In it the two lovers, who were eventually referred to as the Bride and the Bridegroom, are described largely through landscape features. However, the text has a dimension of otherness in addition to its attachment of body to landscape, which is its status as a central text taken from a marginalized community, one eradicated from England in a racial cleansing made national policy in 1290. The expulsion of the Jews was only a symptom of difficulties inherent in appropriating the book of a group both hated as presence and revered as absence. In order to overcome the difficulty of using the sacred book of those who were considered bearers of blood-guilt, the 'analogic' interpretation was put forward by Augustine[7] and others, which transformed the Written Law into a series of prefigurations of the coming of Christ. However, Jews continued to live and write in the Christian world, and their views were persistently hovering, just out of reach and occasionally uncomfortably within it, instancing a classical situation of cultural ambivalence regarding the community of their texts. Resolution was sought in argumentation; the Hebrew texts remained a battleground, especially that of *Song of Songs*, upon which both Christian and Jewish theologians and mystics dilated endlessly.[8] So that in addition to the otherness outlined above, the otherness of this text as one which is foreign and problematic also promotes the diversity and novelty of the conversation on love and marriage which springs up *sub rosa* in January's lively *hortus conclusus*.

The enclosed garden of the *Tale* is built by January, an old and lecherous knight of Pavia, as a playground for his new young bride, May:

> He made a gardyn, walled al with stoon
> So fair a gardyn woot I nowher noon.
> For, out of doute, I verraily suppose
> That he that wroot the Romance of the Rose
> Ne koude of it the beautee wel devyse
> (2029–33)

Given this literary parentage, January's garden is a love garden, or more accurately, a variety of sex garden, where the adventurous lover goes to pick out and eventually pluck a young tender bud as the dreamer so ardently hopes to do in Guillaume's *Roman de la rose*.

However, it is also the garden of the *Song of Songs*, and not only because it is walled, but because of the words used within it by January to woo May. He implores her to 'Com forth' in the yearning words of the *Song*, which were by the twelfth century part of well-known Marian Assumption hymns. He describes his juicy young bride in words used to address the Virgin – 'my white spouse' (2144). With these words January not only reveals himself as a poor judge of character (underscored by his esteem for young Damyan who handily takes his place), but of course he places himself in a landscape where he does not belong – sacred in Christian terms, but characterized at other times and places as not only sacred but sexual, an explosive concept which acts as another lens through which to view the *Tale*.

Yet if the enclosed garden were merely the site of a young wife mistaken for the Virgin, the *Tale* would be a satire, but a simple satire of a garden variety sort of delusion, about ridiculous old age, the *senex amans* theme replayed yet again. An old man deludes himself – he thinks that he can find happiness with a young wife. In this reading one form of human silliness simply underscores the next. January is as silly to call his wife the Holy Virgin as he is to accept her explanation that his sight was returned through the cure of her sexual act up a pear tree with young Damyan. His blindness is just blindness to plain common sense. But others have seen more to it than that. Robertson's early article alone, in proposing the *Tale* as a sort of hypertext to the Biblical discussion of *caritas*, has rescued it from ever being seen as nothing more than an expanded version of a clever and naughty French *fabliau*.

The tale is certainly about delusion, but not simply the old saw that an aged man should not believe he can satisfy a young woman. Rather, it takes up the received idea that the body of woman is possessable and available, that it can be secured and shut away for personal enjoyment as one does to flowers by building a garden with a wall, a door, a lock, and the inevitable 'clycket'. All this sounds the note that will be repeated throughout the tale, which is that in all realms – physical, emotional, metaphysical – there is not only a reaction to every action, but actions going on initiated by wills and forces which an egotist such as January cannot imagine or perceive. He is under the very widely experienced delusion that he can initiate, plan, and carry out a marriage more or less by himself. Reciprocal desire never enters his mind. He feels he can buy a fresh and pretty wife, and in the *Tale* the exchange of wealth for the body of woman will bring two people into a bed, but the convincing, procreative sexual act occurs elsewhere, up a tree, fuelled by reciprocal human lust. The wifely body is possessable on a literal level, but her desire is difficult to elicit and secure.

Moreover, these delusions on the possessibility and will-less body of woman rest, in the *Tale*, very clearly on received and perpetuated literary conventions. The *Tale* offers a send-up of the whole courtly convention of attaching the body of woman to landscape, of attempting to transform it into something elusive and disappeared. This is the literary technique of the dreamer in Guillaume's *Roman* (which includes its own internal critique of the strategy it proposes) whereby the dreamer, searching for his Rose, finds her in a walled garden, down a well, in a reflection, hedged about by other roses, and therefore utterly out of reach. Unfortunately, she is still available to sight and smell. This turns out to be provocation enough to torture the dreamer through the following thousands of lines.

The distancing attempt is also the literary technique chosen by the narrator of the *Knight's Tale*, where Emily's inaccessibility is handled in the first instance by transforming her into a jewelled springtime garden within the garden of the castle. After she is erased this way, her erstwhile admirers supplant her with male competitiveness; their fight is only peripherally about her as time goes on. In the *Kingis Quair* the lady is simply 'floure', another jewelled garden. As such she is the emblem of the narrator's hopes, fears, ambitions, plans, deliverance. This fusion of the lady into landscape, most often accomplished by having her assume a floral presence, is a convention of courtly literature. Such courtly literature conventions are spoofed continuously by Chaucer in *Merchant's Tale*, in his constant duplications of language from the earlier tale ('For, pitee renneth soone in gentil herte', *Knight's Tale*, 1761) and in the contrast between Emily and May. They are also spoofed in his use of the courtly garden of love. In previous literature, when the body is absorbed into the language of trees and flowers, it is disembodied. But here May's body is altogether resistant to this erasure, awake to its own desires and supported by a fully individuated will.

If the *Tale*'s use of landscape constructs a commentary first upon the nature of human love, and then of courtly literature, it also spills into a larger discussion on the nature of the universe itself by using the most devotional phraseology of love from *Canticles*. In the hymns and prayers using the poem, the Virgin is closed and shut, the incarnate version of an inviolate Church. In this world view the love of God is extremely high and distant, and its intercessor is shut and untouchable. It is here that the text's own resistance to this paradigm substitutes a universe where the love between humans is uncontainable, where the body is a garden and the universe is a body, sexual, procreative, and creative.[9] Theseus' great chain of love has melted into something more fluid and multi-directional.

What, then, are the characteristics of the *Song of Songs* and its attendant commentary, which made it the vehicle for so much information? On its face, it is a love and sex song, used at some time as a drinking song since there is a specific Talmudic prohibition against doing so,[10] but which was none the less included in the canonical texts of the Hebrew Bible and characterized as not only sacred, but, echoing its title, as the holiest of holies. This appellation is characterized in rabbinical tradition as a transcription, verbatim, of the outcry of the foremost rabbi of his generation, Rabbi Akiba. It is not found in a tractate on the scroll itself, but in a Talmudic tractate dealing with ritual cleanliness called *Yadayim* (*Hands*), a discussion of problems arising from physical contact with sacred books. The fervour behind Rabbi Akiba's insistence is palpable. 'The whole world is not as worthy as the day the Song of Songs was given to Israel,' he declares, 'for all the writings are holy but the Song of Songs is the holy of holies.'[11]

Yet the *Song* seems a strange candidate for this enthusiasm. It is a poem, or collection of poetic fragments,[12] in which three or four parties are involved, the two prominent voices belonging to male and female lovers, who on the best evidence have consummated this love and fall to admiring each other, and asking each other to resume a love interrupted at the outset by miscommunications. The poem is narrated by her, although sometimes using the persona of her lover as well as the others, who are a chorus of her sisters, or her sisters and brothers. It is also a poem which attaches the body to landscape in nearly every line. The bodies of the lovers are constructed through references which move immediately into landscape as neither static nor disconnected, but existing in the impossible liminal territory of the word in conjunction with the free imagination, where bodies are potentialities joining anatomical references and landscape features, and also the movements of loss and desire that connote a mentality and emotionality for the colossal figures moving in perpetual time and space.

Moreover, these bodies, for all their pure physicality, are difficult to locate. It is often impossible to ascertain who is speaking at any given moment. Meek comments, 'much of the syntax is unusual; for example, the frequent substitution of masculine for feminine forms in pronouns, verbs and suffixes'.[13] The confusion of speakers points to the flowingness and exchange which characterize the *Song*. And although Julia Kristeva identifies the female voice as 'the amorous wife . . . who speaks and sets herself up as equal, in her legal, named, unguilty love, to the other's sovereignty',[14] there is nothing within the poem to suggest legalities, nor, on the part of the woman, an insistence upon the sovereignty of her lover. The poem is not an enunciation of differences but an exchange of likenesses of powers and desires spoken out by the lovers, whoever they are at any given moment.

In addition to the constant exchange of epithets, there is a further attachment of body/landscape into world/landscape since the adjectives applied to the lovers are applied also to the 'surroundings'. The lovers move in landscapes of vineyards, nut gardens, lilies, hyacinth, pomegranate, honeycomb, apples and apple trees, palm trees, fig trees, cypress, aloe and aromatics such as saffron, frankincense and myrrh, as well as watery places including fountains, floods and flowing streams. All these terms are also applied to the lovers. This allows the text to flow effortlessly from body to body to world, and back.

The very physicality of the *Song*, not to mention its overt sexuality, make it a strange choice as a central text for either Judaism or Christianity. The tenor of the discussion in *Yadayim* makes it apparent that several positions on it had been held over some time[15] and there are other indirect proofs about attitudes towards the *Song*, of varying reliability.[16] What is important is that after Rabbi Akiba's vehement utterance, the poem could not be dismissed, and in order to understand it, Jews had to investigate its *derash* (deep, hidden) meaning rather than its *peshat* (plain, literal) meaning. It was henceforth an allegory, a point underlined in another tractate, *'Abot de-Rabbi Natan* in which the poem, along with other sexual material from Proverbs and Ecclesiastes, is said to be only open to allegorical interpretation.[17] All this released it from the prevalent Judaic, and later Christian, admonition, that Scripture be treated if possible *ad litteram* (literally) to unfold first its *peshat* (plain)[18] meaning. This was obviously not possible in the case of the *Song*. Thus from this point on, and possibly for centuries before, the volatile conjoining of the sacred and the sexual would be accomplished through forceful and highly imaginative commentary.

For Jewish exegetes the *Song* became *hieros gamos* (sacred union). It recorded God's love for the Jewish people; his 'kisses' were the Law, the consummation was the giving of the Law at Sinai. Certain early exegeses of *Shir Ha-Shirim* are redacted in the *Midrash Rabbah, Midrash Shir Ha-Shirim* and other sources[19] but the most important medieval scholar, whose commentary is considered definitive is Rashi (Rabbi Shlomo (Solomon) ben Isaac, 1040–1105). He was not only important to Jewish exegesis, but fed into the Christian tradition directly. His biblical commentaries formed the basis for those of Nicholas de Lyra (1270–1342), including those on the *Song*. Also, Aryeh Grabois offers a convincing argument that members of Rashi's school at Troyes came to the Cistercian community at Citeaux in 1190 at the request of founder Stephen Harding to help correct the disparate bibles on hand.[20] In Harding's *Monitum* to the monks he says he is doing so to establish a single line of truth, from one 'Hebraica veritas' through Jerome to them. The *Monitum* relates how 'The Jews, unrolling a number of their scrolls in front of us, and explaining to us in French what was written . . . we completely erased all the unnecessary additions.'[21] There is no mention of copying commentary here, but a complete translation of Rashi's commentary on *Song of Songs* was attempted, with appropriate, often subtle adaptations to the Vulgate version, in the mid-thirteenth-century *Expositio Hystorica Cantici Canticorum Secundum Salomoneum*.[22]

It is a twist of the argument that of all commentators, Rashi is considered most *peshat* – therefore in this instance his genius lies in his ability to comment on his nation's history and the sacred marriage while maintaining the poem's intimacy. For instance, in his commentary on 'Under the apple-tree I aroused you' (8:5) he offers a paradigm of human love-play as a way of describing Israel's memory of Sinai. Rashi comments:

> So she says in the request of the affection of her beloved:
> 'Under the apple-tree I aroused You.' That is the expression of the affection of the wife of one's youth, who arouses her beloved at night when he is asleep on his bed, and embraces and kisses him.[23]

The utter sweetness is evident. Also obvious is his great distance from Christian writers in his approach to sexuality. For Judaism, marriage began and remained the sacred model. Celibacy was not encouraged; in fact, it was not allowed. In this tradition the body is created and possessed by God. The attempt is to make marriage, through ritual, a movement toward purity as well as a reflection of the fecundity and power of God.

It also offers an opposing model to that of the marriage of the tale, since human marriage, though in no way truly comparable to the sacred one, does, through Rashi's love talk, offer a model for reciprocity. But Jewish exegesis as a whole offers something more multidirectional and even interpenetrating as the overarching paradigm for all realities in its polyvalent and endlessly intertextual strategies. If a word is just a word, it may be significant, but it is still simply a term for which some equivalent or partnering word might be found. However, with such far-reaching hermeneutics, each word contains a cluster of attitudes, lessons, values, indications, predictions – so that to have these flow in only one direction would negate the poem's overall allegorical import, that the love which Israel has for God is answered (tenfold!) by the love of the Bridegroom for his Bride – even if she will not open the door for him because she has already washed her feet and turned in for the night. The unlocatable voices, the physicality that constructs abstraction, the accruing of meaning throughout the centuries, all give the *Song* an extremely important position in the scholastic garden, which needs strong yet ambiguous text to enrich its luxuriant growth. The rather tawdry world of the *Tale* is not that of the originary Bride and Bridegroom, nor is Damyan and May's love in any way a reflection of God's love for man. But the constant references to 'Salomon' and the *Song* point out the weaknesses of some of the more totalizing effects of its Christian exegesis. If the world can no longer be the radiant one of the rabbis, where human love shares in some infinitesimal way with the grandeur of divine love, it is also not bound into the bodiless, pure and celibate model of a Church standing at the centre of a culture which has drawn up its bridges and excluded so many that its representative member, an old knight, is more or less left alone with his delusions. His onanistic fantasy life prepares the way for the aridity of his marital exercise; the construction of his unworkable secret garden sets the scene for his grovelling acceptance of May's physical favours. It is through the *Song* references attaching to the Tale's landscapes and bodies that a critique of such a world begins, and the attendant metamorphosis of much conventional wisdom.

The *Song* references in the *Merchant's Tale* fall into three major groups. The first is the attention paid to the *hortus conclusus* which, as delineated above, resonates here with the garden of the *Roman de la rose*. This garden is used to enclose May, and she is expected to become, like Mary,[24] an embodiment of it – secluded, off-limits, but always fresh and available. However, although January locks her into the garden, both she and it easily open themselves to permit infiltration and welcomed occupation.

The next group is a subset of the previous one, for January attaches himself to landscape as well:

> Though I be hoor, I fare as dooth a tree
> That blosmeth er that fruyt ywoxen bee;
> And blosmy tree nys neither drye ne deed
> I feele me nowhere hoor but on myn heed;
> Myn herte and alle my lymes been as grene
> As laurer thurgh the yeer is for to sene. (1461–6)

Here January moves himself into the position of future bridegroom, so that through his attachment to landscape and wooing of his wife with Solomonic words, he is by analogy the Hebrew king, but because Solomon is analogically Christ as the Bridegroom in the *Song*,[25] he is also the King of Kings. This makes him totally ridiculous, for he is in no sense Christ-like, and his marriage (like any other marriage) cannot be a 'paradys terrestre' (1332).

By mentioning the laurel, he also attaches himself to the female enclosed garden, and in fact he selects a nice phallic representation:

> The beautee of the gardyn and the welle
> That stood under a laurer alwey grene. (2036–7)

It is not strange that he define himself as a tree, nor an evergreen one, because he is gleefully unaware of the age belied by his crackling voice and shaking neck folds (1849–50). However, in the *Roman* it is a pine tree which shades the well. The laurel, on the other hand, is associated with one of the great stories of forced love in Ovid's *Metamorphoses*; the tale of Apollo and Daphne. When Apollo attempts to take her, Daphne snatches victory by surrendering her humanity. She becomes a laurel tree. Ovid relates how when Apollo swears he will use the laurel as a sign of victory, her leafy arms wave, perhaps in acquiescence, a gesture May would never make. January has again put his foot in things on a literary level – he has identified himself with a god-rapist from the Greek heavens, but transformed himself as well into the victim of that classical moment.

This particular incarnation of January links to another figure who eventually brings up the *Song* again, through references to its purported author, 'Salomon'. This is begun by antiquity's most infamous rapist, Pluto, who shows up in January's garden by way of Claudian (2232). Here, however, he is not the iron-willed King of the Underworld but a sort of Celtic fairy of the green world, presently very much married to a sharp-tongued Proserpina. She, in turn, has surrendered her victim status in this new version of their story. Yet another literary model for love is about to be destroyed. Not only are the disembody-through-description model and the lock-them-up-and-worship-them model done in, but the classical take-and-rape model is here deflated by laughter as well. As four hundred years later Offenbach would take the tragedy out of the Orpheus-Eurydice story by making them a bourgeois, bickering couple, Chaucer takes this tragic couple and makes a king and queen of the sprites who spend their time dancing and arguing.

The domestic fairy couple, who replace St Peter and God from one of the closest analogues to the *Tale*[26] make up most of the third set of *Song* references, which are those which seek to quote 'Salomon' as an authority. Earlier in the tale Salomon is to Placebo the giver of outdated advice, since advice, as everyone knows, is never listened to by any lord (1487–1504). Now Pluto, arguing for the right of January to discover his wife's adultery, quotes Salomon on the baseness of women (2242–48).

However, Proserpina knows her Old Testament and recounts Salomon's vices of lechery and idolatry (2291–2304). In fact, she demotes Salomon further by bringing up famous good women from Christian and Roman history (2276–85). Like the Wife of Bath, as sick as she is of the language of dominance and authority, she is a mistress of its rhetoric. She begins,

> 'What rekketh me of youre auctoritees?
> I woot wel that this Jew, this Salomon,
> Foond of us wommen fooles many oon.' (2276–80)

yet ten lines later she is using him as her own authority,

> 'Though that he seyde he foond no good womman
> I prey yow take the sentence of the man;
> He mente thus, that in sovereyn bontee
> Nis noon but God, but neither he ne she.' (2287–90)

She knows that the sovereign good lies only with God. Her formulation bonds the sexes in the burden of sin, as the tale amply illustrates. For her this is the 'sentence' or import of the old Jew's words – that God is good, but man and woman have each other to deal with. The back-and-forth banter of the fairy king and queen, their domesticity compared with both analogue and source, all contribute to the closeness and reciprocity of the sexes for whom each argues in their war of words. And although there is certainly a verbal war of the sexes in January's garden which is already removed from the distant passionate exchanges of the *Song* lovers, at least there is in Proserpina's version of the relationship of woman and man a give and take to which January is indeed blind.

January conceives of his need for a wife out of his private lusts, needs and fantasies. When he wants to find one, he does not even bother to look for a real woman, but goes 't'espien' (1257, 1410, 1413) in the mirrored marketplace of his mind's eye for 'many fair shap and many a fair visage' (1580) like the lover in the *Roman* who looks into the mirror of the well and sees a 'rosier chargiez de roses'[27] (a rosebush heavy with roses) – the splendid male prerogative of choice enacted again and again, and finalized here with an exchange of money. In the *Tale* this understanding is underscored by the authorial voice (which is often thought of as the Merchant's)[28] pointing out that while lands, rents, and goods are gifts of Fortune, a wife is God's gift (1311–15). This conflation by contrast of woman and thing is followed by some commonplaces about Eve and her role as the helpmate of Adam (1331) and yet the lines are interestingly mixed. For Eve is not only helpmate but 'lyk to hymself' in God's words (1329), whereas the authorial voice insists she is not only 'helpe' and 'confort' but also 'paradys terrestre' and 'his disport' (1332). M. Teresa Tavormina has the last as meaning 'comfort' but the word's primary connotation is 'amusement'.[29] In the choice of words we can see how the concept of woman is shifting; she is a gift, of God, yes, and like Adam, but she is also in some ways like lands and lamps; she is a help and comfort, no, more an earthly paradise, an amusement . . .

It is not surprising that this last term was used by January as he wooed May with Solomonic address, 'Com forth' for one line ends, 'and lat us taken oure disport;/ I chees thee for my wyf and my confort' (2147–8). He sees her as exactly this, a commodity, and desire is expressed, for the authorial voice reappearing in the next lines as well as January, in the *Song* language now designated as 'olde lewed wordes'. January gets to live in the world his understandings construct. Again using *Song* language, he asks for a kiss as a covenant, a moment of the utmost mystical reverence for both Jews and Christians in the original *Song* opening verse, 'Let him kiss me with the kisses of his mouth', as Damyan sneaks into the garden right under his nose. This is immediately followed by the spontaneous appearance of classical springtime, a review of the ravishing of Proserpina, whereupon the fairies' marriage debate begins, the May–Damyan affair is consummated, the cure effected, the bride and bridegroom reunited, all ending with a prayer that God and lastly his mother, Saint Mary, bless the listeners. They might well expect a can-can to break out.

The ludicrous quality of this marriage is underscored from beginning to end by the *Song* references, and the tenuousness of the literary models on which it is based by the teller is highlighted by the brilliant beam projected from the distant past by a poem about what love once was. It is left to other married couples to find more reciprocal, heartfelt unions, as in the *Franklin's Tale*. But more than that the *Tale* is an earthly victory for the others of the tale, the sexual and most likely procreative entities Damyan and May, the body of woman here operated quite well by its owner, the landscapes escaping their conventions to become at least a cuckoo's nest and perhaps a true sexual paradise. Looked at from the

giddy heights of metaphysical constructs for the universe, it is also a
victory for the *Song* text, its ancient voices singing in the flowering
desert of a universe which at all moments bursts the bounds of any static
definition. It is interesting that the *Song of Songs* became for medieval
kabbalists the vehicle for the veneration of the Shechinah, the Presence,
androgynous and evolving, so that the ancient poem indeed carried the
open, changing body,[30] mystical and actual, forever forward against the
resistance of any vision attempting to construct a closed system of reality.

In the *Tale* the paradoxes presented by the strong appearance of
marginal communities remain in play. Woman (as property, as amatory
body), Jews (as kings and shadows), Jewish text (as authority and
outdated Law) are never forced into settled significations. Rather, their
ambiguities become a subtext of the *Tale*. These groups offer insoluble
and inescapable paradoxes to the *Tale*'s central personality, January. For
the knight, the female body is perennially exciting and disturbing. It
is both possessable and adamantly other. So in the *Song* itself, which
locks the amatory body away by naming it a 'garden enclosed' whilst
offering it as the luxuriant, anatomically specific, quite tangible garden
of delights. The body of woman resonates in the tale with the others
who also come paradoxically to serve as authorities. Their authority
derives from two texts: the *Song* and to a lesser extent, *Metamorphoses*
and *De raptu Proserpina*. The communities of others get to use these
texts to confront the interests of the centre which January represents,
and to dismantle it through the language and concepts the texts provide,
namely, sexuality and change. Translated into rhetoric and action, the
margin comes to centre. Sex replaces marriage, a Jew and various
pagan characters replace the Christian figures from the fabliau, the body
of woman attaches to an effective voice. The strength of the suppressed,
its seductions, become self-evident. It is, after all, January himself who
'calls forth' the woman through his high fantasy. The attractions of the
others of the tale and the unsettled position of these communities, is only
temporarily (although highly satisfactorily) resolved in belly laughter.

Notes

[1] Muscatine, *Chaucer and the French Tradition*, 230 ff.
[2] For instance, *Song of Songs* 8:9 'if she [our sister] be a wall, we will build
upon her a silver turret' is interpreted by Rashi and others as an injunction
against intermarriage. Bernard of Clairvaux's Sermon XIV uses 1:3 '. . . your

name is oil poured forth' as a chance to review the difference between Church and Synagogue as that of compassion against judgement, and dilates at length upon the failure of the Old Law.

3 A good working definition comes from Rose in *Sexuality and the Field of Vision*: 'Located by Freud at the point where the woman is first seen to be different, this moment can then have its effects in that familiar mystification or fetishisation of femininity which makes of the woman something both perfect and dangerous or obscene (obscene if *not* perfect)', 127.

4 One might cite the entire *'école Freudienne'* and Lacan for discussions of absence as a concept attached to perceptions and representations of gender. My use of it is not strictly Lacanian, since it does not attach to language *per se*.

5 The original work on landscape was done by Curtius and his discussion of this figure can be found in *European Literature and the Latin Middle Ages*, the chapter 'Ideal Landscape'. For discussions of the *hortus conclusus* in the *Tale* see Robertson, 'The doctrine of charity'; Wimsatt, 'Chaucer'; Matter, *The Voice*.

6 For extensive historical treatment of the Virgin and the Church see Wimsatt, *Chaucer*, and particularly Matter, *The Voice*, 151–77. Both see this particular use of the *Song* as culminating in the twelfth century; both see it initialized in Pseudo-Melito's sixth-century story of the Assumption, picked up in a letter by Paschius Radbertus (mistakenly attributed to Jerome and therefore extremely influential). It is of particular interest here that the Pseudo-Melito legend tells of two assumptions, one of the Virgin's soul, the other of her body. Wimsatt comments: 'The second Assumption is the more extraordinary so that the tradition focuses on this', 'Chaucer', 69. However, I would argue that *Canticles* is the natural vehicle to carry the body – in this case Mary's, to heaven.

7 Augustine, from *De Utilitate Credendi*, III 5: 'The whole Old Testament Scripture, to those who diligently desire to know it, is handed down with a four-fold sense – historical, aetiological, analogical, allegorical . . . According to the analogical sense we are shown that the Old and New Testaments do not conflict.'

8 For exhaustive bibliographies of Hebrew commentaries see Rosenberg, *The Five Megilloth*; *Shir Ha-Shirim. The Song of Songs with a Midrashic Commentary*, trans. Broch; *Shir Ha-Shirim*, ed. and trans. Zlotowitz. For Latin commentaries see Matter, *The Voice*.

9 Another view of this world-building is offered by Shoaf in his chapter, 'The Merchant and the Parody of Creation'. Shoaf discusses the Merchant's hatred of creativity and considers the Merchant typed as 'a nihilist of the sign', in using *Song* language: Shoaf, *Dante*, 185.

10 In *Sanhedrin Tosephta* 12:10; *Sanhedrin Babylonian*, 101. Meek translates it as 'Anathema were those who dared anymore to sing it as a wine song in the banqueting halls': Meek, 'The Song of Songs', 91.

11 *Yadayim* 3:5; also *Tosephta Yadayim* 2:14.
12 For a complete discussion of form see Pope, *Song of Songs*, and Meek, 'The Song of Songs'.
13 Meek, 'The Song of Songs', 92.
14 Kristeva, *Tales of Love,* 99.
15 *Yadayim* 3:5. There is an extended Mishnaic discussion on whether or not *Ecclesiastes* and *Song of Songs* 'render the hands unclean' meaning, whether they are holy and therefore change the ritual status of what they touch. Rendering unclean is a sign of such holiness. It naturally has nothing at all to do with the sexuality of the material.
16 Worries over the *Song's* dangers to the uninitiated persisted into late Christian translations, such as the one attributed by Cedric E. Pickford to Landericus Wabbiano who closes his version with, 'Mais tant requier que cist romanz/ Unkes ne viegne en main d'enfint', a warning that this piece of Scripture should not fall into a child's hands (Pickford, *Song of Songs*, 97).
17 For a flavour of these discussions, chapter 1 of *'Abot de-Rabbi Natan*; the fathers discuss 'Be deliberate in judgement . . .' It also reflects the length and depth of the difficulties with *Song of Songs* and the point that not time but technique (allegory) was necessary to plumb the depths for its true meaning.
18 Steinsaltz, *The Talmud* for *peshat* 147–54. When it is said that one principle of Jewish hermeneutics is that 'a verse does not depart from its literal meaning' (149), we are already in a complex situation. Perhaps the point is that most texts had to be believed as historical fact in some sense. After Rabbi Akiba's comments, this was never a requirement when speaking of the *Song*.
19 For additional information, see Neusner, *Israel's Love Affair with God*, vii; and Rosenberg, *The Five Megilloth,* 36.
20 Grabois, 14, cites D. Kaplan, 'Les Juifs et la Bible de l'abbé Etienne de Citeaux', *Revue des Etudes Juives* 18 (1889), 131–3, for additional evidence.
21 Matarasso, *The Cisterican World*, 11–12.
22 This is a complete 'translation' of Rashi which attempts resolution of two difficulties: to avoid offending Christian doctrinal beliefs and to resolve huge discrepancies between the Vulgate text the translator is using and the Hebrew text on which Rashi bases his commentary.
23 Rosenberg, *The Five Megilloth*, 96.
24 See Galloway in this volume. As imitators of Mary and brides of Christ the physical situation of most religious women (nuns, anchoresses) was one of enclosure, extending to beguines around whom 'high walls, even moats', were eventually constructed.
25 The schemata for the partners in Christian exegesis are variable, even within any given piece of commentary. The pairs are roughly as follows: beginning with Origen's double scheme of Christ and the Church and the Word of God and the Soul, the list goes on to include the Church and God, the Church and the Virgin, God and the Virgin, Christ and the Virgin. It is in the last coupling

that January would find his position. The marriage of Christ and Mary actually begins with Origen's second-century pairing of Christ and the Church since the twelfth-century Marian identification of the Church and Mary simply substitutes one for the other.

[26] Benson and Anderson, *The Literary Context of Chaucer's Fabliaux*, 238–41. Pluto and Proserpina have not been found in any other analogues or sources.

[27] Langlois, *Roman de la rose*, l.1616.

[28] In the *Ellesmere and Hengwrt* manuscripts, a scribe has placed 'auctor' in the margins at various places.

[29] MED s.v. *disport*.

[30] Scholem, *Jewish Gnosticism*, 39. Scholem discusses *Shiur Komah* (closure *c.* fifth century, AD) as a text which describes the godhead in physical terms. He comments:

> The *Song of Songs* – because it contained a detailed description of the limbs of the lover, who was identified with God – became the basic scriptural text upon which the doctrine of Shiur Komah leaned.

Medieval Kabbalists, using *Song* language, added a specifically female aspect; both have survived. One might therefore say *Song of Songs* was the vehicle for preserving the body for Judaism as well.

Bibliography

'Abot de-Rabbi Natan, trans. J. Goldin (New Haven, 1955).

Augustine, *De Utilitate Credendi* in *Earlier Writings*, trans. J. H. Burleigh, (Philadelphia, 1953).

Benson, L. D. and Anderson, T. M., *The Literary Context of Chaucer's Fabliaux* (Indianapolis, 1971).

Chaucer, G., *The Riverside Chaucer*, ed. L. D. Benson (Boston, 1987, London, 1988).

Curtius, E. R., *European Literature and the Latin Middle Ages*, trans. W. Trask (Princeton, 1953).

Epstein, Rabbi I. (ed.), *Yadayim. Talmud Bavli*, trans. I. W. Slotki (London, 1989).

Grabois, A., 'The *Hebraica Veritas* and Jewish-Christian relations in the twelfth century', *Speculum* 50 (1975) 614–34.

Kamin, S. and Saltsmans, A. (eds.), *Expositio Hystorica Cantici Canticorum Secundum Salomoneum* (Ramat Gan, 1989).

Kristeva, J., *Tales of Love*, trans. L. S. Roudiez (New York, 1987).

Langlois, E. (ed.), *Le Roman de la rose of Guillaume de Lorris and Jeun de Meun* (Paris, 1912).

Matarasso, P. (ed. and trans.), *The Cistercian World: Monastic Writings of the Twelfth Century* (London, 1993).

Matter, E. A., *The Voice of My Beloved* (Philadelphia, 1990).

Meek, T. J., 'The Song of Songs: introduction and exegesis' in G. A. Buttrick *et al.* (eds.), *Interpreter's Bible* (New York, 1952).

Muscatine, C., *Chaucer and the French Tradition* (Berkeley, 1969).

Neusner, J., *Israel's Love Affair with God* (Valley Forge, 1993).

Pickford, C. E. (ed.), *The Song of Songs, A Twelfth Century French Version* (London, 1974).

Pope, M. H. (trans.), *Song of Songs: A New Translation with Introduction and Commentary* (Garden City, 1977).

Robertson, D. W., 'The doctrine of charity in medieval gardens: a topical approach through symbolism and allegory' in *Essays in Medieval Culture* (Princeton, 1980), 21–50.

Rose, J., *Sexuality and the Field of Vision* (London, 1986).

Rosenberg, A. J. (ed. and trans.), *The Five Megilloth vol. 1* (New York, 1992).

Scholem, G., *Jewish Gnosticism, Merkabah Mysticism, and the Talmudic Tradition* (New York, 5720/1960).

Shir Ha-Shirim, ed. and trans. M. Zlotowitz (New York, 1977).

Shir Ha-Shirim. The Song of Songs with a Midrashic Commentary, trans. Y. Broch (Jerusalem, 1983).

Shoaf, R. A., *Dante, Chaucer, and the Currency of the Word* (Norman, 1983).

Steinsaltz, A., *The Talmud (the Steinsaltz Edition); Reference Guide* (New York, 1968).

Tavormina, M. T., 'Notes to the *Merchant's Tale*'; see Chaucer, *The Riverside Chaucer*, 884–90.

Wimsatt, J. I., 'Chaucer and the *Canticle of Canticles*' in J. Mitchell and W. Provost (eds.), *Chaucer, the Love Poet* (Athens, Georgia, 1971), 66–90.

7

Communities of Dissent:
The Secular and Ecclesiastical Communities of
Margery Kempe's *Book*

JANET WILSON

SOME sixty years after the discovery of the Mount Grace manuscript of *The Book of Margery Kempe*, controversy concerning the nature and meaning of Kempe's mysticism has continued, reaching avalanche proportions in the last five years.[1] Earlier interpretations of the mystic as eccentric and hysterical have been succeeded by feminist ones which discern in her distinctive voice the emancipation of later female voices, and an uncontainable female presence about to burst forth into modernity.[2] To some late twentieth-century readers the *Book* hovers tantalizingly on the verge of credibility. Kempe was an extraordinary woman who, in demonstrating an extreme form of Carthusian affective piety, ignored the *via negativa* path of mysticism, the traditional province of medieval English mystics like Julian of Norwich and the author of *The Cloud of Unknowing*, to follow that of positive mysticism.[3] Overblown in her reactions to the divine, she was nevertheless earthbound in her devotions. Her conversations with Christ and the Blessed Virgin, and her mystical marriage to the Godhead in Rome, in which she takes him as her husband, symptomize a spirituality that has been variously described as material, literal-minded, and 'incarnational'.[4] As J. A. Tasioulas points out in her essay in this volume this belief in the tangible presence and full humanity of the Blessed Virgin and Christ was not unusual in the East Anglian community to which Kempe belonged; it is also attested in the great N-Town mystery cycle which is associated with that area and which the mystic may have seen in performance.

It is characteristic of these paradoxes that, although time and again the *Book* recounts how Kempe disturbed the lay and ecclesiastical circles among which she moved, major events from her mystical heyday receive no mention in extant ecclesiastical, municipal and civic records other than in the Account Rolls of the Trinity Guild of King's Lynn, Norfolk, to which she was admitted in 1438.[5] The apparent lack of external evidence, and the ambiguity of the *Book*'s textual composition have led at least one recent critic to treat it as a fiction.[6] But Kempe's meeting with Julian of Norwich at which the older mystic corroborated the holiness of her visions and offered spiritual advice does authenticate her account and, in showing Julian's characteristic scrupulousness in interpreting revelation, reinforces the impression conveyed elsewhere in Kempe's *Book* that respected spiritual figures treated her with dignity.

It is undoubtedly Kempe's collaboration with her second scribe, and the assertion of an authoritative voice in response to sceptical discourses, which creates the *Book's* metatextual dimension, bringing spiritual autobiography closer to the craft of writing fiction.[7] Although the question of who authorizes its final signification is unresolved, some literary intent can be adduced from its rhetorical structure, for the text's apparently artless yet self-conscious attention to its processes of construction amply reflects Kempe's disputatious nature.[8] Reading the account from a socio-historical perspective, the evidence it provides of her disruptive influence upon fifteenth-century King's Lynn society points to a deeply disturbed social and religious milieu, one in which incipient dissatisfaction with the church and with contemporary forms of worship may have encouraged anti-clericalism. Such a reading seems to confirm Jennifer C. Ward's view that the public role which noblewomen played in the devotional life of East Anglia was not incompatible with the move towards private devotion in the late Middle Ages; it may also question Tanner's conclusion, from his study of the late medieval church in Norwich, that tension within the church had diminished in the late fifteenth century.[9] If Kempe encouraged her clerical supporters to question institutional forms of worship and to consider more individual forms of communing with the divine, then the discord that she created in King's Lynn by 1420 may exemplify just the opposite tendency: a complex contretemps between secular and ecclesiastical forces. Her account shows her to be a socially divisive character whose behaviour caused the more conservative minded laity to attempt to suppress radical clerical belief according to their own standards of religious orthodoxy.

For centuries *The Book of Margery Kempe* was known only in the form of devotional fragments which Wynkyn de Worde published in 1501 as *A short treatyse of contemplacyon taught by our lorde Jhesu*

Caxton's Flemish woodcut of the Crucifixion used by Wynkyn de Worde in his 1501 text, *A short treatyse of contemplacyon taught by our lorde Jhesu Chryste taken out of the boke of Margerie kempe*, following his colophon on sig. A.4r. It was commonly used in devotional treatises which de Worde and Caxton printed between 1491 and 1502.

Chryste taken out of the boke of Margerie kempe.[10] Typical of 'this practical manual of contemplation' is Christ's promise toward the end of the account, of heavenly reward in return for Kempe's soliciting the worship of the clergy of Lynn.[11]

> Doughter þu hast desyred in thy mynde to haue many preestes in the towne of lynn, that myght synge & rede nyght and day for to serue me, worshyp me, & prayse me, and thanke me for the goodnes þat I have do to the [have done to you] in erth, & therfore doughter I promyse the thou shalt haue mede & rewarde in heuen for the good wylles and good desyres, as yf thou haddest done them in dede.[12]

Christ's monological voice implies that relations between the mystic and clerical authorities in her home town of King's Lynn were harmonious. But elsewhere Kempe's *Book* tells of recurring disputes within her local community which climaxed around the time of the Great Fire which destroyed the Guild Hall of the Trinity on 23 January 1421.[13] The unreconciled voices of the full text which was discovered in 1936 testify to two images of community: the heavenly community based in love and brotherhood which Christ reveals and promises her, to which the different religious orders of Lynn correspond, and the historically-contextualized community comprising the body politic which Kempe's behaviour fractures into conflict and discontent. One might also infer from the *Book* the shadowy and unstable existence in King's Lynn of another, alternative community which Douglas Gray has described as 'friends of Christ' because of a shared interest in an 'interior mystical or devotional closeness with Christ': that of Kempe and her supporters.[14]

In Margery Kempe's remarkable transition from her secular role as wife of John Kempe to her holy calling as beloved spouse of Christ, the support of the religious and ecclesiastical communities of King's Lynn – secular and religious clergy, friars, monks, anchorites – was crucial.[15] From the outset clerical approval and endorsement were necessary for confirmation of her sanctity. The anchorite attached to the Dominican Preaching Friars whom Stanford Meech and Hope Emily Allen describe as a 'fanatical kind of mystic ... the most suitable confessor for her in Lynn', was an influential friend and her principal confessor until the time of his death sometime after her return from Jerusalem in 1415.[16] He was the first holy man from whom Christ commanded her to seek validation of her visions:

> Dowtyr ȝe sowken [are sucking] euyn on Crystys brest, and ȝe han an ernest-
> peny of Heuyn [you have received a pledge of paradise]. I charge ȝow
> receyueth swech thowtys [to receive such thoughts] whan God wyl ȝeue [give]
> hem as mekely & as deuowtly as ȝe kan & comyth to me and tellyth me what
> þei be & I schal, wyth þe leue [permission] of ower Lord Ihesu Cryst, telle
> ȝow wheþyr þei ben of þe Holy Gost or ellys of ȝowr enmy þe Deuyl. (18)[17]

According to the hostile friar at the inquisition at Beverley before the
archbishop of York, the order of Preaching Friars in Lynn had earlier
saved Kempe from the stake (132).

Just as important as the local clergy's role in Kempe's life is its
determining presence upon the literary construction of her *Book*. Claiming
to be written for other 'synful wrecchys' (1), it has also been described
as 'a justificatory treatise' written to counter clerical and lay scepticism.[18]
Equally potent is its crusading purpose of evangelicizing her mystical
experiences to readers to encourage a new community of believers, an
alternative society. This at least seems to be one purpose of the
explanations of the second scribe who revised Liber I following the first
scribe's death in *c.*1432, completing this task in 1438. Certainly the process
of writing down her story involved him in Kempe's struggle to authenticate
herself as a holy woman and to establish her role and status as a mystic
within the community. His comments in the Proem on the lack of order
and the preoccupation elsewhere with the account's structure reflect the
complex relationship between amanuensis and mystic.[19]

> Thys boke is not wretyn in ordyr euery thyng aftyr oþer as it wer don [eve-
> rything after another as it was done], but lych as þe mater cam to þe creatur
> in mind whan it schuld be wretyn for it was so long er it was wretyn [it was
> so long before it was written] þat sche had forgetyn þe tyme & þe order whan
> thyngys befellyn [occurred]. (5)

The underlying rationale for the *Book*'s often idiosyncratic structure
has never been satisfactorily explained, although Anthony Goodman's
description of the *Book* as a 'series of self-contained episodes and
contemplations loosely linked in which autobiographical material . . . has
been shaped in a sophisticated and highly selective way' is generally
accepted.[20] Kempe dictated her memoirs to the second scribe some
twenty years after the revelations occurred and relied both on her
memory and his guidance in recording them. But his scepticism at her
behaviour, which he obviously shared with other detractors in Lynn,
made their relationship fraught with tension. The sub-text to the scribe's

aesthetic concerns about the ordering of the material, therefore, is his growing recognition that in recording his personal crises of faith about his task and her controversial mysticism he was also shaping her narrative in more than editorial fashion.[21] His responses function meta-textually to draw attention to the process of self-validation with which the *Book* is principally concerned. Through a rhetorical structure of conversion created by strategic departures from the chronological order of events – in which he twice moves from the role of sceptic to that of believer – he reproduces metonymically the form of the controversies which she generated. His accounts of his lapsed faith, in dialogue with Kempe's account of her life in God, and her voice, epitomize the other confrontations between the mystic and her sceptics which appear in the *Book* and which exemplify the divisive impact of her personality. The technique of rhetorically validating the process of conversion also occurs in the hagiography of Old English saints, but Kempe and her scribe adapt this strategy – of exhorting readers to believe in her sanctity – to the purpose of authenticating her voice through the written word.[22]

Kempe's marginal status as a mystic in the clerical and secular communities of King's Lynn, the question of her orthodoxy, the related questions of her 'voice', and the construction of her subjectivity have already received critical attention.[23] Although the ecclesiastical authorities considered her disruptive, theatrical devotions as a challenge to their autonomy, they usually indulged them. For all her excesses she remained devout, and the controversies over her ambiguous status enabled her to convince even the most sceptical of her religious orthodoxy. The accusations of heresy she incurred during her pilgrimages around the north of England after persecution of Lollards increased following the failure of Oldcastle's uprising in 1414 confirm that the label of Lollardy was used loosely for any kind of nonconformity.[24] Widespread confusion about her identity led to some accusers' belief that she was overstepping her wifely status. As Karma Lochrie, David Aers and others have noted, their hostility also masked discomfort at the enigmatic spectacle she presented as a transgressive, free woman whose emotional excesses resisted any easy classification.[25] Patriarchal accusations of religious heterodoxy were founded on such assumptions. From this point of view Kempe was seeking more than approval and toleration of her extreme piety; as a marginal woman mystic she was defending herself against traditional antifeminism using scriptural, revelatory, and verbal resources.

The clerical and social controversies which the *Book* records inevitably affect the form of Kempe's revelations and therefore her mystical image which was based on continental mystics like St Bridget, Blessed Dorothea of Montau, and St Elizabeth of Hungary and the beguine, Mary of Oignies, both of whom also had the gift of tears.[26] It is now widely accepted that Kempe consciously modelled her mystical life as a 'competitive' *imitatio* upon St Bridget (who died in 1373, the year when Kempe was probably born), whose *Revelations* were available in English from 1391, the year she was canonized, although this was not promulgated until 1419, and she probably believed she had inherited Bridget's spiritual graces.[27] Her *Book* imitates Bridget's pattern of voyage to spiritual fulfilment by wearing a hair shirt, taking vows of chastity, making pilgrimages to holy sites, and in a mystical marriage to Christ. The influence of the saint and her cult appears from several allusions to her and 'Bridis boke' in the *Book*: Kempe's scribe read to her from St Bridget's *Revelations* (143); she visited St Bridget's chapel in Rome in 1414 in a period of 'near-identification with the saint', and the Bridgettine Monastery in Syon in 1434.[28] The pseudo-Bonaventuran treatise translated by Nicholas Love, *The Mirror of the Blessed Life of Jesus Christ*, is another likely devotional model – of *imitatio Christi* – especially for her meditations on the Passion, but Kempe's *Book* differs from these tracts of affective piety in its repeated assertion that persecution validates the rightness of her path.[29] Furthermore in representing an extended controversy over her piety which polarized the clergy and the devout laity in King's Lynn, it fractures the structure which these quasi-hagiographical, quasi-autobiographical models provide.

An eminent Franciscan friar, possibly William Melton, who 'had an holy name and gret favour of the pepyl' (152), preaching in Lynn for several years from 1420, spoke out against Kempe and her supporters in his sermons, turning many of them against her.[30] The scribe's account of how he lost faith in her at this time stresses the seriousness of the accusations which dragged her standing to its lowest ebb, and created ripples of ill feeling throughout the community. The generic criteria of the saint's life, the life of a holy woman or the *imitatio vitae christi,* therefore, only partially define Kempe's *Book* which incorporates the structure of social discord as hostility to her mysticism rebounded against her and her supporters.[31] More significantly the scribe's crisis demonstrates a reflexive self-consciousness about textualizing his and Kempe's responses as an act of self-authorization and self-empowerment. His confessions of wavering faith not only provide eye-witness verification; they also contribute to a rhetorical design which ultimately endorses Kempe's mysticism and guarantees an image of saintliness based on her similarity to other holy women like St Bridget, Elizabeth of Hungary and Mary of Oignies.

Early in the *Book* the reader encounters Kempe's mentors – influential seculars, Benedictines, Dominicans and Carmelites – from whom at Christ's behest she sought approval of her visions. The illustrious Carmelite friar, Aleyn of Lynn, doctor of divinity from Cambridge, who offered to write down her experiences for her, was probably the most distinguished in scholarly terms and had compiled indices for the *Revelations* and *Prophecies* of St Bridget; his validation of her powers first acquired authority.[32] When Kempe was almost crushed to death after a stone beam in the church of St Margaret fell on her back as she was praying, he measured and weighed the beam and pronounced her escape a miracle. His public conversion in the face of opposition from some townspeople shows the outlines of arguments used in later controversies over her holiness:

> And this worshepful doctowr seyd it was a gret myracle & ower Lord was heyly to be magnyfied [praised] for þe preseruyng of þis creatur aȝen the malyce of hir enmy, and teld it mech pepyl, & mych pepyl magnyfied mech God in þis creatur. And also mech pepyl wold not leuyn [believe] it but raþar leuyd [preferred to believe] it was a tokyn of wreth & veniawns [vengeance] þan þei wold leuyn it was any token of mercy or quemfulnes [favour]. (22)

It is not surprising, therefore, that in Kempe's darkest period, the priest's prior, Thomas Netter, opposed his association with her and forbad him to speak to her.

The holy Richard Caister, vicar of St Stephen's in Norwich, whose grave in the yard of St Stephen's Church became a local shrine for pilgrims, was another spiritual advisor whom Kempe met on several occasions, and who defended her in an examination by the bishops' officers in 1413.[33] Margery may have subscribed to the cult which sprang up after his death on 29 March 1420, for she recounts how in that year on a pilgrimage to his tomb she 'fel down with boistous sobbyngys, wepyngys, & lowde cryes besyden þe graue of þe god Vicary' (147). In a rhetorical clustering of meetings with holy people from Norwich, she adds an account of interviews with the Carmelite friar, William Southfield (41–2) who received visions including a revelation of the Blessed Virgin, and advised her to accept God's gifts; and the several days she spent just before 1415 with Dame Julian of Norwich, whose words on the action of the Holy Ghost she records.[34] Julian verified her holiness, and confirmed Christ's claim that tears of compunction, devotion and compassion are the greatest gift (66). These assurances are strategically followed by reference to the prophecies of Kempe's confessor, the anchorite (chapter 19), concerning her visit to the Holy Land where she would receive her gift of tears; they anticipate the critical importance of authenticating her weeping in the episode of 1420.

Kempe's confessor, the unidentified recluse attached to the Dominican house at Lynn who first verified her holiness, predicted a hunch-backed man would support her on her travels.[35] After his death when she was in Jerusalem he was succeeded by another, 'sharp' confessor, identified as Robert Spryngolde, parish priest of St Margaret's Church. Naming Spryngolde as her executor, Kempe struck a bargain with the Lord that the priest should receive as reward half the tears and good works that Christ wrought in her (216; cf. 20).[36] A bachelor of law and much versed in the Scriptures, he supported her in times of crisis, and Meech and Allen note his growing appreciation of Kempe and the sensitivity he displays in conflicts within and among the religious and lay communities.[37] Both received confessions of her entire mystical experience. Her relationships with these mentors contrast with her husband's diminished role after their exchange of vows of celibacy and with Christ's disembodied presence, manifested mainly through the discourse of revelation. They show her spiritual life emerging from her quotidian, pious activities.

Such attachments as these, formed before 1413 when Kempe made her first journey to Rome, the Holy Land, and Assisi, helped her endure later persecutions. New religious figures in her life who appear after 1413 are generally not named, either from a desire to preserve anonymity because of their association with Kempe, or because they played a relatively minor part in her drama. These include the priest whom Christ sent to Lynn in 1413 in answer to her plea for greater knowledge, who read to her from works of pious devotion for seven to eight years, and whose illness encouraged her to make her pilgrimage to the grave of Richard Caister in Norwich.[38] He with 'anoþer good preyste' (150) intervened on the first occasion when the Franciscan friar banned her from his sermons. There was the parish priest of St James who supported her weeping on the same occasion (149);[39] and the priest at the Gesine Chapel at St Margaret's Church, which held a representation of the Nativity, whom she met there in her darkest hour after being deserted by all her supporters, the third one in Lynn to whom she confessed her entire mystical life (169).[40]

The level of controversy that her sobbing and roarings at sermons generated during these years when the Franciscan set the town against her is apparent from the number of mentors mentioned: a worthy cleric who was a doctor of divinity (164); a parson who had taken a degree (165) who urged the congregation to tolerate her gift of tears; the Dominican, Thomas Constance, who attended the Chapter of the Preaching Friars at Lynn in 1404 and perhaps in other years (165);[41] another doctor of divinity who tolerated her weeping (166) and an Augustinian friar (169). They advised her on spiritual matters, defended her reputation, and provided extra-parochial facilities for worship when popular feeling against her ran high. Despite the risk of ostracization, local clerical support apparently wavered only rarely, although on one occasion an anchorite and earlier supporter, the Benedictine monk Thomas Brackleye, overwhelmed by negative public opinion, perhaps from the influential circle in Norwich to which he belonged, chided her on her return from pilgrimage (103);[42] while on another, when local opposition was at its height, two priests took her into the country away from any audience to test her sincerity, where she 'brast owt in boistows [loud] wepyng & sobbyng & cryed as lowde er ellys lowder as sche dede whan sche was amongys þe pepil at hom' (200).

The religious milieu in East Anglia during Margery Kempe's lifetime was so richly diverse and tolerated such individuality in devotional practices that the loyalty of her mentors is less surprising than it would otherwise seem. The period of her mission from 1411–36 corresponds to a golden age of religious architecture and art in a culture that was characterized by a hybrid blend of monastic and lay spirituality. This popular, devotional movement developed local, vernacular features, and was directed principally at the laity.[43] The East Anglian monastic houses, for example, which had extensive temporal possessions, retained close ties with the laity, performing many extra-parochial roles for them.[44] They remained munificent patrons of popular drama: of miracle and morality plays, and probably of the famous N-Town mystery cycle which J. A. Tasioulas describes in this volume.[45] Connections with the friaries were equally close. Despite their predominantly rural character, Norfolk and Suffolk had a higher density of churches than any other county in England and the fifteenth century saw a rise in the numbers of secular and beneficed clergy. The city of Norwich had a large number of parish churches, places to hear sermons, say confessions, be buried, find executors for wills.[46] Nevertheless individual piety was also respected. Norman Tanner points out that Norwich contained more hermits and anchorites, including the famous Dame Julian of Norwich, than any other town in England; furthermore it was the only town which harboured among its pious confraternities communities of lay religious women closely resembling the continental beguinages.[47]

The culture was known for the entrenched conservatism of its monastic and lay piety, and owed much of its vitality to the continuity of the older clerical institutions, but the proximity of many East Anglian towns to the continent and the maintenance of commercial links with Flanders and the Low Countries made it unusually receptive to religious change. Norfolk and Suffolk became the breeding ground for non-conformity and the 'most troublesome area of non-conformist thought in fifteenth century England'.[48] In this society in which clergy and laity explored a variety of religious options, extreme forms of piety like Kempe's which were labelled Lollard in other parts of the country were treated leniently. Toleration of non-conformity, for example, is suggested by the evidence that Bishop Alnwick's heresy trials of fifty-one men and nine women Lollards held in Norwich in 1428–31 were prompted by the paranoia of the London courts following Oldcastle's rebellion rather than by local militancy. These trials of lay and clerical Lollards of whom all but three abjured, show that Lollardy, or 'a Lollard-like individualism of conscience' was rampant in the diocese.[49] Although several women Lollards were tried there is no explicit evidence or endorsement of women preaching – this was one of the charges laid against Kempe in York.[50] No further organized episcopal opposition to heresy in East Anglia occurred for almost a century.

The toleration of Kempe's mysticism in King's Lynn until the Franciscan's visits may have been due to the perception that local patterns of belief were non-sectarian and therefore not threatening to clerical autonomy. Strong belief in the Eucharist, for example, might co-exist with an interest in the vernacular Scriptures or scepticism about purgatory.[51] The Latin will of Richard Caister who, according to John Bale was a Wycliffite and disapproved of clerical abuses, also suggests the coexistence of unorthodox and Lollard beliefs.[52] Apart from a bequest of ten pounds to be given to his parishioners' church for antiphoners, he left everything else to the poor. His will's lack of provision for masses, prayers, and alms for the dead suggests a scepticism about purgatory, yet he was locally venerated as a saint, as the evidence of later wills, some of which made provision for pilgrimages to his grave, and his appellation as *Bonus* by Bale and Pits attest. These signs of his cult suggest that in the popular mind his 'radical, even marginally heretical' views may have contributed to his reputation as a 'devout and apostolic priest'.[53]

Kempe may also have devalued orthodox practices associated with purgatory because her views on the after-life were dominated by Christ's guarantee that on her death she would have safe passage directly to heaven. Although like her role models, St Bridget of Sweden and Mary of Oignies, she proclaimed direct communication with God, and insisted on chastity within marriage, to the popular mind these traits may have positioned her dangerously on the edges of religious heterodoxy.[54] Like women Lollards her lack of literacy (she was read to and educated by priests) was compensated for by her powerful memory, and an ability to recount scriptural anecdotes.[55] This gift and Kempe's forthrightness seemed on occasion to subvert clerical authority, and her assertion before the archbishop of York of the right to teach despite the charge of illicit preaching was probably familiar in Lollard circles.[56] The vows of chastity which she and her husband made before the bishop of Lincoln were not unusual in East Anglia at that time, but their domestic arrangements appear to have become controversial in King's Lynn especially after her husband suffered a near fatal fall and Kempe was obliged to nurse him.[57] The evidence of lay and clerical resentment at their separation suggests that any favourable reception of her mystical presence occurred only through the concerted efforts of her supporters. In the crisis which began in 1420 the friar's opposition created a climate in which lay pressure was finally brought to bear on her clerical mentors to withdraw their support.

Kempe's second scribe, who often recorded her experiences with mixed feelings, belonged to this milieu in which closer, more personal relationships with the divine were being explored. Kempe claims a prior, affectionate acquaintance with him and Meech and Allen have identified this scribe as a priest of her parish church, St Margaret's, where Robert Spryngolde was parish priest.[58] His two major interpolations into the drama of her tribulations (apart from the Proem, the Preface and conclusion to Book I) which prove that her spiritual powers overcame his scepticism, reflect popular responses to Kempe. Introduced strategically, these interpolations not only reinforce the *Book*'s dominant rhetorical structure modelled on St Bridget of Sweden's revelations and the theme, that the more persecution she endured for Christ's sake the greater the fulfilment of the divine purpose; they also contextualize and highlight the process of writing as an independent response to persecution which enabled her 'voice' to acquire a distinctive presence.

In the first interpolation in chapter 24 the priest restages his reluctance to act as amanuensis, a reluctance which he initially describes in the Proem as a means of testing Kempe's prophetic powers:

> The prest whech wrot this boke for to preuyn [in order to prove] þis creaturys felyngys many tymes & dyuers [different] tymes he askyd hir qwestyons & demawndys of thyngys þat wer for to komyn, vn-sekyr & vncerteyn as þat tyme to any creatur what xuld be þe ende [things of which the outcome was unsure and uncertain], preyng hir, þei sche wer loth & not wylly to do swech thyngys, for to prey to God and . . . tellyn hym how sche felt, & ellys wold he not gladlych a wretyn þe boke [*or else he would not have gladly written this book* – my italics]. And so þis creatur, sumdel for drede [in part out of fear], þat he wold ellys not a folwyd hir entent [he would otherwise not have followed her desire] for to wryten þis boke, compellyd, dede as he preyd hir & telde hym hir felyngys what xuld befallyn in swech materys as he askyd hir . . . & ȝet he wold not alwey ȝeuyn credens to hir wordys, & þat hyndryd hym in þis maner þat folwyth [in the following way]. (55)

This interpolation belongs to a sequence of anecdotes which collectively illustrate Kempe's spiritual powers. Chapter 23 tells how her gifts of revelation affected parishioners of St Margaret's. In chapter 24, in order to prove the 'truth' of her premonitions, the scribe tells stories against himself of how he was deceived by strangers. The sequence culminates in chapter 25, which narrates a conflict which occurred some years later in 1432 over the status of the chapels of St Nicholas and St James annexed to St Margaret's parish church. Wealthy parishioners attempted to build purifications and fonts and to acquire the sacramental privileges of baptism, matrimony and purification, but they failed in this endeavour after rejecting the offer of the bishop of Norwich, William of Alnwick, which had certain conditions attached.[59] Kempe's power of prayer, her foreknowledge due to revelation that the status quo would continue, are considered to influence this outcome and the story is told as proof of these special graces.[60] The episode is out of chronological order, as the scribe admits:

> Ferthermore her folwyth a rygth notabyl matere [a very notable instance] of þe creaturys felyng, & it is wretyn her for conuenyens in-as-mech as it is in felyng leche to þe materys þat ben wrytyn be-forn [like the matters which have been written before], notwythstondyng it befel [happened] long aftyr þe materys whech folwyn. (p.58; ch.25)

The second interpolation occurs in chapter 62 when the scribe undergoes a personal crisis of faith precipitated by the Franciscan friar's preaching against her, causing:

... many of hem þat pretendyd hir frenschep turnyd abakke for a lytyl veyn drede [hung back out of a little vain dread] þat þei haddyn of hys wordys & durst not wel speken wyth hir of þe whech þe same preyste was on [among whom was the same priest] þat aftirward wrot þis booke & wes in purpose nevyr to a levyd hir felyngys aftyr [resolved never again to believe her feelings]. (152)

The scribe's doubts, bending to the prevailing hostility towards Kempe of some members of the community, contrast to the sustained loyalty of other clerical supporters and confessors. He overcomes them by discovering in the life of Mary of Oignies and later St Elizabeth of Hungary models of sanctity to which he sees Kempe's life as correlating, and by allowing the superior authority of the written text to refute the friar's authority.[61] Again he constructs his dilemma as representative by claiming that other people who had loved her also returned to her in the course of time. Like the earlier confession, this incident belongs to a sequence of doubt and scepticism which culminates in Kempe's demonstration of her spiritual value to her society. Her special powers of prayer apparently caused a snowstorm that extinguished the Great Fire in 1421 before it could destroy St Margaret's Church. This episode (chapter 67) follows the account of how the Lord took her crying away from her (chapter 63) although in reality it preceded the latter.[62] The scribe draws attention to the unusual chronology in order to emphasize the rhetorical importance of the Great Fire episode in vindicating Kempe's piety, and in undermining the Franciscan's imperiousness. Chapter 67 concludes that the friar was blind in his belief that she had the devil within her '& was nothyng mevyd from hys opynyon but raþar defendyng hys errour' just as chapter 25 ended by 'proving' the superiority of Kempe's spiritual powers to those of the wealthy burgesses of Lynn.

In these framebreaking interpolations the scribe foregrounds his doubts in order to re-establish Kempe's religious authority and to validate her mysticism. On the first occasion, in order for the collaboration to continue, he tests her integrity by exploiting his role as amanuensis to forge a relationship of greater trust. Her evident inner powers, surpassing those of temporal, ecclesiastical authorities, authorize him to continue his task. On the second occasion his renewal of faith due to the timely discovery of evidence of other holy women blessed with the gift of tears by reading about Mary of Oignies, seemingly by chance but in fact due to the guidance of another cleric, and then about Elizabeth of Hungary, enables him to empathize with her and complete the narrative. His loss of faith during this crisis reinforces the confessional mode, but on this occasion his recovery leads him to elevate her as a holy woman. The traditions of feminine saintliness to which he turns create a vital point of intersection with the forces of social disorder. Out of this crisis of confidence emerges a more resolved and 'saintly' image of Kempe.

The rhetorical function of these interpolations – to magnify the importance of Kempe's mission and her indispensability to her society – emerges in the broader context of her mystical life. Prior to the first sequence of chapters 23 to 25 and the scribal interpolation are described events which occurred between 1411 and 1413. In these years Kempe and her husband sought and gained audience with high-ranking clergy outside Lynn in order to verify her sanctity, her decision to live a holy life, and to endorse their vows of celibacy. In these ambitions she was only partly successful. Philip Repyngdon, bishop of Lincoln, suggested she write down her experiences, but refused to grant her requests for symbols of chastity, the mantle and the ring, and to wear white clothes (69). The archbishop of Canterbury, Dr Arundel, granted her weekly communion and the power to choose her own confessor, but at this point her *imitatio* of a saintly life had scarcely begun; Christ's promises had not yet been fulfilled. These included the wearing of white raiment and the acquisition of the gift of tears of which he says:

> And þerfor take hem mekely & þankingly [meekly and gratefully] whan I wyl send hem & suffyr pacyently whan I wythdrawe hem & seke besyly [earnestly] tyl þow mayst getyn hem, for terys of compu[n]ccyon, deuocyon & compassyon arn þe heyest & sekerest ȝyftys þat I ȝeue in erde. (31)

Christ's advice that she dress in white, however, is associated with his demand that she make a pilgrimage, and the assurances that she will both finance herself and return safely. These promises, which correspond to St Bridget's revelation in vision that she would travel safely on pilgrimage to Rome and Jerusalem, are deferred for two years.

> And dowtyr, I xal go wyth þe in euery contre & ordeyn [provide] for þe; I xal ledyn þe thyder & brynge þe a getyn in safte [back again in safety], & noon Englysch-man schal deyn [die] in þe schyp þat þow art in. And, dowtyr, I sey to þe I wyl that þu were clothys of whyte & non oþer colowr, for þu xal ben arayd [you shall be dressed] aftyr my wyl. (32)

Nevertheless the fulfilment of these prophecies in 1413–14 on Kempe's pilgrimages to the Holy Land and to Rome, where she visited the same places as Bridget, constitutes the turning point of her life in

Christ and guarantees the successful outcome of her mission.[63] Sometime in early 1414 at the Mount of Calvary at the moment of her vision of Christ's crucifixion she received the gift of tears of compassion, the roars and screams which were to disturb so many who heard her, and which lasted for ten years or more.[64] Additional trials, however, were to be endured before she could acquire the promised white raiment. Kempe's stages of spiritual growth are coded rhetorically into the text in a structure of prophecy and fulfilment. Christ once more assures her after she was abandoned by her companions in Venice, that white clothing will guarantee her safe passage to Rome and return to England (76). At the moment she consents to wear it she encounters the broken-backed man whom her confessor, the nameless Dominican anchorite, had earlier prophesied would escort her to safety on her travels (44). The prophecies made before she left England about her safety on the pilgrimage and her financial welfare, therefore, are linked to her readiness to be clad in white. Yet despite the reassurances with which they were delivered, further conflict followed. The enhanced spirituality Kempe acquired was fraught with tribulation, because dressed henceforth as the bride of Christ she emerged as a figure of social controversy.

Undoubtedly white clothing often suggested, in Kempe's case inaccurately, virginal status or celibacy, but it is also associated with martyrdom, special virtue or holiness as in the case of mystics like Mary of Oignies who wore a coat and mantle of white wool. It could also include 'persecuted innocence . . . penitence . . . and the remission of sins'. In Kempe's visionary life white raiment combined a number of symbolic functions: when linked with her ring it was a kind of bridal dress; it also symbolized the 'comprehensive purity' by which she fulfilled Christ's definition 'þu art a mayden in þi sowle' (52).[65] White is also the colour of clothes worn in heaven.[66] It is often linked with the Blessed Virgin Mary, whose handmaiden Kempe describes herself as being, as a symbol of the swaddling clothes of motherhood and intercession. Her *imitatio Mariae* strikingly parallels that of St Bridget and, according to Tasioulas, of the N-Town cycle author. Mary appears to Margery Kempe in visions clad in 'fayre whyte clothys & kerchys for to swathyn in hire sone' (19); and holding 'a fayre white kerche in hir hand' (209).[67] The wearing of white was tolerated on the continent, but was controversial in England where it was associated with closed religious orders like the Carthusians or with radical forms of continental piety such as the sect of the Flagellants which was proscribed in 1399.[68] Certainly when Kempe first appears in white at Rome (chapter 32), the English priest's disapproval appears as a form of disgust at this apparent exhibitionism, and it accentuates the collective sense of shame that other countrymen in her party felt about her:[69]

> ... & euyr hir owyn cuntremen wer obstynat, & specyaly a preste þat was amonx hem. He steryd meche pepyl a-ȝen hir [he stirred up many people against her] & seyd mech euyl of hir, for sche weryd white clothyng mor þan oþer dedyn whech were holyar & bettyr þan euyr was sche as hym thowt. (84)

The parallels between Kempe's story here (82) and St Bridget's *Liber Celestis* are striking.[70] This English priest persuaded her confessor, 'þe Duche prest' (82) called Wenslawe, to command her to return to her black clothes (84).[71] Before she could convince the German confessor around Christmas 1414 of the truth of Christ's message (92) Kempe was to perform penance by caring for an old woman, 'a pour creatur in Rome' (85), to undertake her mystical marriage to Christ, and receive further tokens of holiness – sounds of melodies, visions of angels, and the flame of the fire of love in her breast. Once more the prophecy's fulfilment is linked to the presence of the broken-backed man and financial considerations, for she gives away his money in response to the Lord's commands that she should render herself destitute (92).[72] The prophecy continued on her return to England when a man from Norwich bought white clothes for her, and she was confessed wearing them on Trinity Sunday in Norwich Cathedral (103–4).[73]

The *Book*'s skeletal chronology illustrates the marked difference in her social relationships that these emblems of a growing intimacy with Christ create. In the period from 1411–13, before she left England and acquired the white clothes and tears of compunction, she suffered sporadic abuse on at least three occasions. This might be interpreted as envy as, for example, when she is summoned to appear before the bishop of Norwich's officers (40) and is delivered by Richard Caister; or as idiosyncratic as in the case of the malicious attack by the woman dressed in a pilch (a garment made of skin dressed with hair),[74] saying 'I wold þu wer in Smythefeld & I wold beryn a fagot to bren þe wyth; it is pety þat þow levyst' (36); or as patriarchal suspicion of the unaccompanied, outspoken woman as in the dramatic encounter with hostile monks, priests and members of the laity which occurred at Christ Church, Canterbury, sometime before 18 October 1416.[75] Kempe's knowledge of scripture provokes one to say: 'I wold ȝow wer closyd in an hows of ston þat þer schuld no man speke wyth þe' (27); but it is her spirited defence in telling a tale against them that fuels their anger and leads them to accuse her of Lollardy. Her persecutors' malevolence foreshadows her sufferings on pilgrimages to the north of England between 1417 and 1421, but the randomness of these attacks contrast to the episcopal and municipal inquisitions organized at York, Beverley and Leicester caused by her wearing of white and her loud sobbing and crying in places of worship.[76] These visits were made anyway during a time of greater severity towards all signs of religious heterodoxy. Tougher measures passed against Lollards following the failure of Oldcastle's rebellion enabled the authorities to jusify their persecution: all unusual religious conduct was subject to scrutiny. Margaret Aston points out that after the parliament which met at Leicester in 1414:

> Heresy hunting [became] a normal duty of the Chancellor, treasurer, justices, and all local officials . . . Secular courts were authorised to receive indictments for heresy, and the justices were henceforth to be commissioned with full powers of enquiry into the activities of all who in sermons, schools, conventicles, congregations and confederacies, as well as by writing, were maintaining heresy.[77]

Often accused of being a heretic and a Lollard, and on one occasion labelled Cobham's (Oldcastle's) daughter (129, 132), Kempe was persecuted because whiteness had become associated in the popular mind not with purity but with its opposite: disruption to social order and a threat to the norms of gender. In the spectacular meeting in the church of All Saints at Leicester in 1417 before the abbot, the dean, the mayor, sundry friars and priests, and 'so meche pepyl þat þei stodyn vpon stolys for to beheldyn hir & wonderyn vpon hir' (114), her white clothes, solitary status, and clear articulation of the articles of the faith would have been an extraordinary phenomenon. They considered that she might lead their wives astray, a belief which subsequent inquisitions in the north of England suggest was widespread.[78] In Beverley she was alleged to have encouraged Lady Westmorland's daughter (the duke of Bedford's cousin) to leave her husband (133). Yet these investigations into her piety enabled her to display her verbal, defensive skills in ways which were not possible in the disputes in Lynn. In an intimidating inquisition from the archbishop of York, Henry Bowet, who interpreted white clothes as a sign of virginity, and called her a heretic for claiming she was married, Kempe deftly retaliated to his prohibition against teaching in the diocese, by arguing that the Gospel gave her leave to do so.

Nay, syr, I xal not sweryn . . . for God al-mythy forbedith not, ser, þat we xal speke of hym. And also þe Gospel makyth mencyon þat, whan þe woman had herd owr Lord prechyd, sche cam beforn hym wyth a lowde voys & seyd, 'Blyssed be þe wombe þat þe bar & þe tetys þat ȝaf þe sowkyn.' Þan owr Lord seyd a-ȝen to hir, 'Forsoþe so ar þei blissed þat heryn þe word of God and kepyn it.' And þerfor, sir, me thynkyth þat þe Gospel ȝeuyth me leue to spekyn of God. (126)

It is a measure of the more corrosive vilification that she suffered in her home town that Kempe could not recover her reputation by verbal retaliation, but was forced instead to seek refuge from her opponents. The narrative accentuates the disorientation of her devotional life by clustering incidents which occurred at different times into a few chapters, loosely linking them with the Franciscan's persecution and so reinforcing the sense of chaos and mental distress which it caused her. The renewed fervour of Kempe's devotions following a lengthy illness clearly provoked local hostility; but ironically this occurred at a time when Lollards were being burnt in Norwich for their denial of the sacrament. The confusion that arose about her activities, as to where she should say her devotions, take communion or be confessed – according to Archbishop Chichele's letter this should be as often as she wished – contributes to the sense of dislocation which culminated in a crisis of desolation.[79] Her tumultuous weeping led to her being given communion secretly in the Prior's Chapel (138) beyond the hearing of the people; then a monk's opposition to her sobbing led Dom Thomas Hevyngham, prior of Lynn, to arrange for her to take communion in St Margaret's Church once more (139), but she again fled to the Chapel to escape slander after the Great Fire (164). She was removed to the Prior's Cloister to take air following her exertions one Good Friday (140) and here the Lord promised to take away her tears and ordered her to return to the church (155). The Gesine Chapel of Our Lady (155) was another sanctuary where the priest would hear her confession when Spryngolde was unable to (169). It was this priest who comforted her after she had been deserted by all her other supporters. Not surprisingly, the spiritual significance of eviction from places of worship is revealed to Kempe when the Dominican, Thomas Custance, tells a story about Mary of Oignies; this anticipates her acceptance within her community (165–6).

The Franciscan's extremely harsh treatment of Kempe and her supporters fanned public outcry in what appears to have been a dynamic, complex relationship between reactionary and radical forces within Lynn society.[80] He encouraged the belief that her gifts were diabolical so that even when her tears were taken away she was condemned for hypocrisy.

> þan meche pepil leuyd [many people believed] þat sche durst no lengar cryen for [because] þe good frer prechyd so a-ȝeyn hir & wold not suffyr [tolerate] hir in no maner. þan þei helden hym an holy man & hir a fals feynyd ypocrite. & as summe spoke eyuyl of hir aforn [before] for [because] sche cryed so summe spoke now euyl of hir for sche cryed not. (156)

Her supporters' attempts to restore her to favour after she was excluded from his sermons, and ostracized by some clergy and townspeople indicate loyalty if not autonomy and community spirit. The good priest who often read to her with another good priest, talked unavailingly to the grey friar to permit her to attend his sermons; so did Master Aleyn and Mr Spryngolde; and finally a most worthy burgess who a few years later was to become mayor of Lynn. Aleyn and Spryngolde redoubled their efforts at the friar's intransigence:

> So owr Lord of hys mercy, liche [just] as he had promysyd þe seyd creatur þat he xulde euyr prouydyn for hir, steryng þe spiritys [stirring the spirits] of tweyn good clerkys þe whech longe & many ȝerys had knowyn hir conuersacyon and al hir perfeccyon, made him mythy & bolde to spekyn for his party in excusyng þe seyd creatur, bothyn in þe pulpit & besyden [outside it] wher þei herd any-thyng meuyd aȝen hir, strengthenyng her skyllys [their arguments] be auctiteys of Holy Scripture sufficiently, of whech clerkys on was a White Frer, a doctowr of diuinite. þe oþer clerk was a bacheler of lawe canon, a wel labowred man in Scriptur. (167–8)

But Thomas Netter, the provincial of the White Friars, urged by 'sum envyows personys' (168) who believed Aleyn of Lynn was instructing Kempe in Scripture, forbade him to see her and only relaxed this prohibition some years later. Netter's antipathy towards Kempe's cryings may have developed during visits to Norwich in 1421, *c.*1425 and 1428. As a vigorous opponent of Lollardy he may have disliked any signs of radical piety; but in any event he disapproved of women drawing attention to themselves, although he was known to support women recluses.[81] His official boycott seems to have extended to her other supporters, so that Kempe lamented 'Maister Robert dar vnethys [hardly] spekyn wyth me. Now haue I in a maner no comfort neiþyr of man ne of childe' (168–9) and the priest of the Gesine Chapel commented: 'Anethe [scarcely] is þer any man þat heldith wyth ȝow [on your side] but I alone' (155).[82] But if the dispute did broaden beyond the question of Kempe's holiness to include suspicions of heresy, one might argue that they were coerced into deserting her rather than that they were disloyal or treacherous. The fact that she refused to leave town at the urging of friends because feeling ran so high against her (154) suggests an instinct of how to ride a crisis that had become political in nature.

The deeply ambiguous nature of Kempe's collusion with the communities of Lynn has been pointed out by Deborah Ellis who comments on her dual ambitions for 'inclusion (acceptance by the townspeople) and exclusion (repelled recognition of her special status)'.[83] Lay hostility extended to disapproval of her unusual domestic arrangements – of living apart from her husband – due to scepticism that they had kept vows of celibacy, and criticism that her refusal to look after him had led to his near-fatal accident. On the other hand the laity looked upon her spiritual gifts with favour when they were required in times of domestic and public crisis to say prayers for the sick and dying, or to pray when St Margaret's Church was nearly burnt in the Great Fire of 1421.[84] Such ministrations are rhetorically highlighted after Christ promises to take away the gift of tears (chapter 63), when the violence of her devotions diminishes, and a more saintly and spiritual image of her emerges. In the spirit of hagiography the account turns to the theme of Kempe's indispensability to her local community and stresses the ascendancy of her powers as she performs gratuitous acts of mercy particularly for other afflicted women. Chapters 74–6 describe how she kisses lepers and heals a woman suffering from post-partum psychosis (from which she herself had suffered after the birth of her first child); the sequence culminates in the most compelling answer to her social critics: caring for her sick husband at the end of his life.[85]

The enhanced spirituality of Kempe's status as she tends the sick, the dying, lepers and other social outcasts is also suggested, towards the conclusion of Book I (200–202), by her association with an order of nuns who sought devotional strength, and the abbess of Denny, a house of Poor Clares, and a strictly enclosed order as Jennifer Ward points out. The abbess's urgent and repeated demands for the mystic to visit them suggests a spiritual crisis, and her willingness to relax her Rule shows an entirely different relationship between the religious community and devout laity than that described by Ward in this volume. But it was Kempe's acceptance into the Guild of St Trinity in 1438, as prestigious in King's Lynn as in Coventry according to Ward, out of public respect for her spiritual aid, that ultimately vindicated her mission: devotion to 'The Trinity' had been paramount from the outset, and had anticipated the extent of her achievement according to Christ's revelation: 'For I haue ordeyned þe to knele be-for þe Trynyty for to pray for al the world, for many hundryd thowsand sowlys schal be sauyd be þi prayers' (20). Norwich Cathedral was dedicated to the Trinity, as was the Merchants' Guild of Lynn, of which her father had once been alderman, so this official recognition, coming at about the time of her dictation of *Liber* II, enabled her triumphantly to bridge the two ultimate sources of power, both temporal and ecclesiastical, within the town of Lynn.[86]

The conflicting perspectives on Kempe's mission cannot be easily contextualized because her anomalous status as a lay female mystic would have been problematic from both secular and ecclesiastical points of view. Her account suggests that the citizens of Lynn were volatile and bowed to what they perceived as the Franciscan's superior religious authority. In the popular imagination her behaviour may also have been associated with a more general drift away from the pulpit and clerical control towards the experience of grace for its own sake, and hence with Lollardy and anti-clericalism.[87] Furthermore it can be argued that Kempe's conspicuous public presence – her desire for official ecclesiastical approval, her disruptiveness, her abandoned marriage, her pilgrimages – which reduced opportunities for privacy in her life, caused her to blur the boundaries between her inner life and the external world of Lynn. The *Book*'s presentation of the need to care for her husband as a response to social disapproval and the conscious designation of a private space suggest that friction between the private and public spheres had existed.[88] Nevertheless her symbiotic relationship with the town that reviled her for hypocrisy and for threatening social stability gave her a wider stage on which to play out her mission. Public condemnation inspired her to action, while persecution provided her with a means of self-justification.

Despite the lack of documentary evidence for these controversies, the *Book*'s rhetorical projection of the scribe's vacillations about Kempe's sanctity indicates the scale of the social conflict which she aroused. His narrative interpolations illustrate the pattern of distrust, scorn, and eventual conversion experienced by many religious and lay devout who encountered Kempe. His renewed belief in her 'true' status through discovering models in Mary of Oignies and Elizabeth of Hungary, furthermore, anticipates her 'saintly' image, although Kempe herself would have assisted in this process by consciously modelling herself on St Bridget. By claiming that her gift of tears was divinely inspired the scribe attacks prejudice and enables a semiotic reading by linking her with other holy women: the tears are symptomatic of her personal asceticism; the wearing of white clothing, and a ring suggests that she is either an order unto herself or has affiliations with the conventual life.[89]

This interaction between mystic and scribe is the most innovative aspect of Kempe's *Book;* it creates a mystical autobiography which records her disruption of the religious and social order and her threat to prevailing ideologies while simultaneously enacting them in its structure. If *The Book of Margery Kempe* is to be identified with the genre of the holy woman's life, the controversies that Kempe provoked might be interpreted simply as vindications of her vocation in Christ. Yet the involved interactions between the mystic and the lay and ecclesiastic communities of King's Lynn suggest that her mission became involved in a wider conflict among different beliefs, factions and ideologies.[90] The controversy's duration and its effects on her supporters suggest that the local clergy were prepared to endorse her extreme piety in the face of lay hostility because they wished to consider different agendas and were willing to jeopardize their traditional authority in order to do so. Some of these mentors – educated, radical clerics, anchorites, holy figures, and confessors – may have already been dissatisfied with ecclesiastical forms of worship. If they were exploring alternative forms of spiritual contact, then their acceptance of her mysticism may be one symptom of an invisible, but large-scale crisis of faith. Certainly Thomas Netter's rebukes to Aleyn of Lynn suggest that institutional authority was reaffirmed in the face of considerable clerical discontent with the status quo. That is, in profoundly challenging social, sexual, as well as religious orthodoxies Kempe seems to have provoked dissent on a wide scale. The rupture of the apparently calm surface of the religious and secular communities in East Anglia which her pietistic excesses caused may in fact have exacerbated underlying tensions over the efficacy of conventional forms of worship, so contributing to that crisis of the faith which acquired shape through the often organized sectarianism of the Lollards.

Notes

[1] For descriptions and histories of the manuscript originally owned by the Charterhouse of Mount Grace in Yorkshire and found in the possession of the Butler-Bowden family, now BL Add MS 61823, see Kempe, *Margery Kempe,*

ed. Windeatt, 9, 298n.; Kempe, *Margery Kempe*, eds. Meech and Allen, xxxii–
xlvi; Atkinson, *Mystic*, 18–21.

[2] Negative responses are recorded in Partner, 'Reading', 31–3, 62–3, n.55;
Bremner, 'Margery Kempe and the critics'; Aers, 'Margery Kempe', 73–5;
Beckwith, 'Problems', 176–8 (175 n.11); Delany, 'Sexual economics', 72ff.
See also Bosse, 'Tarnished reputation' for a revisionist view; Long, 'Mysticism and hysteria'; and Atkinson, *Mystic*, 195–220 for an overview. Kempe's
incipient modernity is noted by Robert Gluck in a review of Staley's *Dissenting Fictions* in the *TLS* (4 August 1995), 4.

[3] On *via negativa* mysticism as the 'superior mystical mode' see Beckwith, 'Material mysticism', 39; Long, 'Mysticism and hysteria', 100.

[4] A term used by Gibson, *Theater*, 16; see also 65, 78–9; Beckwith, 'Material
mysticism'.

[5] Kempe, *Margery Kempe,* eds. Meech and Allen, Appendix III, i, 358–9; there
is no proof that this is the 'creature' of the *Book*. Owen's *The Making of
King's Lynn* provides no independent record of her existence.

[6] Staley, *Dissenting Fictions,* 3–5, 11, 171–4.

[7] On Kempe's voice see Lawton, 'Voice', 101–6; Beckwith, 'Problems', 180–
2, and Finke, *Feminist Theory*, 99–103, discuss mystical 'double voicedness'.

[8] See Finke, *Feminist Theory*, 99, on issues of reading the mystical text; Smith,
Poetics, 50 and Mueller, 'Autobiography', 12, on textual self-consciousness.

[9] Tanner, *Church,* 169; Gibson, *Theater,* 31. See Gray's comment on Tanner,
'Popular religion', 28.

[10] Kempe, *A shorte treatyse, STC* 14924. De Worde's treatise survives in a single copy in the Cambridge University Library. It was reprinted by Henry
Pepwell in 1521 (*STC* 20972).

[11] Holbrook, 'Margery Kempe and Wynkyn de Worde', 41; Glasscoe, *Games of
Faith,* 26.

[12] Kempe, *A shorte treatyse*, sig. A2v. See Kempe, *Margery Kempe*, eds. Meech
and Allen, xlvi-xlviii. They reprint de Worde's treatise with variants from
Pepwell's edition in Appendix II, 353–7 (355); this extract occurs 203–4.

[13] On the clerical community's heterogeneous responses to Kempe see Aers,
'Margery Kempe', 109; cf. Goodman, 'Piety', 357; on clerical, political conflicts in Lynn, Delany, 'Sexual economics', 75.

[14] 'Community' may be defined as a group living together, like a monastic body,
religious society, practising, more or less, community of goods (close to the
ideal of a heavenly community) (*OED*, sv. 8); or as 'a body of people or-
ganised into a political, social or municipal unity' (*OED,* s.v. 7) including
groups which have in common circumstances of belief, pursuit, religion which
may not be shared by those whom they live among (*OED* s.v. 7c). See Gray,
'Popular religon', 15, 18–22 for a discussion of liminal '*communitas*', and
Ellis's definition, 'Margery Kempe and King's Lynn', 151, of 'a new tran-
sient group' centred on Kempe. Cf. Staley's concept of a new society built

from love through 'a system of relationships defined in language' which bridges the active and contemplative spheres, and demarcates an 'arena for charitable action', *Dissenting Fictions*, xii, 100, 121–3, 184–7, 191–3.

[15] See Atkinson, *Mystic*, 120; quoted in Aers, 'Margery Kempe', 108.

[16] Kempe, *Margery Kempe,* eds. Meech and Allen, 168, 264n., 279n., 285n.; they claim his influence on her was formative.

[17] *Ibid.* Page references are henceforth included in the body of the text.

[18] Goodman, 'Piety', 348–9.

[19] Kempe, *Margery Kempe*, eds. Meech and Allen, 1–6. Kempe, *Margery Kempe,* ed. Windeatt, 33–8, divides this material into Proem and Preface.

[20] Goodman, 'Piety', 348–9; see Beckwith, 'Problems', 173–4; Kempe, *Margery Kempe*, ed. Windeatt, 23; Lawton, 'Voice', 101; Staley, *Dissenting Fictions*, 87–8; Gray, 'Popular religion', 24–6.

[21] Atkinson, *Mystic*, 29–32; she claims, 112, that Kempe's answers to her accusers in the north of England may also have been shaped by the scribe; see Gray, 'Popular religion', 10–11.

[22] The best example of such hagiography is Aelfric's 'Life of St Edmund', I, 76, 82, and II, 94, 114 .

[23] Staley, *Dissenting Fictions*, 85ff. Beckwith, 'Material mysticism', 48–9, and 'Problems', 174–5, notes that Christ's words licensed Kempe to refashion a divided self 'due to the perception of identity as a choice not as destiny'('Problems', 174). See also Lochrie, 'Marginal woman's quest', 34–5, on Kempe's insistence on literary authority; Aers, 'Margery Kempe', 83–116.

[24] See Tanner, *Heresy Trials*, 41ff; Thomson, *Later Lollards*, 123; Atkinson, *Mystic,* 106–7, 111–12; Gibson, *Theater*, 30; Aston, *Lollards and Reformers*, 195, 207, on Kempe's illiterate bookishness sometimes identified as a sign of Lollardy.

[25] Lochrie, 'Marginal woman's quest', 40; Aers, 'Margery Kempe', 100.

[26] On Kempe's models see Kempe, *Margery Kempe*, ed. Windeatt, 14–22; Lawton, 'Voice', 93–115; Despres, *Ghostly Sights,* 27–37.

[27] Cleeve, 'Margery Kempe', 164, 171, 173; see Watson, 'Julian of Norwich', 653–5, on works on and by continental women visionaries which appeared in England in *c.*1390; for Bridget's influence on East Anglian piety see Staley, *Dissenting Fictions,* 179; Gibson, *Theater,* 20–1, 97–8; Atkinson, *Mystic,* 35.

[28] Cleeve, 'Margery Kempe', 166–77 (168); Lochrie, *Translations,* 77–8; Kempe, *Margery Kempe*, eds. Meech and Allen, 95, 245–6, 348–9 and notes.

[29] On Love's *Meditations* see Lawton, 'Voice', 99–100; Staley, *Dissenting Fictions*, 91, 118; Gibson, *Theater*, 49–60.

[30] Melton's name, recorded in the margin of the manuscript, is of doubtful authority, although Atkinson, *Mystic,* 143, has corroborated this identity; see Kempe, *Margery Kempe*, eds. Meech and Allen, 321n.; Kempe, *Margery Kempe*, ed. Windeatt, 322n. This controversy and Kempe's part in it are not mentioned in any surviving records.

[31] My point is that the need to record social controversy fractures the devotional models; cf. Staley, *Dissenting Fictions*, 4, 155, who argues that this is due to Kempe's growth in subjectivity.

[32] Bale attributed to Aleyn of Lynn four original works, and fifty-one indices; Kempe, *Margery Kempe*, eds. Meech and Allen, 268.

[33] On his cult see Tanner, *Church*, 231; on other radical vicars of St Stephen's, 124–5, 232; on Bale's attribution of sainthood and miracles at his tomb, Kempe, *Margery Kempe*, eds. Meech and Allen, 276n., 320n., 322n.

[34] Watson, 'Julian of Norwich', 681, comments on the view that the conversation recalls fragments of Julian's *Revelation of Love*. According to his suggested redating of the Short and Long texts, Julian would have been revising her book as late as 1415.

[35] See note 16 above.

[36] See Kempe, *Margery Kempe*, eds. Meech and Allen, Glossary s.v. 'Spryngold'; Appendix III.iv. for his appearance in Norwich and Lynn records. He was still alive when Margery dictated the second version of *Liber* I in 1436.

[37] Kempe, *Margery Kempe*, eds. Meech and Allen, 340n.; see chapters 57, 61, 63.

[38] *Ibid.*, 142–3, 147, 320n. He recovered upon her return.

[39] *Ibid.*, 329–30, Appendix III.v, identify the priors of these priests as Thomas Hevyngham and John Derham.

[40] *Ibid.*, 324n. From OFr. *gesine*, 'childbed'; on feast days officials of the Guild of Holy Trinity carried the image in processions.

[41] *Ibid.*, 327n. They record assemblies in 1344 and 1365; but there were undoubtedly others.

[42] *Ibid.*, 307n.; Brackleye belonged to the College of the Chapel in the Fields in the parish of St Stephen in Norwich. His will was proven on 16 July 1417.

[43] Gibson, *Theater*, 23; Tanner, *Church*, 167.

[44] Tanner, *Church*, 2–5, 28–32.

[45] See also Gibson, *Theater*, 20, 23; on the monastic theatre, 107–35.

[46] Tanner, *Church*, 10–15; Gibson, *Theater*, 20.

[47] Tanner, *Church*, 14, 57–9, 64–6, 168–9, 198–203. On the beguines, see Penelope Galloway's essay in this volume. 92–115.

[48] Gibson, *Theater*, 21.

[49] *Ibid.*, 30–1; Tanner, *Church*, 163–6; *Heresy Trials*, 7–10; Thomson, *Later Lollards*, 120–31, 237.

[50] Aston, *Lollards and Reformers*, 8, 207–8; Cross, 'Women Lollards', 362.

[51] Gibson, *Theater*, 29–30, mentions cases of heterodox piety in the early sixteenth century.

[52] Tanner, *Church*, 136, 231–3, claims Bale's claim is unsubstantiated, but endorses Caister's radicalism (232); see Gibson, *Theater*, 31; Kempe, *Margery Kempe,* eds. Meech and Allen, 276n.; Gray, 'Popular religion', 15.

[53] Tanner, *Church,* 232.

[54] See Watson, 'Julian of Norwich', 657, on the conservatism of late medieval English spirituality; Tanner, *Heresy Trials*, 10–22; on the belief in unmediated communication with God (*ibid.*, 20); Thompson, *Later Lollards,* 127 (on Lollard opposition to the sacraments).

[55] See McSheffrey, 'Literacy and the gender gap', 164–5.

[56] Watson, 'Julian of Norwich', 665–6, n.71; Aers, 'Margery Kempe', 111; for other readings of Kempe's 'Lollard' tendencies see Lochrie, 'Marginal woman's quest', 42–5; *Translations*, 107–13; Staley, *Dissenting Fictions*, 5–10.

[57] Virginity was identified with holiness and chastity was negotiated by married holy women; see Cleeve, 'Margery Kempe', 165–6; Gray, 'Popular Religion', 13 n. 45.

[58] Kempe, *Margery Kempe,* eds. Meech and Allen, 4; they claim, viii, 58, that he was in Lynn as a young man by 1413.

[59] See Kempe, *Margery Kempe,* ed. Windeatt, 311n.; Kempe, *Margery Kempe,* eds. Meech and Allen, 1, 284 n., Appendix III, vii; Atkinson, *Mystic,* 113–14, on an earlier request in 1378 which was opposed by John Brunham, Kempe's father, then Mayor of Lynn, and John Kempe, probably her father-in-law.

[60] See Aers, 'Margery Kempe', 82, 198n.; Gray, 'Popular religion', 23–4.

[61] See Ellis, 'Margery Kempe's scribes', 161–75; Barratt, 'Margery Kempe', 189–201, on the identification of these women and their *vitae.*

[62] See Kempe, *Margery Kempe,* eds. Meech and Allen, 148, 321n., which records that persecution had begun by 1420 and persisted after the subsequent defence. This episode is made to coincide with the discrediting of the 'good friar'.

[63] Cleeve, 'Margery Kempe', 167–8; Kempe, *Margery Kempe,* ed. Windeatt, 29. Windeatt dates this first pilgrimage as between October 1413 and May 1415.

[64] Kempe, *Margery Kempe,* ed. Windeatt, 29, 313 n.8. He points out that the text distinguishes between earlier fits of crying and these which occurred later in life; see Atkinson, *Mystic,* 60–5.

[65] See Gray, 'Popular religion', 22n.; Cleeve, 175–7 on parallels between Kempe's and St Bridget's missions as brides of Christ.

[66] On whiteness as a sign of virtue and virginity see Kempe, *Margery Kempe,* eds. Meech and Allen, 273n., 274n.; the symbolism of white clothing in heaven is also found in the *Life of St Teresa.*

[67] Bridget, *Liber Celestis*, 485–7; Cleeve, 'Margery Kempe', 173–4; Gibson, *Theater,* 51–60, on swaddling clothes and shrouds in the late Middle Ages and their origins in the *Meditationes Vitae Christi.*

[68] Kempe, *Margery Kempe,* eds. Meech and Allen, 314–15n.

[69] See Gray, 'Popular religion', 15–16, on foreigners' greater appreciation of Kempe.

[70] Cleeve, 'Margery Kempe', 168–9.

[71] Kempe, *Margery Kempe,* eds. Meech and Allen, 293–4n. on the confessors in Kempe's party; Glossary s.v. 'Wenslawe' on the priest of German origin.

72 Bridget, *Liber Celestis*, 436; Cleeve, 'Margery Kempe', 168.
73 Kempe, *Margery Kempe,* eds. Meech and Allen, 308n.; it was the Patron's Day of the Cathedral.
74 Kempe, *Margery Kempe,* ed. Windeatt, 308n.; this image of bestiality invokes Christ's tormentors.
75 Kempe, *Margery Kempe,* eds. Meech and Allen, 270n.; this dates the death of one of the monks, John Kynton.
76 Atkinson, *Mystic*, 107–12.
77 *Lollards and Reformers*, 42–3; significantly, strong lay support was given to the Church authorities; on Kempe's involvement see Thomson, *Later Lollards*, 220–1.
78 Kempe, *Margery Kempe*, eds. Meech and Allen, 116; Aers, 'Margery Kempe', 100–1; Wilson, 'Margery and Alison', 223–37; Atkinson, *Mystic*, 108–10.
79 See Kempe, *Margery Kempe*, eds. Meech and Allen, 319n.; 324n.
80 Atkinson, *Mystic,* 64.
81 See Kempe, *Margery Kempe*, eds. Meech and Allen, 328n., 329n.; Kempe, *Margery Kempe*, ed. Windeatt, 324n. Netter was elected as Provincial Prior of the Carmelites in 1414. On the opposition to Lollard women preachers in his *Doctrinale*, see Aston, *Lollards and Reformers*, 65–6.
82 An exception is the Dominican Thomas Custance: see Kempe, *Margery Kempe,* eds. Meech and Allen, 327n.
83 Ellis, 'Margery Kempe and King's Lynn', 139.
84 *Ibid.*, 153–5; Atkinson, *Mystic,* 62–5.
85 This incident is out of chronological order; the date of her husband's accident is not known, but he is believed to have died in 1431. See Kempe, *Margery Kempe*, eds. Meech and Allen, 1; 342n.
86 *Ibid.*, 266n.; 322n.; see note 5 (above).
87 Dickman, 'Continental tradition', 165–6.
88 See Ellis, 'Margery Kempe and King's Lynn', 150, 154–5.
89 Kempe, *Margery Kempe*, eds. Meech and Allen, 297n. on Kempe's ring; Cleeve, 'Margery Kempe', 169–70 on its links with the Order of the Holy Saviour founded by St Bridget.
90 These approaches are most recently explored by Staley, *Dissenting Fictions*; Beckwith, 'Problems'; see also Aers, 'Margery Kempe', 73ff. and his reference to Delany's and Atkinson's work; Despres, *Ghostly Sights*, 62.

Bibliography

Aelfric, 'Life of St Edmund' in W. W. Skeat (ed.), *Aelfric's Lives of Saints* (London, 1890), I–II.

Aers, D., 'The Making of Margery Kempe: individual and community' in *Gender and Community and Individual Identity: English Writing, 1360–1430* (London, 1988), 73–116.

Aston, M., *Lollards and Reformers: Images and Literacy in Late Medieval Religion* (London, 1984).

Atkinson, C., *Mystic and Pilgrim: The Book and the World of Margery Kempe* (London, 1983).

Barratt, A., 'Margery Kempe and the King's daughter of Hungary' in S. McEntire (ed.), *Margery Kempe: A Book of Essays* (New York, 1992), 189–201.

Beckwith, S., 'A very material mysticism: the medieval mysticism of Margery Kempe' in D. Aers (ed.), *Medieval Literature: Criticism, Ideology and History* (Brighton, 1986), 34–57.

Beckwith, S., 'Problems of authority in late medieval English mysticism: language, agency and authority in *The Book of Margery Kempe*', *Exemplaria* 4 (1992), 172–99.

Bosse, R. B., 'Margery Kempe's tarnished reputation: a reassessment', *Fourteenth Century English Mystics Newsletter* 5 (1979), 9–19.

Bremner, E., 'Margery Kempe and the critics: disempowerment and deconstruction' in S. McEntire (ed.), *Margery Kempe: A Book of Essays* (New York, 1992), 117–35.

Bridget, St, *The Liber Celestis of St Bridget of Sweden*, ed. R. Ellis (Oxford, 1987).

Cleeve, G., 'Margery Kempe: a Scandinavian influence in medieval England?' in M. Glasscoe (ed.), *The Medieval Mystical Tradition in England V* (Woodbridge, 1992), 163–78.

Cross, C., '"Great Reasoners in Scripture": the activities of women Lollards, 1350–1530' in D. Baker (ed.), *Medieval Women* (Oxford, 1978), 359–80.

Delany, S., 'Sexual economics: Chaucer's Wife of Bath and *The Book of Margery Kempe*' in R. Evans and L. Johnson (eds.), *Feminist Readings in Midde English Literature: The Wife of Bath and all her Sect* (London, 1994), 72–87.

Despres, D., *Ghostly Sights: Visual Meditation in Late Medieval Literature* (Oklahoma, 1989).

Dickman, S., 'Margery Kempe and the continental tradition of the pious woman' in M. Glasscoe (ed.), *The Medieval Mystical Tradition in England II* (Woodbridge, 1984), 156–72.

Ellis, D. S., 'Margery Kempe and King's Lynn' in S. McEntire (ed.), *Margery Kempe: A Book of Essays* (New York, 1992), 139–59.

Ellis, R., 'Margery Kempe's scribes and the Miraculous Books' in H. Phillips (ed.), *Langland, The Mystics and the Medieval English Religious Tradition: Essays in Honour of S. S. Hussey* (Cambridge, 1990), 161–76.

Finke, L. A., *Feminist Theory, Women's Writing* (London, 1992).

Gibson, G. M., *The Theater of Devotion: East Anglian Drama and Society in the Late Middle Ages* (Chicago and London, 1989).

Glasscoe, M., *English Medieval Mystics: Games of Faith* (London, 1993).

Goodman, A. G., 'The piety of John Brunham's daughter, of Lynn', in D. Baker (ed.), *Medieval Women* (Oxford, 1978), 347–58.

Gray, D., 'Popular religion and late medieval literature' in P. Boitani and A. Torti (eds.), *Religion in the Poetry and Drama of the Late Middle Ages in England* (Cambridge, 1990), 1–28.

Holbrook, S. E., 'Margery Kempe and Wynkyn de Worde' in M. Glasscoe (ed.), *The Medieval Mystical Tradition in England IV* (Woodbridge, 1987), 27–46.

Kempe, M., *A shorte treatyse of contemplacyon taught by our lorde Jhesu Chryste taken out of the boke of Margerie kempe* (1501) *STC* 14924; (reprinted 1521) *STC* 20972.

Kempe, M., *The Book of Margery Kempe*, eds. S. B. Meech and H. E. Allen (London, 1940).

Kempe, M., *The Book of Margery Kempe*, ed. and trans. B. Windeatt (London, 1985).

Lawton, D., 'Voice, authority and blasphemy in *The Book of Margery Kempe*', in S. McEntire (ed.), *Margery Kempe, A Book of Essays* (New York, 1992), 93–115.

Lochrie, K., '*The Book of Margery Kempe*: the marginal woman's quest for literary authority', *Journal of Medieval and Renaissance Studies* 16 (1986), 33–55.

Lochrie, K., *Margery Kempe and the Translations of the Flesh* (Philadelphia, 1994).

Long, J., 'Mysticism and hysteria: the histories of Margery Kempe and Anna O' in R. Evans and L. Johnson (eds.), *Feminist Readings in Middle English Literature: The Wife of Bath and all her Sect* (London, 1994), 88–111.

McSheffrey, S., 'Literacy and the gender gap in the late Middle Ages: women and reading in Lollard communities' in L. Smith and J. Taylor (eds.), *Women, the Book and the Godly* (Cambridge, 1995), 157–70.

Mueller, J., 'Autobiography of a new "Creatur": female spirituality, selfhood, and authorship in *The Book of Margery Kempe*' in M. B. Rose (ed.), *Women in the Middle Ages and Renaissance* (New York, 1986), 155–71.

Owen, D. (ed.), *The Making of King's Lynn: A Documentary Survey* (London, 1984).

Partner, N. F., 'Reading *The Book of Margery Kempe*', *Exemplaria* 3 (1991), 29–66.

Smith, S., *A Poetics of Women's Autobiography: Marginality and the Fictions of Self Representation* (Bloomington, 1987).

Staley, L., *Margery Kempe's Dissenting Fictions* (Pennsylvania, 1994).

Tanner, N. P. (ed.), *Heresy Trials in the Diocese of Norwich: 1428–1431* (London, 1977).

Tanner, N. P., *The Church in Late Medieval Norwich, 1370–1532* (Toronto, 1984).

Thomson, J. A. F., *The Later Lollards: 1414–1520* (Oxford, 1965).

Watson, N., 'The Composition of Julian of Norwich's *Revelation of Love*', *Speculum* 68 (1993), 637–83.

Wilson, J. M., 'Margery and Alison: women on top' in S. McEntire (ed.), *Margery Kempe: A Book of Essays* (New York, 1992), 223–37.

8

English Noblewomen and the Local Community in the Later Middle Ages[1]

JENNIFER C. WARD

IN examining the English medieval economy, historians have found that the nobility were the takers, recipients and beneficiaries of profits and wealth. Methods of exploiting estates changed over the Middle Ages, but they continued to receive rents, issues of jurisdiction and other forms of income from their manors and towns. Studies of individual estates and of noble households have inevitably tended to separate the nobility from the communities where they lived. Yet they were by no means cut off from these communities, and it is important to evaluate their relationships with the people around them, and their participation in local life. Much of the illustration for this paper refers to eastern England in the fourteenth and fifteenth centuries, since many of the surviving household accounts for noblewomen describe their activities in that region. However, these activities mirrored what was going on in other parts of England.

The term 'community' had a variety of meanings in the Middle Ages, and, in addition, modern historians have given it certain specialized connotations.[2] In this paper, 'community' has been taken in the first instance to denote the village or town where the noblewoman resided and over which she often exercised lordship. Yet in several cases the local community has rather to be thought of in the sense of neighbourhood or region over which the lady had influence and on whose resources she and her household relied. For great noblewomen travelling periodically between residences, the impact on a particular locality was spasmodic rather than permanent. Women of the knightly and gentry groups often had a closer identification with their neighbourhood, as evidenced by their wills; Katherine Peverel's bequests in 1375 to Sussex monasteries, friaries and hospitals showed that her religious interests centred on the county.[3] A parallel can be drawn between these women and townswomen whose community was based on their own locality, as Janet Wilson shows in her discussion of Margery Kempe. A different but related use of the word 'community' denoted a group of people of similar status or lifestyle: hence the description of a monastery as a religious community, or the modern term, 'county community', to describe the élite of a particular shire. The noble household itself also constituted a community. In this paper, the relationships of the noblewoman to the local community will be investigated with reference to both places and people, and will concentrate on relationships outside the normal bonds of lordship; tenurial and jurisdictional ties will not be considered.

There is no doubt that the nobility got more out of all their possessions than they put back into the community. However, their need to provision their households meant that they were dependent on the local community, and their reliance on food supplies purchased for cash increased in the later Middle Ages, as can be traced through household rules and accounts. In the rules said to have been drawn up by Robert Grosseteste for the countess of Lincoln *c*.1241, it was assumed that most of the household's provisions would be supplied from the lady's demesne manors; at this time, it was usual for the nobility to be exploiting their manors directly, rather than leasing them out. Articles such as wine, wax and spices would have to be purchased, and this could be done at the great fairs, as at Boston and St Ives.[4] The fourteenth century, however, saw the decline of these fairs, the growth of importance of London and several provincial towns, and the growing practice after *c*.1370 to rent out manors, a policy which continued into the sixteenth century. Moreover, it became far less usual to have frequent changes of residence. The noble household therefore relied increasingly on securing its foodstuffs by purchase, and this is reflected in household accounts. Margaret de Brotherton, living at Framlingham, Suffolk, in the 1380s, made use of merchants in Ipswich and Norwich, and of local fairs. Anne Neville, duchess of Buckingham, obtained only her meat from her demesne manors, and bought all her other provisions: wine, fish and spices from London, and items such as grain and ale from traders close to her residence. While she was living at Writtle in Essex in the 1460s, she found Chelmsford a convenient shopping centre. When Alice Chaucer, duchess of Suffolk, was living in London, Thomas Cartere of Wingfield, butcher, was driving oxen to London for her household; Wingfield was her main residence in Suffolk. The general reliance on purchases is reflected in the household rules of Cecily, duchess of York in the late fifteenth century; proclamation was to be made four times a year in the market towns around Berkhamsted, Hertfordshire, to discover whether her purveyors, caterers and others were making true payment for the goods they received.[5]

Cecily Neville's proclamation makes it clear that it was not necessarily the place of residence which would see the largest amount of business. It was particular tradesmen who benefited rather than the place as a whole, and household officials drew on a whole region for their supplies, sometimes going to considerable distances. When Elizabeth de Burgh was living at Clare, Suffolk, and Great Bardfield, Essex, in the first half of the fourteenth century, her officials made the occasional purchase in Clare or Bardfield market,[6] but much of the grain and meat which the household needed was supplied from her demesne manors, and many other provisions were bought much further afield, in spite of transport costs. For instance, in 1350–1, 154 gallons of red wine were bought at Clare from Matilda Mone to mix with vinegar, but the bulk of the wine purchases was made at Ipswich, Colchester and in London; salt was purchased at King's Lynn, and at Reach, Wisbech, and Stourbridge Fair, Cambridgeshire; spices were bought in London from the Italian grocer, Bartholomew Thomasin. It is clear from Elizabeth's household accounts that once a trader secured her custom she normally remained loyal to him for years, and several, including Bartholomew Thomasin, wore her livery.[7] Less wealthy noblewomen, such as Alice de Bryene in the early fifteenth century, tended to shop nearer home, but even they often looked towards London or a major provincial town for items such as wine and spices. Alice, living at Acton Hall in Suffolk, made use of local markets, such as Sudbury and Lavenham, but her wine, spices and some of her fish came from London, Ipswich, and Stourbridge Fair at Cambridge.[8]

In addition to generating business, the noble household also provided employment. The problem here lies in seeing how many of those employed came from the local community. It is relatively easy to trace the career patterns of the most important officials as they moved between the households of the nobility, ecclesiastics and the Crown. The same is true of the local gentry who in the fourteenth and fifteenth centuries came to be appointed increasingly as stewards, auditors, legal experts and councillors, as well as feoffees and executors of wills; their appointment strengthened the links binding local landed society together, and they became part of the affinity. What is much more difficult is to discover the background of the household servants, the esquires, yeomen, grooms, pages, and ladies who made up the majority of the household's personnel. In wealthy households the number could be considerable, such as the fifty-one grooms and fourteen pages on Elizabeth de Burgh's livery list of 1343.[9] It is likely that these men were recruited locally, probably on personal recommendation; Walter Mildmay who was serving Anne Neville, duchess of Buckingham, in 1465–6 came from a yeoman's family living a few miles from Anne's residence at Writtle.[10] However, the practice of identifying servants by their work and occasionally not even giving a Christian name often makes it impossible to trace their origins; Elizabeth de Burgh's livery list of 1343 included among the pages Adam page of the poultry, Adam page of the bakery, and the nameless page of the palfreys.[11] Household service presumably represented an acceptable career pattern, offering long-term work, if one was fortunate, and some possibility of promotion; this was certainly the case in Elizabeth de Burgh's household. Reward took the form of board, wages and livery; in addition there was the chance of gifts, tips and a bequest in a will.

The practices of provisioning and employment applied to any noble huusehold, whether headed by a lord or a lady. It is, however, important to stress the number of households in the later Middle Ages under the control of women on a temporary or permanent basis, during absences of husbands, or during widowhood. These women had an important part to play in the context of noble and gentry society; through their use of hospitality, the exchange of gifts, and the development of social contacts, they exercised influence on behalf of their families, households and the communities around them.

Hospitality and the exchange of visits gave the nobility and gentry the opportunity to enjoy a busy social life. The noblewoman was able to build up a circle of friends and acquaintances in the neighbourhood of her residence.[12] Visiting and entertaining within one's own locality and social group were as popular in the Middle Ages as in more recent times, and the networks established tied in with affinities and business contacts. Interests were furthered by the growing practice in the later Middle Ages of the nobility spending part of the year in London. Social activities undoubtedly provided enjoyment, but also had deeper significance.

In these circumstances, the wife who was left at home while her husband was away at war or on business had a vital role to play, and it was usually taken for granted that she was capable of doing this. Neither Elizabeth Berkeley nor her husband, Richard Beauchamp, earl of Warwick, accepted the entail which prevented her from inheriting Berkeley Castle in Gloucestershire. While her husband was engaged in the Hundred Years War in 1421, it was Elizabeth who had to present her case before the king's council.[13] In the mid-fifteenth century, in the absence of her husband, John Paston I, his wife Margaret had to run the household, supervise his lands, and protect his interests; this involved the physical defence of his possessions as when she was expelled from the manor house at Gresham by Lord Moleyns in January 1449. Through the summer of 1465 she was keeping her husband informed of the situation at Drayton and Hellesdon, the latter seized by the duke of Suffolk in October. Such responsibilities entailed an intimate knowledge of county politics, and the women's actions inevitably had an impact on the places concerned. Elizabeth and Margaret were not isolated figures, as other wives are found acting locally in their husbands' interests; about 1481, Margery Brews, the wife of John Paston III, was proposing to make a personal intervention with the duchess of Norfolk on behalf of her husband, and she promised to choose her words carefully.[14]

Families like the Pastons needed the backing of lords, and such lordship was offered by noblewomen both in conjunction with their husbands, and on their own as widows.[15] A few noblewomen like Joan de Bohun, countess of Hereford and Essex, emerged as the leading figures of their counties. Joan was widowed in 1373 and the Bohun inheritance was divided between her two daughters who married Thomas of Woodstock, duke of Gloucester, youngest son of Edward III, and Henry Bolingbroke, the future Henry IV. With the murder of the duke of Gloucester in 1397, and the accession of Henry IV two years later, and in the absence of other prominent nobles in Essex in the early fifteenth century, Joan was responsible, along with leading gentry, for quelling disorder and maintaining royal interests. Members of the gentry were happy to belong to the lady's affinity, and must have felt that her lordship would bring them tangible gains. Fees and liveries were given to retainers, and relationships were fostered by the exercise of patronage and by gifts. Hospitality provided the setting for the formation of new relationships, and service to a lady like Elizabeth de Burgh enabled the retainer to meet many of the leading nobles of the time. Elizabeth, like Joan de Bohun, had wealth, status, and close ties with the royal family, and was in an excellent position to be able to further the interests of her dependents. About a hundred years later, Alice, duchess of Suffolk, was a formidable figure in East Anglian politics, as the Pastons found to their cost.[16]

Lordship implied a two-way relationship between the lady and local gentry: patronage and reward on the one side, and service and loyalty on the other.[17] Similarly, the relationship with religious communities conferred benefits on both lady and convent. However, the importance attached to the prayers offered by the house for the salvation of the souls of the lady's family and for her own well-being and good estate distinguishes this relationship from that enjoyed with lay people. A distinction also has to be drawn between noblewomen's relations with religious houses and those of women such as Margery Kempe who had spiritual benefits to confer on the convent; for instance, Margery was summoned by the abbess of Denny to give her nuns spiritual comfort.

In extending hospitality to religious communities in their locality, noblewomen were usually still moving within the same social group, although an element of choice can be detected as to whom they chose to entertain; they by no means entertained all the religious houses of the vicinity. In 1265 Eleanor de Montfort entertained the Cistercian nuns of Wintney in Hampshire. Elizabeth de Burgh entertained the Augustinian friars at Clare when she was at Clare castle, and the Minoresses when she was at her London house which was in the outer precinct of the convent; when she was in residence at Usk, she entertained the nuns of the Benedictine priory whose history is discussed in Jane Cartwright's paper.[18] Both the nunneries were known for their noble inmates. The entertainment offered could be lavish, and papal indulgences were secured to allow guests from religious houses to eat meat.[19]

In return, the nobility were admitted into confraternity in religious houses; Marie de St Pol, countess of Pembroke, in her will of 1377 wanted her executors to inform all religious houses where she had been received into confraternity of the date of her death, and she wished each to have one of her relics, vestments, or images for the greater remembrance of her soul.[20] Members of the nobility were granted indulgences to enter religious houses, such as that granted to Marie de St Pol in 1333 to enter nunneries once a year with a retinue of six matrons.[21] Such visits might create disturbance, at least for some nuns; in 1364, Matilda of Lancaster, countess of Ulster, who had been professed as a nun at Campsey priory in Suffolk, asked to be transferred to the Minoresses' house at Bruisyard in order to escape the number of nobles coming to Campsey.[22] The mutual exchange of gifts reinforced the links between the noblewoman and the religious house. Noblewomen's gifts were reciprocated; on 21 April 1465 Anne Neville, duchess of Buckingham, received three capons from the college of Pleshey, Essex, a token reminder of the connection between the college and the Stafford family.[23]

There is more evidence for close connections with religious houses than with local churchmen. However, individual clerics were also entertained. Alice de Bryene at Acton Hall gave hospitality to friars from East Anglian houses on their journeys as well as to local priests, and Elizabeth Berkeley, countess of Warwick, made it a habit to invite the parish priest to Sunday dinner, wherever she happened to be residing.[24]

As with lay society, hospitality, visits and gifts had a deeper significance. Noblewomen exercised patronage over parish churches and certain religious houses, and had responsibilities for appointments and custodies. Appointment to benefices was a way of rewarding officials and others, but the right of patronage could also be used to endow a religious or educational foundation, as in the case of the Cambridge colleges founded by Marie de St Pol and Elizabeth de Burgh. Very little is known about how the lady carried out her duties over patronage, but an agreement survives in which Elizabeth de Burgh clarified her rights over Anglesey priory during a vacancy in the office of prior.[25]

On the religious level, the depth of the relationship depended on what the lady herself wanted and how close she wished to be to the religious life. Certain women, like Matilda of Lancaster, chose to enter the community as nuns. Others remained in the world but had a close sympathy with the conventual life; Marie de St Pol had her own chamber in the abbey for Minoresses which she founded at Denny, and her will specified that she was to be buried in the choir of the abbey church, clothed in the nun's habit.[26] The house which Elizabeth de Burgh built in the outer precinct of the Minoresses' convent outside Aldgate in London came to be the home of several noble ladies.[27] It gave them contact with the religious services of the nuns, and the opportunity to enjoy a busy social life in the capital.

Many noblewomen founded or were included in chantries established in religious houses which celebrated requiem masses on behalf of themselves and their families. Their choice of religious house was often due to family tradition, but the popularity of the friars gave founders a large number of possible options. While Marie de St Pol and Elizabeth de Burgh favoured the Minoresses, Elizabeth Lady Despenser in her will of 1409 wanted to be buried between her husband and son in the abbey church of Tewkesbury, and arranged for seven chaplains to celebrate masses for the salvation of her soul for a year after her death; they were to be the most honest that could be found and each was to receive £5.[28] The Despensers were lords of Tewkesbury, and it was usual for members of the family to be buried there in the fourteenth and early fifteenth centuries. Taking all the evidence together, there was great variety in the relationships between noblewomen and religious houses, but there is no doubt that the contacts were regarded as important on both sides.

Hospitality to the poor and almsgiving were duties expected from the nobility throughout the Middle Ages, as is brought out by Patricia Skinner's paper in this volume, and J. A. Tasioulas emphasizes the importance of the Virgin Mary as a role model for the dispensing of charity. Depictions of the seven works of mercy and didactic treatises, such as that of the Knight of La Tour Landry for the education of his daughters, show that charity was especially expected from women.[29] Few sources however make it clear whether the relief was specifically targeted at poor men or poor women. All noble families distributed leftovers of food to the poor outside the gates, a practice emphasized in the Rules of St Robert,[30] and it is likely that all gave hospitality to strangers. Alice de Bryene's Household Book of 1413 gave particulars of all those present at dinner and supper, including nameless strangers.[31] Other types of relief varied from one household to another. Although the criticism can be made that far less was spent on relief than on the noblewoman's own comforts and pursuits and that the noblewoman was only making a symbolic gesture, it appears likely that many women gave their responsibility towards the poor serious thought. Some, like Joan de Valence, countess of Pembroke, and Katherine de Norwich, gave regular relief to poor people within their households.[32] Others provided especially for the poor on certain anniversaries, as Elizabeth de Burgh did on St Gregory's day, the anniversary of the death of her third husband. Towards the end of her life, she regularly set aside a certain sum of money for the relief of the poor at her place of residence and certain other manors.[33] Sometimes, relief took the institutional form of founding or supporting a hospital or almshouse, as with Margaret Lady Hungerford and her hospital at Heytesbury.[34]

Maundy Thursday was a regular occasion for almsgiving, recalling Christ's washing of the disciples' feet after the Last Supper. On Maundy Thursday 1352, £1. 17s. 6d. was distributed to fifty poor people by Elizabeth de Burgh; each received 9d. and a further £1. 4s. 6d. was given to her almoner for distribution. Mary de Bohun, countess of Derby, distributed gowns and hoods of russet to eighteen poor women on Maundy Thursday 1388, together with 9s. in money.[35] It is not clear in either case whether the ladies washed the feet of the poor, but there is a link between the number of the poor and the age of the lady, although Elizabeth de Burgh in 1352 was aged fifty-six.

Distribution to the poor at funerals was virtually an invariable practice among the nobility, the prayers of the poor for the speedy passage of the soul through purgatory being especially highly valued. In addition, many wills left money to relieve particular groups of poor people, the choice of groups often being gender-specific, and sometimes related to the lady's estates. Joan Beauchamp, lady of Abergavenny, in her will of 1434, wanted 100 marks to be distributed to the poor at her funeral, and left 200 marks for her poor tenants in England, £100 for the poor in her lordships by way of clothing, bedding, horses and oxen, £100 for the marriage of poor maidens in her lordships, and £40 for poor prisoners.[36] As Skinner points out, some groups of women were particularly vulnerable. Women of the late as well as the early Middle Ages were driven into poverty when they lacked resources of land or wealth which they could exploit, or were unable to secure adequately paid work to bring up their families. Both men and women are found suffering from poverty either temporarily or permanently, but girls with no prospect of marriage and destitute widows were groups especially at risk.

The evidence on hospitality and relief indicates that the noblewoman engaged with the local community at her own social level and among the poorest members of society. What about the people in between? Here it appears that occasional formal entertainment was offered, although it is likely in view of the strength of medieval ideas on social hierarchy that both the noblewoman and her guests felt that there was a deep gulf between them. On 1 January 1413 Alice de Bryene gave a dinner for, among others, 300 tenants and other strangers, a far larger number than she entertained at any other time in the year. The presence of a harpist indicates that music formed part of the entertainment. The social gulf is typified by the food served, with wine, geese, capons, rabbits and piglets for the more important guests who included members of the local gentry, and ale, two pigs and two sheep for the rest. Two swans were served at the 'top table'.[37] This type of occasional formal entertainment is found with other noblewomen, as when Elizabeth de Burgh entertained the 'gild of Clare' in 1344; unfortunately it is not known who belonged to the guild.[38] There was good reason for Eleanor de Montfort to entertain the burgesses of Sandwich and Winchelsea in the summer of 1265, as she wanted to ensure their support for her husband against Henry III.[39]

With these entertainments being essentially occasional, the links between the lady and most people in the local community were probably limited to business contacts and to the lady's exercise of lordship over her tenants. In exceptional circumstances, tenants might petition the lady for the redress of a specific wrong,[40] and it is likely that many noblewomen followed the practice of Cecily, duchess of York, in giving audience for an hour after dinner to all who had any business with her.[41] A noblewoman with extensive connections at court as well as in the county was an asset to the local community in securing privileges and pardons, and in defending the community against competition from elsewhere. Intercession was regarded as an acceptable activity for women in the treatises of the time, and was a way in which the gap between the locality and the centre could be bridged. Women like Elizabeth de Burgh and Margaret de Brotherton, duchess of Norfolk, were active in petitioning the king on a variety of matters affecting communities on their lands. In 1359, an agreement concerning Sudbury and Long Melford was reached in Elizabeth de Burgh's household at Clare, a few miles away.[42] Intervention took place at the papal court as well as at the royal court, and was on behalf of individuals as well as communities; thus in 1352 Elizabeth de Burgh petitioned the pope for the priory of Thremhall in Essex to be allowed to appropriate the church of Stansted Mountfichet in order to help it to clear its debts.[43]

Further possibilities of contact were to be found in the religious sphere, especially in connection with parish churches and confraternities. In recent historical work, emphasis has been put on the private, individual nature of religious practice among the nobility and gentry, and this is borne out by the importance attached to the household chapel, and by the widespread possession of books of hours, relics and other religious objects.[44] Worship within the household and private prayer were not, however, incompatible with attachment to the local church and to religious groups, although noblewomen's involvement in public worship was likely to be less frequent than for townswomen, as evidenced by Margery Kempe's presence at services in the church of St Margaret at King's Lynn. Details in household accounts and wills certainly point to a willingness to give local churches financial support. In some cases this was deliberately done to bring the presence of the lord and lady perpetually to the memory of the community. In her accounts of 1453–4, Alice Chaucer, duchess of Suffolk, recorded a contribution of 20 marks towards building the bell-tower of the church of Eye, so that there should

be a permanent memorial among the lady's tenants for the benefit of the
soul of her most dear lord, William duke of Suffolk, and for the good
estate of the duchess herself and their son John.[45] The building of the
church at Poynings in Sussex in the later fourteenth century was financed
by the complementary bequests of Sir Michael de Poynings and his wife
Joan. He bequeathed 200 marks to build a new church at Poynings; she
added 100 marks, and left a further 100 marks to her son Thomas which
she wanted to be used on the building of the church when he came of
age.[46]

   Casual aid to churches is also recorded. Among the donations made
by Isabel Lady Morley in 1463–4 were 20d. towards the fabric of St
Andrew's Church in Norwich. Many noblewomen's wills recorded
bequests to parish churches as well as religious houses. Isabel Lady
Morley left money and a whole vestment of black velvet with the orfreys
that she had made for it to the church of Swanton Morley.[47] Elizabeth
de Bohun, countess of Northampton, who died in 1356, left a pair of
vestments from her chapel to the parish church of Rochford, although
her money bequests were devoted to houses of friars. Similarly
Elizabeth de Burgh left money and a cloth of gold each to the parish
churches of Clare, Great Bardfield, Standon and Bottisham, although her
bequests to religious houses were far more impressive.[48]

   Women like Elizabeth de Bohun and Elizabeth de Burgh belonged to
the higher nobility, and although their gifts benefited parish churches their
own interests lay much more with religious houses. It was the women
of the lesser nobility, like Isabel Lady Morley and Alice de Bryene, as
well as of the gentry whose attention was more focused on the parish
church, who chose to be buried there and whose chantries were to the
benefit of the parish. Isabel planned her tomb at Hingham before her
death and it is recorded in her accounts of 1463–4. Alice de Bryene's
brass survives in Acton church. Margaret de Thorp in 1347 left specific
items to the church of Thorpe near Newark where she was buried: one
silver cup to serve as a chalice at the altar of the chapel of the Holy
Trinity, and her psalter to serve as long as it would last.[49] The parish
church of Helmsley in Yorkshire was among several to benefit in terms
of clergy and possessions from the will of Beatrice Lady Roos of 1414.
She bequeathed £50 to two chaplains celebrating mass there daily for
five years after her death for the salvation of her own soul, the soul of
her second husband Thomas Lord Roos, and the souls of all the faithful
departed. She also left the parish church a vestment of chequered red
and white velvet.[50] Whether parish churches benefited from gifts and

endowments depended very much on the noblewoman's wishes; as a result, some were enriched considerably, and others not at all.

It is rare to have evidence of women's attendance at the parish church as this was a matter which seldom needed to be recorded. Elizabeth de Burgh's chamber account of 1351–2 recorded the offerings made at Mass, and show that although she normally attended her own chapel she went to the parish church at Clare on a number of festivals, often giving money to children who were baptised in her presence. Occasionally she engaged a friar to preach at these services. Parish churches were also used to sing requiem masses for officials who had died.[51] It is probable that other noblewomen acted similarly.

There was therefore some contact between the noblewoman and the community where she was living via the parish church, but this contact was occasional and spasmodic rather than regular. With the rise of new cults, especially that of Corpus Christi in the fourteenth century, noblewomen became involved in the great confraternities associated with major towns, probably finding in them a common religious focus with wealthy merchant families; the social and political aspects of the fraternity also had their appeal to landed families.[52] The feast of Corpus Christi epitomized the centrality of the Mass in late medieval religion and focused devotion on the Body of Christ in the form of the Host. The Corpus Christi fraternities were primarily to be found in the towns but attracted noble and gentry families living in the country, and both wives and widows were eligible as members. St Helen's guild at Colchester was refounded in 1407 by the wealthiest men of the borough to maintain five chaplains who were to pray for Henry IV and the members of the guild; the sixty-five members of 1418 included Joan de Bohun, countess of Hereford and Essex.[53] The guild of Holy Trinity, St Mary, St John the Baptist and St Katherine at Coventry attracted the élite of the town, local nobility and gentry, and some of the leading nobles of the realm; it was usual for the wife to join as well as the husband, as in the case of Sir John Arundel and his wife Eleanor, received in 1379.[54] The ordinances for the Corpus Christi guild at York laid down that no lay person was to be admitted unless he or she was of good character. The lay members had no share in the government of the guild. All brothers and sisters of the guild were to say yearly the Psalter of the Virgin for the souls of brethren who had died, and to attend Mass on the Sunday in the octave of the feast of Corpus Christi and contribute 2*d.* each for the support of the guild. The requiem mass for deceased members took place on the Monday. This guild attracted the same range of members as Holy Trinity guild at Coventry, and again it was usual for wives to become members at the same time as their husbands. Widows were also eligible to join, such as Alice Neville, Lady Fitzhugh, who became a member in 1473 shortly after the death of her husband, her children Richard, Roger, Edward, Thomas and Elizabeth joining at the same time. Other well known northern families, such as the Scropes, Constables and Parrs were among the brethren of the guild, rubbing shoulders with the York merchants.[55]

It is likely that it was the religious benefits of the confraternity that members primarily appreciated. Such benefits were gained whether members were present at services or not, and, if they lived at a distance from the town, it is probable that they were usually absent.[56] The confraternities, however, were a possible means of facilitating social contact between nobles, gentry and merchants outside the framework of their business relationships, although there is no record of such socializing between individuals during meetings. Margery Kempe, as a member of the Trinity Guild at King's Lynn, may well have seen Norfolk notables without having the opportunity to converse with them.

Looking at the roles that the noblewoman played in the various types of local community, it is apparent that they were derived far more from their position and status than from gender, and the widow, and the wife with an absent husband had a much more prominent part to play than the wife whose husband was at home. Women were not passive spectators of the local scene. They contributed to the well-being of the places where they lived through the business and employment which they provided, their religious and charitable benefactions, and sometimes through their ability to intercede and to secure privileges from king or pope. Contacts with groups below them in the social hierarchy were occasional and formal, as were the connections which many noblewomen had with their parish church. They took the duties of hospitality, almsgiving and intercession seriously, but preferred to associate with social equals and people of wealth, whether these were to be found in county society, religious houses or the principal towns. The preservation of the social hierarchy was regarded as vital, although it is likely that the growth of confraternities in the fourteenth and fifteenth centuries extended their range of contacts.

The situation has strong similarities with the writings of Jane Austen and Anthony Trollope at a much later date. In their works there is the same stress on social hierarchy, the desire to mix with the right people, a feeling of responsibility for the poor but few points of contact with those whose birth and fortune placed them between the rich and the destitute. Emma Woodhouse, to name but one example, enjoyed the company of her equals and was charitable to the poor, but had no time for the tenant-farmer Robert Martin.

Notes

¹ I would like to thank the members of the Gender and Medieval Studies Conference in 1995 for their questions and comments which have enabled me to develop a number of points in this paper.

² The use of the term 'community' by historians is discussed by Rubin, 'Small groups', 132–5.

³ Lambeth Palace Library, Register of Simon Sudbury, fo. 90r-v. The will is printed in translation in Ward, *Women of the English Nobility and Gentry*, 224–6.

⁴ Lamond, *Walter of Henley's Husbandry*, 144–5.

⁵ BL Add. Roll 17,208, m. 1, 3, 4; Ridgard, *Medieval Framlingham*, 86–128; BL Add. MS. 34,213, fos. 7r, 7v, 8r, 21r, 24v; BL Egerton Roll 8,779, m. 9; *A Collection of Ordinances and Regulations*, 38.

⁶ For example, PRO E101/92/7, m. 1–3; Ward, 'Elizabeth de Burgh and Great Bardfield', 56.

⁷ PRO E101/93/8, m. 5, 6, 8; E101/92/23, m. 2. A large part of Elizabeth de Burgh's wardrobe account for 1350–1 is printed in translation in Ward, *Women of the English Nobility and Gentry*, 162–79. Elizabeth's purchases in London are analyzed in Ward, 'Elizabeth de Burgh, Lady of Clare', 33–7.

⁸ Redstone, *Household Book of Dame Alice de Bryene*, 119–20.

⁹ PRO E101/92/23, m. 3.

¹⁰ BL Add. MS. 34,213, fo. 20r; Grieve, *The Sleepers and the Shadows*, I, 90.

¹¹ PRO E101/92/23, m. 3.

¹² Ward, *English Noblewomen*, 105–7.

¹³ Nicolas, *Proceedings and Ordinances of the Privy Council*, II, 287, 289, 295–6.

¹⁴ Davis, *Paston Letters and Papers*, I, nos. 73, 128–31, 180–90, 194–6, 418; Watt, '"No writing for writing's sake"', 125, 134–5.

¹⁵ For discussion of the affinities of noblewomen, see Ward, *English Noblewomen*, 133–42.

¹⁶ Archer, 'Women as landholders and administrators', 153–6.

¹⁷ The nature and importance of the service ethic is discussed by Horrox, 'Service', 61–78.

¹⁸ Turner, *Manners and Household Expenses*, 6, 11; PRO E101/93/4, m. 5; E101/93/18, m. 2, 5.

[19] As granted to Elizabeth countess of Northampton in 1343, and to Elizabeth de Burgh in 1345; Bliss, *Calendar of Papal Registers. Petitions, 1342–1419*, 27, 102.

[20] Jenkinson, 'Mary de Sancto Paulo', 434.

[21] Bliss, *Calendar of Papal Registers. Papal Letters, 1305–42*, 393.

[22] Bliss, *Calendar of Papal Registers. Papal Letters, 1362–1404*, 37–8; *Petitions, 1342–1419*, 488.

[23] BL Add. MS. 34,213, fo. 11v.

[24] Redstone, *The Household Book of Dame Alice de Bryene*, 3–5, 62, 79; Ross, 'The household accounts of Elizabeth Berkeley', 94.

[25] BL Harley Charter 47 E.38; Loyd and Stenton, *Sir Christopher Hatton's Book of Seals*, no. 242; printed in translation in Ward, *Women of the English Nobility and Gentry*, 206–7.

[26] Gilchrist, *Gender and Material Culture*, 120. Jenkinson, 'Mary de Sancto Paulo', 432.

[27] Bradley, 'Lucia Visconti, Countess of Kent', 81–2.

[28] Lambeth Palace Library, Register of Thomas Arundel, fos. 108v–109r.

[29] I would like to thank Anne Dutton for drawing my attention to the miniatures of Margaret of York, duchess of Burgundy, performing the works of mercy in Finet, *Benois seront les miséricordieux*, fo. 1r; Hughes, 'The library of Margaret of York', 60–2; Weightman, *Margaret of York*, 203–4. Margaret is shown feeding a cripple and an orphan, visiting prisoners and the sick, clothing the naked, and giving alms to a pilgrim.

[30] Lamond, *Walter of Henley's Husbandry*, 135.

[31] Redstone. *The Household Book of Dame Alice de Bryene*, 4, 7, 18, 46, 79.

[32] PRO E101/505/25, m. 10; BL Add. Roll, 63, 207.

[33] PRO E101/93/4, m. 14; E101/93/18, m. 2.

[34] Dugdale, *Monasticon Anglicanum*, VI, 725–6; Hicks, 'Piety and lineage', 100.

[35] PRO E101/93/12, m. 4; DL28/1/2, fos. 20v, 25v, 26r. The gowns and hoods took 35¼ yards of russet cloth, and the making up cost 7*s*. 6*d*.

[36] Jacob, *The Register of Henry Chichele*, II, 535–6.

[37] Redstone, *The Household Book of Dame Alice de Bryene*, 28.

[38] PRO E101/92/24, m. 7.

[39] Turner, *Manners and Household Expenses*, 47–8, 50, 62.

[40] For example, PRO S.C.6/1110/25, m. 1.

[41] *A Collection of Ordinances and Regulations*, 37.

[42] PRO E101/94/1, m. 3.

[43] Bliss, *Calendar of Papal Registers. Petitions, 1342–1419*, 229–30.

[44] Catto, 'Religion and the English nobility', 43–55; Mertes, *The English Noble Household*, 139–60; Richmond, 'Religion and the fifteenth-century English gentleman', 198.

[45] BL Egerton Roll, 8,779, m. 8.

[46] Lambeth Palace Library, Register of William Whittlesey, fos. 99r-v, 100v–101r. The mark was a unit of account and was worth 13*s*. 4*d*., two-thirds of £1.

[47] BL Add. MS. 34,122A, m. 2; Carthew, *The Hundred of Launditch*, I, 82.

[48] Lambeth Palace Library, Register of Simon Islip, fo. 122r-v. Nichols, *Wills of The Kings and Queens of England*, 33; the first three churches were left £3 each, and the fourth £2.

[49] Borthwick Institute of Historical Research, York archiepiscopal register, 10, fo. 330r; Raine, *Testamenta Eboracensia*, I, 36–7; printed in translation in Ward, *Women of the English Nobility and Gentry*, 222.

[50] Borthwick Institute of Historical Research, York archiepiscopal register, 18, fos. 357v–358v; Raine, *Testamenta Eboracensia*, I, 375–9; printed in translation in Ward, *Women of the English Nobility and Gentry*, 227–30.

[51] PRO E101/93/12, m. 1–3, 2d, 4d.

[52] Rubin, *Corpus Christi*, 232–43.

[53] Morant, *Colchester*, 150n.; Cooper, *Victoria County History of Essex*, IX, 64. According to the text, the 'countess of Hertford' was a member, but, as this title did not exist in 1418, it is likely that it is a mistake for the countess of Hereford.

[54] Harris, *The Register of the Guild of Holy Trinity, Coventry*, I, 28.

[55] Skaife, *The Register of the Guild of Corpus Christi in the City of York*, vi–vii, 63, 69, 86, 89, 97, 121.

[56] Swanson, *Church and Society*, 282–3.

Bibliography

A Collection of Ordinances and Regulations for the Government of the Royal Household (London, 1790).

Archer, R. E., '"How ladies … who live on their manors ought to manage their households and estates": women as landholders and administrators in the later Middle Ages', in P. J. P. Goldberg (ed.), *Woman is a Worthy Wight. Women in English Society c. 1200–1500* (Stroud, 1992), 149–81.

Bliss, W. H. (ed.), *Calendar of Entries in Papal Registers relating to Great Britain and Ireland. Papal Letters, 1305–42, 1362–1404; Petitions, 1342–1419* (London, 1895–1902).

Bradley, H., 'Lucia Visconti, Countess of Kent (d.1424)', in C. M. Barron and A. F. Sutton (eds.), *Medieval London Widows 1300–1500* (London, 1994), 77–84.

Carthew, G. A., *The Hundred of Launditch and Deanery of Brisley in the County of Norfolk*, I–III (Norwich, 1877–9).

Catto, J., 'Religion and the English nobility in the later fourteenth century', in H. Lloyd-Jones, V. Pearl and B. Worden (eds.), *History and Imagination. Essays in honour of H. R. Trevor-Roper* (London, 1981), 43–55.

Cooper, J. (ed.), *Victoria County History of Essex*, IX (Oxford, 1994).

Davis, N. (ed.), *Paston Letters and Papers of the Fifteenth Century*, I–II (Oxford, 1971–6).

Dugdale, W., *Monasticon Anglicanum*, eds. J. Caley, H. Ellis and B. Bandinel, I–VI (London, 1817–30).

Finet, Nicolas, 'Benois seront les miséricordieux' (Brussels, Bibliothèque Royale, MS 9296).

Gilchrist, R., *Gender and Material Culture. The Archaeology of Religious Women* (London, 1994).

Grieve, H., *The Sleepers and the Shadows. Chelmsford: a Town, its People and its Past*, I–II (Chelmsford, 1988–94).

Harris, M. D. (ed.), *The Register of the Guild of Holy Trinity, St Mary, St John the Baptist, and St Katherine of Coventry*, I (Dugdale Society 13, 1935).

Hicks, M., 'Piety and lineage in the Wars of the Roses: the Hungerford experience', in R. A. Griffiths and J. Sherborne (eds.), *Kings and Nobles in the Later Middle Ages: a Tribute to Charles Ross* (Gloucester, 1986), 90–108.

Horrox, R., 'Service', in R. Horrox (ed.), *Fifteenth-Century Attitudes. Perceptions of Society in Late Medieval England* (Cambridge, 1994), 61–78.

Hughes, M. J., 'The library of Margaret of York, duchess of Burgundy', *The Private Library*, 7, 3rd ser. (1984), 53–78.

Jacob, E. F. (ed.), *The Register of Henry Chichele, Archbishop of Canterbury, 1414–43*, I–IV (Canterbury and York Society, 1937–47).

Jenkinson, H., 'Mary de Sancto Paulo, foundress of Pembroke College, Cambridge', *Archaeologia* 66 (1915), 401–46.

Lamond, E., *Walter of Henley's Husbandry together with An Anonymous Husbandry, Seneschaucie and Robert Grosseteste's Rules* (London, 1890).

Loyd, L. C. and Stenton, D. M. (eds.), *Sir Christopher Hatton's Book of Seals* (Northamptonshire Record Society 15, 1950).

Mertes, K., *The English Noble Household, 1250–1600. Good Governance and Political Rule* (Oxford, 1988).

Morant, P., *The History and Antiquities of Colchester* (2nd edn., Chelmsford, 1815).

Nichols, J., *A Collection of All the Wills of the Kings and Queens of England* (London, 1780).

Nicolas, N. H. (ed.), *Proceedings and Ordinances of the Privy Council of England*, I–VII (London, 1834–7).

Raine, J. (ed.), *Testamenta Eboracensia*, I (Surtees Society 4, 1836).

Redstone, V. B. (ed.), and M. K. Dale (trans.), *The Household Book of Dame Alice de Bryene, 1412–13* (Ipswich, 1931).

Richmond, C., 'Religion and the fifteenth-century English gentleman', in R. B. Dobson (ed.), *The Church, Politics and Patronage in the Fifteenth Century* (Gloucester, 1984), 193–203.

Ridgard, J. (ed.), *Medieval Framlingham. Select Documents, 1270–1524* (Suffolk Records Society 27, 1985).

Ross, C. D., 'The household accounts of Elizabeth Berkeley, countess of Warwick, 1420–1', *Transactions of the Bristol and Gloucestershire Archaeologi-
cal Society* 70 (1951), 81–105.

Rubin, M., *Corpus Christi. The Eucharist in Late Medieval Culture* (Cambridge,
1991).

Rubin, M., 'Small groups: identity and solidarity in the late Middle Ages', in J.
Kermode (ed.), *Enterprise and Individuals in Fifteenth-Century England*
(Stroud, 1991), 132–50.

Skaife, R. H. (ed.), *The Register of the Guild of Corpus Christi in the City of
York* (Surtees Society 57, 1871).

Swanson, R. N., *Church and Society in Late Medieval England* (Oxford, 1989).

Turner, T. H. (ed.), *Manners and Household Expenses of England in the Thirteenth and Fifteenth Centuries, illustrated by original records* (London, 1841).

Ward, J. C., *English Noblewomen in the Later Middle Ages* (London, 1992).

Ward, J. C., 'Elizabeth de Burgh and Great Bardfield in the fourteenth century',
in K. Neale (ed.), *Essex Heritage* (Oxford, 1992), 47–60.

Ward, J. C., 'Elizabeth de Burgh, Lady of Clare (d. 1360)', in C. M. Barron and A.
F. Sutton (eds.), *Medieval London Widows 1300–1500* (London, 1994), 29–45.

Ward, J. C. (ed. and trans.), *Women of the English Nobility and Gentry, 1066–
1500* (Manchester, 1995).

Watt, D., '"No writing for writing's sake": the language of service and house-
hold rhetoric in the letters of the Paston women', in K. Cherewatuk and U.
Wiethaus (eds.), *Dear Sister. Medieval Women and the Epistolary Genre*
(Philadelphia, 1993), 122–37.

Weightman, C., *Margaret of York Duchess of Burgundy 1446–1503* (Stroud,
1989).

9

Gender and Poverty in the Medieval Community[1]

PATRICIA SKINNER

TO what extent did being a woman increase the chances of experiencing poverty in the Middle Ages? The theme of the poor, vulnerable woman demanding support from the wider community may be so well-rehearsed that another investigation is not merited. However, little detailed empirical work has been done to illustrate the truth behind the theory that poverty was gendered.[2] This study, whilst in no way pretending to be an exhaustive survey, sets out to discover the evidence for that assumption.

The standard study of medieval poverty by Michel Mollat highlights some of the problems associated with trying to reveal the effect of gender on levels of wealth.[3] Mollat rarely mentions or discusses women, which may be attributable to their invisibility in the majority of texts, nor does he raise the question of different experiences of poverty. Bronislaw Geremek, similarly, fails to address the problem of gender in his work on the medieval poor.[4] The same author's study of the underclass of late medieval Paris, exploiting sources which might have been expected to reveal more of women's lives, is also notably lacking in any discussion of the effects of gender. It deals with women only in a specific context – prostitution.[5]

Historians of medieval women have long been familiar with their fleeting appearances in the documents: they are, for much of the time, obscured by the men in whose households they live, be it the father or husband. Young, unmarried women, for example, are a rare sight in the medieval documentation, apart from the odd appearance alongside their parents or in wills. Wives have a more active role, but almost always as companions to their husbands, agreeing to a transaction because the law requires their assent, but with little identity of their own.[6] Nevertheless, in medieval discussions about poverty certain women, in particular widows, appear disproportionately frequently as a vulnerable group. In this survey I shall consider where this discourse originated, examine whether women themselves believed what was said of them, and finally attempt to reconcile this with the experiences of women in one well-documented area, southern Italy to around 1200.

'All historical reconstruction can only be a contemporary construction.'[7] That is, historians are a product of the age in which they write, and project their own experiences on to the history they write, so we are unlikely to reach the reality, if there is such a thing, of the medieval pauper's existence. No text can present anything more than one of a series of realities – a phenomenon discussed by Robert Chartier[8] – an important point to bear in mind when considering whether poverty was gendered in the Middle Ages. Our sources were not written by the poor, but by those who by turn assisted, protected or despised them. Different narrative sources present the varying expectations, stereotypes and downright prejudices of those who wrote and preached about the poor. They can, however, be read against other types of primary source – charters, wills, late medieval tax records – which both support and present an alternative view to the constructs present in narrative material. From these our task is to reconstruct, if not always the actual experiences, then at least the factors conditioning the perception of the poor and needy in medieval sources.

What exactly was poverty to the average medieval man or woman? Was it a state of extreme need, to the extent that daily life consisted of finding enough to eat and little more? Or was poverty relative – those with one-storey houses coveting the high-rise luxury of a neighbour's two-storeyed construction, for example? A working definition for this paper is a state in which a person was forced involuntarily to live in a certain manner or do things which a certain amount of money or the items it could buy would have alleviated. Thus different people existed at different levels of 'poverty'. Some protestations of poverty by women in medieval southern Italian documents I have examined seem entirely unjustified, as we shall see, but those who made the protests clearly believed they were poor and acted upon that belief.

Besides these considerations, the well-rehearsed one of male authorship of most of the written sources must concern us too.[9] The ways in which men and women viewed and experienced poverty may have been very different, particularly if there was a difference of opportunity to alleviate their need. Even though female authors appear on charters, the charters themselves were written by male notaries and often follow formulaic patterns.

Mollat's study provides us with an entry point to and several examples of the trend in medieval texts to single out lone women as a poverty-stricken group. Almost universally, narrative sources portray the ideal ruler as one who helps widows and orphans.[10] The charitable bishop was a familiar feature of early medieval urban life, as Gregory of Tours shows us. He reports the deeds of bishop Maurilio of Cahors, who 'as it is written in the book of Job', singled out widows, the blind and the lame as vulnerable groups.[11] That is, a *topos* which was as old as the bible still had relevance to a cleric described in the sixth century, and indeed would later become a central tenet of developed canon law.[12] Ratherius of Verona, writing in the tenth century, listed widows and orphans alongside the infirm and the blind as most likely to experience indigence.[13] In a similar way, the *Liber Pontificalis*, a potted biography of every pope from St Peter onwards compiled in the ninth century and continued to the twelfth, stresses the care of widows and orphans among the admirable qualities of many of its subjects.[14] The vulnerability of widows is also underlined by the bishop of Metz. In a warning to the aldermen of that city in 1179, he reminded them to defend the rights of widows and orphans.[15]

For our purposes, establishing whether any of these figures actually did help those in need is less important than the fact that such actions were recognized as praiseworthy and worth assigning as an exemplary quality of the individual being written about. The powerful ruler's attitude to the poor could establish his character in a text.[16] Gregory of Tours includes in his condemnation of the Merovingian King Chilperic the opinion that the king 'hated the poor and all they stood for'.[17] The Council of Paris in 829 called upon the Frankish royal ministers to help the servants of God, widows, orphans and all other poor and indigent people.[18] Bishop Liutprand of Cremona, writing in the tenth century, praises King Hugh of Italy for relieving the needs of the poor and being solicitous for the welfare of the church, and later condemns Berengar for forcibly collecting money from these same sources.[19] According to his biographer, the pious Louis IX, king of France, entertained old and crippled men, gave alms to 'men and women of gentle birth in need, to homes for fallen women, to poor widows and to women in labour, also to poor craftsmen who through age or sickness could no longer ply their trade.'[20]

Many of the sources mentioned so far emanated from public institutions or learned men whose writing served specific functions. Clerical authors, in particular, were keen to associate literally Christian qualities with the figures they admired or supported. Joinville's biography of Louis fuelled the campaign for the king's canonization: it was almost to be expected that such a pious man would help the poor. We must be wary of trusting such rhetoric as a reliable way of identifying needy groups. Rosemary Morris has demonstrated that tenth-century Byzantine legislation apparently protecting the poor had very little to do with actual concern for that group, even though, like St Louis in Joinville's work, the emperors were praised for their charity. Rather, the laws sought to limit the political ambitions of the emperors' most powerful subjects by promoting the interests of humbler groups.[21] If such sources' main objective is not to inform us about the poor, the picture they present may be generic. In the case of poor widows, therefore, we must then 'look behind the text'[22] to find out whether they really were vulnerable, and to decide why the theme remained so strong.

That the genre survived at all, of course, suggests that it still reflected the groups the authors thought to be poor, or that their readers would accept as such. The main sources of information for comparison are private charters, particularly wills, where donations to charitable causes became increasingly common up to the twelfth century. Even this evidence may be conditioned by formulaic expectations. In 1138 a bequest to charity by one man, John of Trani, specified that his largesse be distributed to 'poor widows, orphans and clerics'.[23] John's document is symptomatic of a prevailing attitude that women were incapable of supporting themselves after their husbands' deaths, and were as vulnerable as children. Indeed, a child was commonly called an orphan when its father died, regardless of the fact that its mother was still alive to care for it. The *Liber Pontificalis* assigns this status to the young Pope Stephen II, and Abbot Guibert of Nogent states that he himself was orphaned by the death of his father.[24]

The ability of lone women to support themselves was particularly important in an agricultural context. St Gerald of Aurillac's charitable works included giving money to a poor woman he saw using a plough so that she might hire a labourer (her husband was ill).[25] Whether or not the story is apocryphal, the message is that heavy fieldwork was not suitable for women. Here a class issue arises, for peasant women would have had little choice but to work in the fields. Nevertheless, the underlying tendency in the higher social strata seems to have been to assume that women were unable to, or should not, work. Widows in Ledesma, in medieval Spain, were considered poor and tax-exempt if they had neither son nor son-in-law to work their property.[26]

The *Life of Saint Louis* underlines this attitude: the men he gave alms to were old or crippled, or unable to continue working. That is, apart from monks, very few of these men were able-bodied. Yet women's poverty is identified on grounds of their sex and marital status: widows, 'fallen' women and pregnant women. Nowhere is their ability to work commented upon. The very fact of their being women implies that they are, by definition, unable to support themselves.

It is possible to argue for certain areas of medieval Europe, like southern Italy, that women's economic capacity was limited by legislation, to the extent that even those who were not actually poor might still find themselves in need. Liquidating landed property, for example, could be a particular problem for a woman on her own, as bad as having no property at all. The early medieval Lombard laws equated women with children, with no legal identity of their own and thus unable to continue to run their deceased husbands' estates without intervention from a male family member, the *mundoald*, or a public official acting in this capacity.[27] Sales of certain types of women's property, moreover, were normally considered forbidden and needed extremely clear justification in order to go ahead. The very unusual sale by the widow Wiletruda of her *morgengab*, her portion of her husband's lands which was designed to be kept to support her, occurred in such exceptional circumstances: the city of Salerno where she lived was under siege by the Saracens, and she had no food.[28]

That these limitations on their activities caused real difficulties is suggested by the fact that almost all protestations of poverty or hunger made in southern Italian charters from our period came from women living in areas where Lombard law continued to prevail, especially widows with children, and their response was often to ask permission to sell off property. The problem was not one of actual poverty, but simply the inflexibility of the law which left women with lands which they could not exploit for one reason or another. A widow's economic activities depended not only on the legal consent of her *mundoald*, but also on her ability to negotiate with her own and her late husband's family whose intentions for the properties left in her hands might differ greatly from her own plans. This difficulty might become particularly acute if the woman found herself unable to exploit property whilst disagreements continued.

There was a solution, however. In 1040 Nibia of Nocera, 'formerly' the wife of Lando (often meaning widowed), asked and received permission to sell off three pieces of land to alleviate her poverty and that of her two young sons.[29] In other documents of this type, the *children's* need is consistently stressed as the primary factor in the transaction, even though their mother might be suffering equal deprivation. In 938, for example, Selletta, a widow from Conversano, and her young son Iaquintus, together with her two sons-in-law, sold off their portions of a vineyard near that town. The sale was made in the presence of the judge of Conversano, and the price set by independent assessors. The boy, it was recorded, had sold his portion through poverty.[30] A key point to note in this document is that great care was taken to ensure that the boy was not disadvantaged by the sale of his property. Thus a fair price was set for it, and it was his poverty, not his mother's, that was cited as the reason for the sale. Another document from Conversano follows the same pattern. In 994, the underage Beneaggi sold off land because he was unable to support himself and Antofana his mother. Again, the judge before whom they came appointed men to set a fair price.[31]

The reason for the stress on the child's poverty lies in the Lombard laws. Mothers faced difficulty when trying to sell off property independently, but a child was permitted to alienate its property in times of need. (It would seem that both girls and boys could do this.) In 735 King Liutprand of the Lombards had prohibited any sale of children's land except in circumstances of impending starvation.[32] Significantly, the law had included the provision that such sales were to be explicitly attributed to poverty in the documentary record, and thus it is found cited in many later charters. However, the citation may not be so much an indicator of the law's continuing sway over practice, but a manœuvre designed to allow a woman greater freedom in her affairs. Lombard legislation, in effect, provided a loophole which women could exploit to enable them to alienate at least some property. Two centuries later, little had changed within Lombard society, and the provisions of the edict were still useful to allow the mothers of Beneaggi and Iaquintus a way to escape a time of need. Strikingly, it may also have functioned as a way that women could retain their property and force the sale of their children's. Thus legislation which has often been seen as limiting women's options may in fact have been very beneficial to their interests.

In other parts of Europe, much research has concentrated in the same way on stressing women's rights in relation to property.[33] Heath Dillard considers the variety of circumstances in which a Spanish widow might find herself. Even if the Church regarded her as especially vulnerable, in Spain 'the municipal widow . . . was not invariably a charity case'.[34] There is evidence elsewhere, however, that women's enjoyment of their property could still be limited. The Byzantine world acknowledged the vulnerability of women by providing the dowry, customarily a protection against indigence when widowed. However, as in Lombard Italy, its alienation was made extremely difficult in the eleventh and twelfth centuries, again requiring exceptional circumstances.[35] For example, a married woman in Byzantium in 1112 sold her dowry lands, citing as the reason the unusual and repeated failure of her husband's crops.[36] Here we meet a situation which must have been very common throughout medieval Europe: a married woman with property having to relinquish it (willingly or otherwise) to help her husband, and thereby storing up problems for herself when widowed.

However, if women were thought to be in need of help, they also played an important role within the community of helping the poor. The image of the pious, charitable noblewoman is as common in medieval texts as her poverty-stricken counterpart. Jennifer Ward's paper in this volume underlines how charity came to be seen as a peculiarly female attribute in the later Middle Ages, but this discourse had a long history. St Jerome praised the widow who borrowed money to give alms, thereby combining both situations.[37] Hospices for the poor in Paris were described as having been built 'with the farthings of old women'.[38] Such charitable works were not limited to the women of the Christian community. The tradition of baking a few extra loaves and doing charitable works, associated with Jewish women in Fustat in Egypt and recorded in the Cairo Genizah documents,[39] was probably just as strong in the Jewish and other communities of western Europe as well. However, we must be wary of pushing this gender specificity too far. In testamentary evidence, which might be expected to show up women's and men's acts of charity, no strong tendency for women to give emerges in the southern Italian material.

There is no evidence to determine whether women directed their charitable efforts specifically at other women, or co-operated in female networks to alleviate the effects of poverty. For example, although dowering poor young girls became a popular act of charity, it seems to be a late medieval phenomenon. The act of adopting children, however, seems to have carried with it gendered assumptions. The mothers of poor and abandoned youngsters were clearly held responsible for their children's state. Early medieval penitentials, for example, generally represent infanticide as a woman's crime, but poverty is allowed as extenuation in the penalties to be imposed.[40] At the end of the eighth century a hospice was founded in Milan where children abandoned by their mothers could be cared for until their seventh year.[41] In the twelfth century, mothers in Anjou, unable to feed their children, were said to have left them at the gates of monasteries.[42] In 1204 Pope Innocent III donated the old and disused *schola* of the Saxons in Rome for children abandoned or thrown into the Tiber by their mothers.[43]

The only two documents from medieval southern Italy which overtly record the giving up of children seem to support the notion that lone mothers were most likely to do so. One was a concubine surrendering her child by a former lover, the other a lone widow in debt.[44] Both the women in these documents were vulnerable, Gemma the concubine because she relied on the goodwill of her new keeper, Marinus, who seems to have been unwilling to support her child by another man, and Asterada the widow because she had no one to help pay her debts. Asterada's very real poverty is signalled by the fact that she appears not to have had landed property to alleviate her distress. Significantly, both women gave up their children to couples, suggesting that a child's future economic security was held to be linked to the presence of an adult male guardian.[45]

Many lone women with children were trapped into this state by the fact that the remarriage of widows, whilst often economically necessary, might be actively discouraged on the grounds of protecting the interests of their late husbands' families and their children. Both Anglo-Saxon and southern Italian wills of men contain clauses making the widow's enjoyment of property conditional upon her remaining single. An Anglo-Saxon example, the will of ealdorman Alfred (871–88), contains his bequest to his wife, so long as she remains unmarried 'as we verbally agreed'.[46] In 968 Boso, from Nocera near Salerno, left instructions that his wife, Iaquinta, was to control his property until his sons came of age. At that point she could take her *morgengab*,[47] but only if she remained unmarried. If not, her share would go to their sons.[48] The condition did not only apply to wives: the concubine of one Astilf of Salerno, mother of his daughter, was similarly restricted in 1023.[49] These examples suggest of course that to remain single after bereavement could be beneficial to the woman, providing her with property to live off for the remainder of her life. We cannot assume, therefore, that the restrictive clauses in men's wills were necessarily negative in their effect, nor that a woman would want to remarry. The cases cited do reveal how widowhood as a status was strongly gendered – any woman who was bereaved, in the absence of precise canon laws on marriage before the twelfth century, was classed as a widow and treated as such. No comparable documentation exists recording the status of bereaved men.

However, a lone woman's economic independence might be hampered by the fact that, even if provision had been made for her in her husband or partner's will (a fairly universal pattern across medieval Europe being for the woman to have use of his property), she might still have to fight relatives in court to secure even limited entitlement. Numerous examples survive of such litigation in southern Italy. A court-case of 1039, for example, records the battle between Alfarana of Bari and her adult son over the patrimony left by Alfarana's late husband, Peter. Alfarana won the case.[50] An almost contemporary English document contains similar evidence of a woman's ability to resist a claim from her adult son and, indeed, to promise it in an oral will before witnesses to a kinswoman. Her case was upheld and her will recorded for posterity.[51]

It was in the interests of her late husband's family and her children, therefore, if a woman did remarry. But then she might face hostility and a threat to her property from her new husband's children, particularly if widowed again. A document from Corato in Italy records the settlement of a property dispute between Paunessa and her stepson Maraldus after he had claimed a portion of his father's estate as his through his own mother Daria.[52]

Elsewhere, Abbot Guibert of Nogent praises his mother for refusing remarriage and continuing to run her estates as a widow before retiring to the contemplative life.[53] However, his account of the pressure she had come under to defend her lands and avoid taking a new husband reveal that widowhood could bring other threats besides poverty. This issue has not hitherto attracted much attention from early medievalists, but forms a major theme of a recent collection of essays on late medieval widowhood.[54] Litigation involving late medieval English noblewomen seems also to have a direct connection with their being left alone to run their estates:[55] one wonders whether opponents chose this time particularly to initiate proceedings.

Further evidence suggesting that the generalized view of the vulnerable widow had currency comes from documents recording the support of ageing parents by their children. It is significant that in her discussion of the attempts by Spanish towns to legislate for the support of ageing parents, almost all of the cases cited by Heath Dillard involve mothers.[56] Similarly, a survey of the southern Italian evidence reveals that the parent who seems to have required support was almost always a widowed mother. Practical measures such as housing and food show up in the documents. For example, in 970 Leo, a monk of the Neapolitan monastery of SS. Sergius and Bacchus, gave to his son Peter almost all of his property, on condition that the younger man feed his mother, Maria, for life.[57] In 1004, Matrona, a widow from Gaeta, handed over her property to her daughter Euprassia, and the latter was to provide the support for her in her old age. The pension that Euprassia undertook to give her mother comprised of twenty *modia* of grain, ten of beans and peas, and thirty jars of wine per year, plus a slave and any clothes that the older woman might need.[58] John of Agrigento stipulated that his widowed mother should have the use of a house donated to St Mary Magdalene for life.[59] It is important to recognize that these elderly mothers were not always poor: Matrona was a member of one of Gaeta's oldest noble families. We do not know whether Euprassia was married. That her mother chose to hand over lands to her suggests that lone stewardship was not such a problem in Gaeta, and here perhaps it was old age that influenced Matrona's decision. Indeed, the prospect of having to support a widowed mother might again have led adult children to bring pressure on her to remarry.

How much truth, therefore, is there in the gendered approach to poverty and charity in medieval texts? Is it simply a paradigm which bore no resemblance to reality? The evidence suggests that the picture of women's vulnerability is·at least partly accurate. This, though, may have been created by a series of restrictions on lone women in medieval custom and culture which combined to prevent them escaping the poverty trap. The women whom I have described in this paper were by no means the poorest members of medieval society. They are better described, then, as temporarily needy, but neediness was gendered too: women were most likely to be found experiencing it. Many could sell property to alleviate their debt, or fought for access to property in the courts. Even the latter process, however, might be fraught with difficulties: women were not always allowed the greatest of access to legal proceedings.[60]

The poverty which widows, in particular, faced seems to fall into one of the categories proposed by Mollat, who divides the poor into two groups. The first consists of those who are structurally poor: their circumstances are unchanging and their lives are governed by the institutions around them, so that they have little control over the poverty in which they find themselves and little prospect of escaping it. The poverty of the second group is conjunctural, that is, they may not have been poor to start with, but a certain combination of events has left them poor. Sudden widowhood would certainly seem to fit this category. There is no reason to believe that conjunctural poverty was any easier to escape.

One cannot do much about a spate of bad weather or the loss of one's crop for the year, but a man might be able to take on further debt to allow him to remedy the situation the next year, whilst a lone woman might face obstacles in doing so. As Mollat comments, conjunctural poverty 'seems to have been particularly common during the so-called dark ages',[61] and, one might argue, afterwards as well. That is certainly the impression given by the source material under examination here. It is important to recognize, however, the ambiguity of the term 'poverty', for *paupertas*, as Rosemary Morris's article reminds us, could be used as the antonym to *potestas* (power). Thus the 'poverty' suffered by some medieval women might be a description of their relatively powerless state, rather than their economic deprivation: the examples in this paper may well fit such a description.

Many of my comments have been about widows, because they are the most visible group of women in the sources. As Jinty Nelson has recently reminded us, not all women were widowed,[62] and so objections might be raised that any discussion of gender and poverty using this group does not reveal the whole picture. However, most of the restrictions and difficulties that widows faced were not a problem for widowers. The status of widowhood, therefore, is an extremely useful one for pointing up gender specificity in medieval society.

It is likely that this division continued among men and women of the very poor. On the face of it they had very similar lives, devoted to the everyday search for food and shelter. Their success in doing so, however, may have depended on their sex. As we saw earlier, King Louis's choice of male paupers to give alms to was dictated by their inability to work, whilst women of all conditions were aided. Could this be an acknowledgement on the king's part (or that of his biographer) that, whether women were able to work or not, they were unlikely to be able to support themselves or their families? The marginal and unskilled nature of much of women's documented paid work has been stressed by Kowaleski and Bennett,[63] and the conflicting demands on a woman of caring for her family and working are still a resonant theme. Even if women gained a certain amount of security within a guild of skilled workers, their status was still likely to be related to their husbands' membership. The possibility that women may have enjoyed a 'golden age' in Europe after the Black Death – itself still hotly debated – does not devalue evidence from other periods for the difficulties they faced. Geremek highlights the low pay of female workers in late medieval France and Italy, at the same level as that of child labourers, and illustrates that the very fact of having to work was seen as socially degrading for a woman.[64] The southern Italian evidence indirectly supports the notion that women found it hard to gain acceptance as workers. In medieval Naples, a community which included a high number of artisanal surnames (for example, smith, harness-maker, soapmaker), only one woman is found with a surname suggesting an occupation.[65]

Another factor in the poverty trap may have been women's perceived or real physical weakness: the story of Gerald of Aurillac and the woman with the plough is explicit in its message that heavy work of this kind was *contra naturam*. However, those documents from southern Italy recording the giving-up of land because the tenants were 'unable to continue working it' feature not lone women but couples.[66] The only instance of a lone woman, Sillecta, reveals her giving up land which she *had* worked after her husband's death only when 'the Lombards came', that is, in exceptional circumstances of war.[67] A document of 1029 reveals a widow, Drosu, and her sons leasing out land to be cultivated.[68] However, Sillecta and Drosu lived in Amalfi, where women's economic opportunities were far wider than in other parts of southern Italy.[69] No such examples of female enterprise can be found elsewhere in the South.

The construction of women as particularly vulnerable in medieval communities has rarely been recognized as an archetype of medieval literature. The assumptions of medieval writers have filtered through into modern historiography. Roberta Gilchrist has recently demonstrated that the assumption that medieval nunneries were always poorer and less numerous than their masculine counterparts rests on the notion that they were founded for similar purposes, and that they 'failed' to attract support, when in fact their function may have been rather different from that of monasteries.[70] Similarly, modern historians frequently reject or fail to recognize the evidence for medieval women engaged in warfare, simply because they have been conditioned by medieval texts into thinking that this was an inappropriate pursuit for the so-called weaker sex. Yet recent work has demonstrated that this assumption, too, is mistaken.[71]

In the same way, the medieval construction of lone women as particularly susceptible to poverty has formed the starting point for many investigations, when it is clear that there is a need to question this inbuilt expectation that being without male support or patronage automatically led to destitution. Can we really be sure, for example, that the loan taken out by Grusa Scannapecu of Ravello on the death of her husband, and recorded later in her will,[72] was due to difficulties after his demise?

For every woman who pleaded poverty in a charter, there were others who managed estates and did not find themselves in difficulties. Both outsiders and family could be a threat to a lone woman's enjoyment of her property but, conversely, early medieval communities could provide a great deal of support. Southern Italian society was centred around the extended family group: a woman might therefore expect to be able to call upon relatives for help if she needed it, even against other relatives. It might be argued that their success in managing their affairs was partly the reason for the pressure some widows found themselves under to remarry: not only were they too successful for men's sensibilities, but also they may well have increased the value of their property by good – dare I say it – husbandry. The notion that charity had to make a special place for lone women became a perpetual feature in didactic texts, however, and whilst it may obscure the reality of many women's efforts to continue to work or manage estates, it probably accurately reflects the difficulties most had in convincing their contemporaries that they were capable of doing so.

Notes

[1] I am grateful to the British Academy and the Wellcome Trust for financial support enabling me to work on medieval southern Italy. This paper benefited from the comments received at two meetings, the Gender and Medieval Studies conference at Gregynog in January 1995 and a colloquium held on *Poverty in the Middle Ages* at the Institute of Romance Studies in London the following month. I would also like to thank Chris Wickham and Jinty Nelson for their critical reading of an earlier draft, and Diane Watt for her skilful editing.

[2] Even the recent, excellent collection of essays edited by John Henderson and Richard Wall, *Poor Women and Children in the European Past*, begins its coverage only in the later Middle Ages.

[3] Mollat, *Poor in the Middle Ages*.

[4] Geremek, *Potence*. He does, however, address the issue of unequal work opportunities: see below, note 64.

[5] Geremek, *Margins of Society*.

[6] Compare Ward, 'English noblewomen and the local community in the later middle ages' in this volume: 'the widow, and the wife with an absent husband, had a much more prominent part to play.'

[7] Gurevich, *Historical Anthropology*, 9.

[8] Chartier, *Cultural History*, 9, calls this 'representation', each group having its own reality.

[9] This issue is not, of course, peculiar to southern Italy: compare Jane Cartwright, 'The desire to corrupt', in this volume, 20–48, who points out that in medieval Wales, too, 'the *vox feminae* is non-existent', as it is in many regions of medieval Europe.

[10] Mollat, *Poor in the Middle Ages*, 43, quotes Jonas of Orléans' *De Institutione Regia* referring to the prince's duty to defend widows, orphans, foreigners and the poor. There are many other examples of rulers being praised in this way.

[11] Gregory of Tours, *History of the Franks*, 5:42.

[12] Brundage, 'Widows as disadvantaged persons', discusses the Church's traditional responsibility for the care of the poor and widows.

[13] Goglin, *Misérables*, 42.

[14] *Lives of the Eighth-Century Popes*, trans. Davis.

[15] Mollat, *Poor in the Middle Ages*, 100.

[16] Not all rulers, of course, were male, but female rulers' positive qualities almost always include charity and mercy, as numerous contributions to a recently published conference, on *Queens and Queenship*, demonstrated. See also Stafford, 'Portrayal of royal women', 147: 'an image of a queen/empress dispensing charity as a handmaiden became common.'

[17] Gregory of Tours, *History of the Franks*, 6:46.

[18] Goglin, *Misérables*, 45.

[19] Liutprand of Cremona, *Antapodosis*, III.19, in *The Works of Liutprand of Cremona*, 77, 147 respectively.

[20] Joinville, *Life of Saint Louis*, chapter 18, in *Chronicles of the Crusades*, trans. Shaw, 342.

[21] Morris, 'The powerful and the poor'.

[22] Gurevich, *Historical Anthropology*, 8.

[23] Prologo, *Le Carte*, document 36.

[24] *Lives of the Eighth-Century Popes*, 53; Benton, *Self and Society*, Book I, chapter 4.

[25] Mollat, *Poor in the Middle Ages*, 37.

[26] Dillard, *Daughters of the Reconquest*, 31.

[27] Rothari's law 204, in Drew, *Lombard Laws*, 92: 'No free woman . . . is permitted to live under her own legal control . . . but she ought always to remain under the control of some man or the king . . .'

[28] Morcaldi, *Codex Diplomaticus Cavensis*, I, document 97 (882). Elsewhere in centro-southern Italy, in the Abruzzi, we do find sales of women's *morgengab*, but these seem to be related to ties of clientage rather than outright poverty. Their effect, however, was still to deprive a woman of a significant source of support: Feller, 'Achats de terres'.

[29] Mongelli, *Abbazia di Montevergine*, document 44.

[30] Coniglio, *Pergamene di Conversano*, document 6.

[31] *Ibid.*, document 27.

[32] Liutprand, law 149, my paraphrase from Drew, *Lombard Laws*, 212.

[33] See, for example, Rivers, 'Widows' rights in Anglo-Saxon law'.

[34] Dillard, *Daughters of the Reconquest*, 99. Her economic security, however, might rest on whether she had children or not. If not, she might come under severe pressure from her in-laws to divide her late husband's property with them, and she might lose everything, even her home: Dillard, *Daughters of the Reconquest*, 103.

[35] Laiou, 'The role of women', 238. The Byzantine pattern is relevant for the parts of southern Italy not affected by Lombard customs, that is, the duchies of Amalfi, Naples and Gaeta in Campania, the southern tip of Apulia and most of Calabria.

[36] Oikonomides, *Actes de Docheiariou*, document 3: my thanks are due to Professor Alice Mary Talbot for giving me this reference.

[37] Mollat, *Poor in the Middle Ages*, 22.

[38] *Ibid.*, 102.

[39] Goitein, *Mediterranean Society*, II, 105–13.

[40] Boswell, *Kindness*, 219–23.

[41] Riché, 'L'enfant', 97.

[42] Mollat, *Poor in the Middle Ages*, 61.

[43] *Ibid.*, 93. Boswell, *Kindness*, 416, note 56, characterizes the story of the hospital's foundation as a legend, but throwing children into the river may well have been an effective means of disposal.

[44] Morcaldi, *Codex Diplomaticus Cavensis* V, document 833 (1031); Filangieri di Candida, *Codice Diplomatico Amalfitano*, document 85 (1090).

[45] However, poverty was not necessarily always linked to the lack of an adult male in the house, and to characterize it as such would be too sweeping a statement. In an interesting inversion of what might be termed the normal situation, one Sellitus of S. Michele Gargano sold off a vineyard, pleading his own hunger and that of his small children and father-in-law as the reason: Camobreco, *Regesto*, document 102 (1192). This exceptional document, nevertheless, proves the more common rule.

[46] Whitelock, *English Historical Documents*, document 97, 537.

[47] Legally, the *morgengab* was set at a maximum of a quarter of the man's property: Liutprand 7; the maximum *usufruct* a widow might enjoy, however, varied according to how many children there were: Aistulf 14; both laws from Drew, *Lombard Laws*, 147 and 234 respectively. I think, since provision was made for Iaquinta's death or remarriage, that it is *usufruct* which is being referred to here.

[48] Morcaldi, *Codex Diplomaticus Cavensis* II, document 257.

[49] Morcaldi, *Codex Diplomaticus Cavensis* VI, document 753. Pierre Toubert has noted a similar opposition to remarriage in Lazio: *Structures*, I, 777.

[50] Nitti di Vito, *Pergamene di S. Nicola*, document 27.

[51] *English Historical Documents*, I, document 135. (I am grateful to Jinty Nelson for alerting me to this parallel.)

[52] Beltrani, *Documenti Storici*, document 65 (1181).

[53] Benton, *Self and Society*, 1: chapter 13.

[54] Mirrer, *Upon My Husband's Death*; see especially, on the theme of this paper, the essay by Barbara Hanawalt: 'The widow's mite'. A recent paper by Jinty Nelson, 'The wary widow', has provided an exemplary guide to tackling the problem of widows and litigation in the earlier period: I thank Jinty for allowing me to read this in advance of publication.

[55] See Jennifer Ward's paper in this volume, 186–203.

[56] Dillard, *Daughters of the Reconquest*, 117.

[57] Capasso, *Regesta Neapolitana*, document 178.

[58] *Codex Diplomaticus Cajetanus*, I, document 110.

[59] Collura, *Più Antiche Carte*, document 26 (1154/71).

[60] Southern Italian society, certainly, seems to have disapproved of female litigants: Skinner, 'Disputes and disparity'.

[61] Mollat, *Poor in the Middle Ages*, 26.

[62] Nelson, 'The wary widow'.

[63] Bennett, *Sisters and Workers*, 12.

[64] Geremek, *Potence*, 88–9.

[65] Anna *medica*, documented early in the tenth century: Skinner, 'Urban communities'.

[66] Filangieri di Candida, *Codice Diplomatico Amalfitano*, documents 13 (987): Ingizzu and Maria; and 14 (990): Peter and Drosu.

[67] Filangieri di Candida, *Codice Diplomatico Amalfitano*, document 31 (1012).

[68] Mazzoleni, *Pergamene*, document 11.

[69] As the numerous examples of women managing their husbands' and sons' business affairs in their absence testify: Filangieri di Candida, *Codice Diplomatico Amalfitano*, documents 21, 42 (significantly, a widow for her adult sons), 45, 48 and 74 (another widow); Mazzoleni, *Pergamene*, document 12 (another widow); Mazzoleni and Orefice, *Codice Perris*, documents 52 (1025), 36 (1039) and 89 (1097).

[70] Gilchrist, *Gender and Material Culture*. The likelihood that women's piety in fact took different forms is illustrated by Jane Cartwright's study of Wales in this volume, 20–48.

[71] McLaughlin, 'The woman warrior'.

[72] Salvati, *Pergamene*, document 97 (1182).

Bibliography

Beltrani, G. (ed.), *I Documenti Storici de Corato* (Bari, 1923).

Bennett, J. (ed.), *Sisters and Workers in the Middle Ages* (Chicago, 1989).

Benton, J. F. (ed.), *Self and Society in Medieval France: the Memoirs of Abbot Guibert of Nogent* (New York, 1970).

Bowsell, J., *The Kindness of Strangers* (New York, 1988).

Brundage, J. A., 'Widows as disadvantaged persons in medieval canon law', in Mirrer (ed.), *Upon My Husband's Death*, 193–206.

Camobreco, F. (ed.), *Regesto di S. Leonardo di Siponto* (Rome, 1913).

Capasso, B. (ed.), *Regesta Neapolitana*, in *Monumenta ad Neapolitani Ducatus Historiam Pertinentia*, II, i (Naples, 1885).

Chartier, R., *Cultural History*, trans. L. Cochrane (Oxford, 1988).

Chronicles of the Crusades, trans. M. R. B. Shaw (Harmondsworth, 1963).

Codex Diplomaticus Cajetanus, I (Montecassino, 1887).

Collura, P. (ed.), *Le Più Antiche Carte dell'Archivio Capitolare di Agrigento* (Palermo, 1961).

Coniglio, G. (ed.), *Le Pergamene di Conversano*, I (Bari, 1975).

Dillard, H., *Daughters of the Reconquest* (Cambridge, 1984).

Drew, K. F., *The Lombard Laws*, (Philadelphia, 1973).

Duggan, A. (ed.), *Queens and Queenship in Medieval Europe* (Woodbridge, 1997).

Feller, L., 'Achats de terres, politiques matrimoniales et liens de clientèle en Italie centroméridionale dans la seconde moitié du XIe siècle', in *Campagnes médiévales: l'Homme et son espace. Études offertes à Robert Fossier* (Paris, 1995), 425–38.

Filangieri di Candida, R. (ed.), *Codice Diplomatico Amalfitano*, I (Naples, 1917).

Geremek, B., *La Potence ou la Pitié: l'Europe et les Pauvres du Moyen Age à nos Jours*, trans. J. Arnold-Moricet (Paris, 1987).

Geremek, B., *The Margins of Society in Late Medieval Paris* (Cambridge, 1987).

Gilchrist, R., *Gender and Material Culture* (London, 1993).

Goglin, J.-L., *Les Misérables dans l'Occident Médiéval* (Paris, 1976).

Goitein, S. D., *A Mediterranean Society II: the Community* (Berkeley, 1971).

Gregory of Tours, *The History of the Franks*, trans. L. Thorpe (London, 1974).

Gurevich, A., *Historical Anthropology of the Middle Ages* (Oxford, 1993).

Hanawalt, B., 'The widow's mite: provision for medieval London widows', in Mirrer (ed.), *Upon My Husband's Death*, 26–35.

Henderson, J. and Wall, R. (eds.), *Poor Women and Children in the European Past* (London, 1994).

Laiou, A., 'The role of women in Byzantine society', *Jahrbuch der Österreichischen Byzantinistik* 31 (1981).

Lives of the Eighth-Century Popes (Liber Pontificalis), trans. R. Davis (Liverpool, 1992).

Mazzoleni, J. (ed.), *Le Pergamene degli Archivi Vescovili di Amalfi e Ravello*, I (Naples, 1972).

Mazzoleni, J. and Orefice, R, (eds.), *Il Codice Perris: Cartulario Amalfitano*, I (Amalfi, 1985).

McLaughlin, M., 'The woman warrior: gender, warfare and society in medieval Europe', *Women's Studies* 17 (1990), 193–209.

Mirrer, L. (ed.), *Upon My Husband's Death* (Michigan, 1992).

Mollat, M., *The Poor in the Middle Ages*, trans. A. Goldhammer (London, 1986).

Mongelli, G. (ed.), *Abbazia di Montevergine: Regesto delle Pergamene*, I (Rome, 1956).

Morcaldi, M. *et al.* (eds.), *Codex Diplomaticus Cavensis*, I–VIII (Milan, Naples, Pisa, 1873–93).

Morris, R., 'The powerful and the poor in tenth-century Byzantium', *Past and Present*, 73 (1976), 3–27.

Mosher Stuard, S. (ed.), *Women in Medieval Society* (Philadelphia, 1976).

Nelson, J., 'The wary widow', in W. Davies and P. Fouracre (eds.), *Property and Power* (Cambridge, 1995), 82–113.

Nitti di Vito, F. (ed.), *Le Pergamene di S. Nicola di Bari: periodo greco (939–1071)* (Bari, 1900).

Oikonomides, N. (ed.), *Actes de Docheiariou* (Paris, 1984).

Prologo, A. (ed.), *Le Carte che si Conservano nello Archivio del Capitolo Metropolitano della Città di Trani* (Barletta, 1877).

Riché, P., 'L'enfant dans le haut moyen age', *Annales de Démographie Historique* (1973).

Rivers, T. J., 'Widows' rights in Anglo-Saxon law', *American Journal of Legal History* 19 (1975), 208–15.

Salvati, C. (ed.), *Pergamene degli Archivi Vescovili di Amalfi e Ravello*, II (Naples, 1974).

Skinner, P., 'Disputes and disparity: women at court in medieval southern Italy', *Reading Medieval Studies* 22 (forthcoming).

Stafford, P., 'The portrayal of royal women in England, mid-tenth to mid-twelfth centuries', in J. Carmi Parsons (ed.), *Medieval Queenship* (Stroud, 1994), 143–67.

Toubert, P., *Les Structures du Latium Médiéval*, I–II (Rome, 1973).

Whitelock, D. (ed.), *English Historical Documents*, I (2nd edn., London, 1979).

The Works of Liutprand of Cremona, trans. F. A. Wright (London, 1930), reprinted with new introduction by J. J. Norwich (London, 1993).

10

Between Doctrine and Domesticity: The Portrayal of Mary in the N-Town Plays

J. A. TASIOULAS

THERE is not much mention of the Virgin Mary in the Bible. The whole of the New Testament merely presented the early Christian community with a betrothed virgin who conceived and bore a child without loss of her virginity, and who was prominent in the short account of her son's infancy, but about whom little was known before or afterwards. By the latter half of the second century there were already attempts to supply this missing information. Stories grew up, mostly in the form of the apocryphal gospels, of the child Mary, her education, her relationship with her parents, and even of her conception itself. There was no detail too small to be of interest to the medieval community and the tales rapidly circulated throughout medieval literature. Of these, the great N-Town mystery cycle gives a particularly full and interesting account. Transcribed between *c*.1468 and the early years of the sixteenth century, it most probably originated in East Anglia, a centre of intense popular devotion to the Virgin:[1]

> In late medieval England, images of the Virgin Mary were rarely out of sight or mind; this was especially true in East Anglia, where to the very eve of the English Reformation, the roads and streets and bridges of Suffolk and Norfolk thronged with men and women who were not only Mary's worshippers, but her pilgrims. These pilgrims journeyed to 'England's Nazareth', the holy shrine at the village named Little Walsingham in the northwest corner of Norfolk, that had become by the fifteenth century not only the most important pilgrimage site in England but an international centre of pilgrimage whose importance was probably rivalled only by Santiago de Compostella in Spain and by Rome itself.[2]

The reason for the area's popularity and its 'Little Nazareth' title was the existence of a little wooden house, supposedly a replica of the

Virgin's own home, which she was said to have instructed one of her female followers to build there in the early twelfth century. The stone chapel built to enclose this house became the site of miraculous healings, and among the church's possessions was a relic which was believed to be particularly powerful, a phial said to contain drops of the Virgin's breast milk, brought by crusaders returning from the Holy Land. These tangible symbols of the Virgin's early life, her domesticity, physicality and motherhood are indicative of this community's interest in the woman Mary. It is no surprise, therefore, that the most complete account of her life to be found in any of the extant mystery cycles should have come from this area. It begins with her conception and ends with the Assumption, giving in between almost every detail which could have appealed to the pilgrims of the Walsingham area.

We know little, of course, about the provenance and auspices of the N-Town cycle, and consequently little about its role in the community. We do know that it was associated with the Feast of Corpus Christi, observed throughout England from 1318 onwards, when the various craft guilds performed plays intended to celebrate God's relationship with his creation. It may be the case that the guilds in fact decreased the labour opportunities for women and that women only rarely formed their own professional bodies. Certainly, the mystery cycles do not show us guilds of women contributing to the proceedings. But as Jennifer Ward points out in this volume, the rise of the Corpus Christi cult meant that noblewomen at least became involved in the great confraternities of the major towns. The purpose of the feast and its celebrations was ultimately that 'every man, woman and child throughout Christian Europe, whether literate or not, was reminded that Christ's Church embraced him in his daily living as well as his church going'.[3] While women, and for that matter children, have often been dismissed as peripheral in the cycle drama, or at most women have been seen to be either portrayed as stereotypically good or evil, N-Town appears to offer a slightly more complicated view of their function. To use Janet Wilson's phrase, the 'heavenly community' being presented in this case in the drama, with its depiction of the early life of the Virgin and her family, may have offered the medieval woman more, and have been more representative of the earthly community than has hitherto been acknowledged.

However, writing the sections of the Virgin's life omitted by the Bible was a dangerous and controversial matter. The Church attempted to suppress many of the apocryphal writings and objected to much of what survived. The greatest controversy was that over the conception of the

Virgin herself: had she been conceived in the normal manner or not? More specifically, had some miracle occurred that meant she had not been created through the sexual union of her parents and had in fact been conceived immaculately? This was by no means a settled matter in the eyes of the medieval Church. It was not until 1854 that Pope Pious IX was to proclaim the Immaculate Conception of the Virgin Mary a dogma of faith. In so doing he brought to an end a debate which had lasted for many centuries and had occupied the mind of every great medieval theologian. And as the debate over this was so important, and as most medieval accounts of the life of the Virgin actually begin before her conception, an examination of her life must begin with her parents, Anne and Joachim.

If the Bible is silent about the early life of Mary, it certainly dwells on the early life of Eve, and consequently upon original sin. As the first couple are expelled from Eden, Eve is told that her punishment will be to bring forth children in pain (Genesis 4:16). Until that point, as we are told by both Augustine and Aquinas, the relations between Adam and Eve were untainted by concupiscence, not flawed by the foreboding of the pains of pregnancy.[4] Other Church Fathers even took the view that Adam and Eve were virgins before the Fall.[5] At any rate, childbirth and all that pertains to it, in the opinion of Augustine and of many other Fathers, including Aquinas to some extent, was inextricably linked to original sin, and the child in the womb was consequently, in the chilling words of St Jean Eudes, 'the shrine of the demon'.[6] The whole lamentable process was neatly summarized by Pope Innocent III in his *De miseria condicionis humane*:

> For behold I was conceived in iniquities, and in sins did my mother conceive me. Not in one such sin, not in one such transgression, but in many sins and in many transgressions ... Who does not know that copulation, even conjugal, is never performed entirely without the heat of desire, without the fervour of the flesh, without the stench of lust? Because of this conceived seeds are made filthy, defiled, and spoiled, from which seeds the soul ultimately imparted contracts the blemish of sin, the stain of guilt, the filth of iniquity, just as an infused liquid is spoiled by a tainted vessel.[7]

In spite of the directive of St Paul, then, that it was better to marry than burn (I Corinthians, 7:9), the sacrament of marriage did not escape accusations of carnal desire. As Chaucer's Parson put it, 'God woot, a man may sleen hymself with his owene knyf, and make hymselve dronken of his owene tonne'.[8] Original sin, according to Augustine, was consequently inescapable, bound as it was to the *concupiscentia carnalis* accompanying all human generation, even that which took place within 'the honourable state of matrimony'.[9] The main problem was that the body of Christ could not be 'defiled through the impurity and filth of the sin of the vessel in which it enters'.

This situation finds a parallel, though not in theological urgency, in the circumstances of the birth of heroes throughout the Bible. Samson, Samuel, Joseph etc. had to be marked out as superior to their fellow men. Thus arose the biblical phenomenon of the miraculously late birth: the heroes who issue from elderly, seemingly barren unions; Sara, for example, was allegedly ninety years old when she gave birth to Isaac.[10] Viewing children as the miraculous product of divine intercession in the lives of those already too old to give birth was a useful way in which the powers of the Lord could be demonstrated while imputing the necessary degree of virtue to the biblical hero. The *Legenda aurea* puts this very plainly when an angel explains to St Anne that it may be God's will that a woman remain childless early in her marriage:

> so that He may open . . . [the womb] afterwards more wonderfully and it may be known that it is not from lust that [the child] is born but as a divine gift.[11]

The Old Testament is consequently full of such 'divine gifts'. The longest list occurs in the angel's address to Joachim in the *De nativitate Mariae,* but the angel in the N-Town Conception play manages to provide a respectably long list for the edification of both Anne and the audience, beginning with the birth of Isaac and proceeding to name Joseph, Samson and Samuel as gifts 'ful mervelyous' rather than as the embodiment of parental sin (ll.181–8). The apocryphal account of the Conception of the Virgin is intended to foreshadow the more wonderful birth of her Son, and is modelled upon just such biblical accounts as the birth of Isaac, whom Sara, contrary to nature, bore in her old age. According to the three apocryphal gospels (the *Protevangelium,* the Gospel of Pseudo-Matthew, and the *Evangelium de nativitate Mariae*), Joachim and Anne grieve over their barrenness, which is seen as a sign of God's rejection. When on these grounds Joachim's offering in the Temple is refused, he withdraws in shame to the country. During this time an angel announces the future birth of Mary to Joachim and Anne in turn, and they rush to meet one another at the Golden Gate of Jerusalem. All accounts reflect Hebraic values in their stress upon barrenness as a curse, and even a fifteenth-century work such as the N-Town cycle retains this to some extent in an attempt to prove the absolute purity of the Virgin.

In medieval accounts of the conception of Mary, therefore, there is an attempt to move away from the implications of the views of such writers as Innocent III, by stressing these older Hebraic values. It is clear in N-Town, for example, that the absence of the natural fecundity displayed everywhere in the play except in the marriage of Joachim and Anne, is more a cause for concern than any possible parental sin. The recreation of church ritual is effective in emphasizing the cursedness of Joachim and Anne's barren state. Indeed, when Joachim's offering is refused by the priest it is this word – 'cursyd' – which is used to rebuff him.[12] Joachim himself draws the same conclusions:

> I am nott wurthy, Lord, to loke up to hefne.
> My synful steppys an vemynyd þe grounde.[13]

There would appear to be a reference here to Adam and Eve whose steps, according to popular belief, remained burnt into the ground when they were driven from Paradise.[14] This subtle equation of Joachim and Anne in their childless state with the first sinful couple enables the author further to emphasize the approval of all at Mary's eventual birth. Traditional medieval associations of childbirth with sin, and more particularly with Eve's sin – the Jean Eudes idea again that all 'children of Adam' are the 'shrine of the demon' – are here reversed so that Anne is likened to the cursed Eve only in her barren state and her pregnancy is consequently blessed.

However, Mary was more than a great Old Testament patriarch who could be proved sufficiently holy if it could be said that his mother did not conceive him until she was ninety. In spite of the success of Anne and Joachim's Hebraic laments on their childlessness they did not go far enough in ensuring the purity of the Mother of God. Today, the views of the Roman Catholic Church on the question of the Immaculate Conception are relatively settled. In the Middle Ages, however, nothing could have been further from the truth. In the simplest of terms the problem was that the vessel which received the Infant Christ had to be absolutely pure. Mary's perfection and freedom from actual sin were generally accepted from about the fourth century; original sin, which for Augustine, of course, was indissolubly bound to the *concupiscentia carnalis* accompanying all human generation, was a far more complex issue.

Augustine fully believed that the Virgin was born in a state of original sin, although protected by grace against its consequences. Bede, on the other hand, broke with the Augustinian conviction of the generic necessity of birth in sin when he argued that John the Baptist was sanctified in the womb at the Visitation. This was of great importance in later treatments of Mary's birth as it was argued that whatever pertained to John the Baptist must apply to her to an even greater degree.[15] The Eastern Church, however, went further than this, advocating belief in an immaculate active generation and the sanctity of the *conceptio carnis*. St John Damascene, for example, deemed Mary's parents to have been purified by the Holy Ghost during her generation, and thus freed from sexual concupiscence. Consequently, even the human element of her origin, the material of which she was formed, was pure and holy. Such a view was certainly not without support in the West, being put forward by, among others, Petrus Comestor in his treatise against St Bernard. Some writers even taught that Mary was born of a virgin and that she was conceived in a miraculous manner when Joachim and Anne met at the Golden Gate of Jerusalem.[16]

Such beliefs raised problems for the medieval Church. At a lesser level, belief in one virgin birth inevitably led to another. If Mary had to be proved pure enough to bear Christ, it soon became clear that St Anne had to be proved pure enough to bear Mary and so on *ad infinitem*. Thus, fantastic legends grew up, for instance, that the mother of St Anne conceived her daughter by breathing in the fragrance of a rose.[17] Far more worrying for the medieval Church, however, was the fact that such beliefs ultimately jeopardized belief in the full humanity of Christ. As, again following the Augustinian view, all natural womanly functions were regarded as the result of original sin, which of course was sexually transmitted, then a woman immaculately conceived would be physiologically incomplete. If Mary had a physiology wholly uncorrupted by the consequences of sin, then her body would have been incapable of nourishing the child Christ in the womb, and of providing milk for the new-born infant.[18] The Dominican approach to the problem was to proudly advance the claims of the lactating Virgin – thus, the vast number of Madonna and Child paintings they supported in which the child Christ is depicted at the breast. The Franciscans, on the other hand, display something of the more popular following of the Virgin. While supporting claims for the Immaculate Conception, they possessed and proudly displayed the mikveh in which Mary allegedly washed away her first ritual 'defilement', without comprehending the implications of what they possessed. Such indiscriminate enthusiasm is reminiscent of the work of Paschasius Radbertus who addressed the problem of the conception of the Virgin in his ninth-century *De partu virginis,* declaring, 'nor, sanctified in the womb, did she contract original sin' a seemingly self-contradictory statement with which he juxtaposes the explanation that the Virgin was purified by the Holy Ghost at the Annunciation.[19] Precision in the matter would appear not to have been as important as a desire to convey firm belief in the complete purity of the Virgin.

One very influential work, the *Liber de Infantia* or Gospel of Pseudo-Matthew (an eighth- or ninth-century compilation although manuscripts date from no earlier than the eleventh century), comes to us with just such a plea for doctrinal tolerance. In order to introduce it to the world under good auspices the compiler (most likely) provided it with credentials in the form of pretended letters to and from St Jerome. One of these reads:

> I believe none of the faithful will deny that, whether this story be true or invented . . . great miracles preceded the holy birth of Mary . . . and therefore this can be believed and read with intact faith and without peril to the soul.[20]

Pseudo-Matthew then proceeds to recount how Anne conceives Mary while her husband is alone in the desert, and even before their meeting at the Golden Gate.

In 1969, André Grabar put forward the idea that iconography was responsible for the promotion of various Church feasts and of certain Christian dogmas. He contended that the Christian image-makers of late antiquity were accustomed to biographical cycles where, before the birth scene, the embrace of the parents was presented in symbolic reference to the conception. Thus, from the biographies of the Judaic kings developed the habit of depicting an embrace scene before the scene of the birth; from this developed the practice of viewing the actual conception in terms of this passionless embrace; which in turn led to widespread belief in an Immaculate Conception which occurred as Anne and Joachim embraced at the Golden Gate of Jerusalem.[21] This venerated iconographic image of Mary's conception which appeared tantamount, in the eyes of St Bernard of Clairvaux in the late twelfth century, to worshipping the copulation of her parents, was not formally banned by the pope until 1677, and consequently must have done much to colour popular belief about the Virgin's birth.[22]

The very setting for this iconographic embrace associates it with traditional images of birth and conception. The closed gate as a figure of Mary's conception of Christ is, of course, a medieval commonplace, deriving ultimately from a passage in Ezekiel (44:2):

> This gate shall remain shut; it shall not be opened, and no one shall enter by it; for the Lord, the God of Israel, has entered by it; therefore it shall remain shut.

Elsewhere too, gate images are frequently associated with birth and conception, the womb being the 'devil's gateway', and the painful birth described in *Mundus et Infans*, for example, being associated with a 'narrow wicket'. As for gold, it was the undefiled metal of the ark of the covenant, in Hebrews 9:4, the substance of the urn which preserved the manna from rottenness, and as such, a reference to the pure and uncorrupted womb of the Virgin. The two concepts are often explicitly joined in connection with the Virgin Birth, as in the Latin metaphor from Pope Gregory's *Liber responsalis:*

> He has entered through the bright region, the ear of the virgin, to visit the palace of her womb; and he has returned through the golden gate of the Virgin.[23]

This metaphor for the physical birth from Mary's womb was a rhetorical commonplace in poetry, hymns and commentaries as well as the liturgy. Its great popularity and early appearance would suggest that references to golden gates in the Middle Ages generally implied some association with the doctrine of the Virgin Birth, and, therefore, that the famous iconographic embrace of Anne and Joachim at the Golden Gate of Jerusalem strongly associates the conception and birth of Mary with the conception and birth of her Son. Such equations were, in fact, facilitated by the very people anxious to refute such claims. As primarily Maculist in outlook, the Dominicans had no desire to promote belief in the miraculous conception of Mary, but they equally had no desire to impugn the Virgin's purity. They consequently continued to use the term 'Immaculate Conception' but applied it to the conception of Christ by Mary. The resulting confusion probably did as much to undermine their case as to strengthen it, as the same term was applied, albeit by different groups, to both conceptions.

It is typical of the ambiguous treatment of this subject that the famous iconographic embrace is frequently retained even by authors who have no interest whatsoever in advocating belief in the Immaculate Conception. *Cursor Mundi* is one such case, retaining the traditional longing of St Anne for her absent husband, and their meeting at the Golden Gate, but making it clear that 'Soone aftir to gider þei lay'.[24] Lydgate, in his *Life of Our Lady*, retains the Golden Gate but dispenses with the embrace, again making it clear that the conception takes place afterwards.[25] And Nicholas Love in his *Mirrour of the Blessed Lyf of Jesu Christ*, a free translation of the Latin *Meditationes vitae Christi* and an example of a standard medieval approach to the lives of the Virgin and of Christ, simply makes no mention of the conception of Mary. Perhaps Love decided that discretion was the better part of valour. Even Aelfric, as Mary Clayton points out in her study of the cult of the Virgin in Anglo-Saxon England, originally refused to write a homily on the nativity of the Virgin for fear of heresy.[26]

N-Town retains a greater level of ambiguity in its Marian plays than any of these. The Golden Gate and the famous iconographic embrace are much in evidence. Even more important, however, is the chaste kiss, the 'kusse of clennesse' which Joachim gives his wife at their meeting, urging her to keep it with her, an implication at least of the Immaculate Conception.[27] So too, when the angel tells Joachim that Anne shall conceive, he juxtaposes her impregnation with Mary's conception of Christ through the intercession of the Holy Ghost: 'And as sche xal be bore of a barrany body, / So of her xal be bore, with-out nature Jhesus'.[28] The implication would appear to be that one birth 'without nature' is the inevitable corollary of another, an idea which verges on a claim for the Immaculate Conception.

The ambiguous tone continues in the next play in the cycle, introduced by Contemplacio:

> Sovereynes, ȝe han sen shewyd ȝow be-fore
> Of Joachim and Anne here botherys holy metynge.
> How oure Lady was conseyvid and how she was bore,
> We passe ovyr þat breffnes of tyme consyderynge.[29]

The meeting at the Golden Gate is described as 'holy' which could be a reference to the notion that Mary was conceived at that very moment. Further, although the third line most probably belongs to the fourth, indicating that the poet, through a professed lack of time, will pass over the conception and eventual birth of Mary which occurred after the meeting, it could only slightly more awkwardly be taken in conjunction with the second line and result in the meaning that, due to lack of time, the poet will no longer dwell on how the Virgin was conceived and born (in the sense of came into existence) as a result of her parents' holy meeting at the Golden Gate. Such ambiguity is typical of the author of the N-Town Marian cycle. Although it appears likely that he is not advocating the idea of the Immaculate Conception it is never explicitly dismissed. Nor does the motivation for this reluctance appear to be a simple Aelfric-like fear of heresy. Rather, he would appear to have used the controversy to his own ends in order to stress the absolute purity of the Virgin while sacrificing nothing of her humanity. The theology is presented to the community in a way which makes the Virgin accessible and comprehensible.

This approach proved successful not only in the case of the conception doctrine but also in the portrayal of the infant Mary. Indeed, N-Town's child Virgin proves to be one of the most successful portrayals of a holy child throughout all medieval literature, uniting as it does the charm of her very real humanity with her unique purity and goodness. A popular medieval practice was to divide man's life into stages, attributing to him certain characteristics as he attained each age. Such *schemas* led to great interest in those exceptional persons who transcended the natural order and achieved in youth, for example, the wisdom proper to old age. This particular *topos* is usually referred to as *puer senex* (aged youth) and the vast majority of medieval saints and a large number of heroes, for example, come into this category. The medieval *puer senex*, however, was not without his critics. In the words of J. A. Burrow:

> It seems that ordinary folk, then as now, were only too ready to admire, or at least to forgive, naughty boys and wild young men, on the grounds that such behaviour was only natural at their age; while they might look on good children and virtuous youths with a certain coolness, suspicion, or even outright hostility.[30]

This hostility is manifested in various medieval proverbs such as 'Soon ripe, soon rotten' and 'Young saint, old devil'. There is similar testimony to hostility of this sort in the N-Town play of *Christ among the Doctors*. The Virgin, anxiously looking for the boy Jesus who is lost, expresses the fear that his precocious goodness and wisdom have made him enemies:

> I am aferde þat he hath fon
> For his gret wyttys and werkys good.
> Lyke hym of wytt forsoth is non,
> Euery childe with hym is wroth and wood.[31]

The talents of holy infants apparently knew no bounds. St Nicholas, for instance, on the day of his birth sat upright in his bath, fasted at the breast, and was in the habit of sleeping in his cradle with his arms outstretched in imitation of the crucifixion.[32] Nor could the courage of any man or woman surpass that of the young martyrs. The *Legenda aurea* praises the child martyr St Celsus in words which could be applied to all the young saints: 'he transcended his boyish years by the virtue of his soul'.[33] Faced with such astonishing, even miraculous virtue, medieval authors would appear to have often had to sacrifice the human, childlike qualities of their subjects.

The childhood of Mary is often treated in a similar manner. According to apocryphal sources, the chief miracle of Mary's early life is her unaided ascent of the Temple steps at the age of three. *Cursor Mundi* provides a concise and typical account of the event: Mary climbs 'Wiþ outen helpe of mon of welde / As she were wommon of elde', and no more is said.[34] The N-Town play of *Mary's Presentation in the Temple* recounts the same miracle, but in a very different manner. To Rosemary Woolf there appeared to be nothing childlike about N-Town's portrayal of the young Virgin:

> Deliberately and in keeping with the tradition no attempt is made to charac-
> terise Mary as a child, the adult gravity of her speeches reflecting her mi-
> raculous power to ascend the fifteen steps of the Temple unaided.[35]

Certainly, Mary's speeches do display an adult gravity, but N-Town scarcely appears to belong to the same tradition as *Cursor Mundi* where Mary is compared to a 'wommon of elde' and subsequently treated as one. In the earliest records the reason people marvelled at the Virgin's ascent of the steps was that the child accomplished the feat without once looking back at her parents; thus in the *Protevangelium*.[36] In the *De nativitate Mariae* Anne and Joachim are not even present, they are changing out of their travelling clothes unaware of what their child is doing.[37] The *Legenda aurea* makes no mention of the Virgin's parents at this point, even dismissing the miracle itself as something accomplished by the child with perfect ease.[38] And although both Anne and Joachim are present in *Cursor Mundi*, their involvement ends there; there is no indication at all that they may be anxious for the safety of their child. In N-Town, however, the emphasis is very much upon the loving attention of Anne and Joachim as they anxiously watch their daughter's progress. The scene is reminiscent of an alabaster at Kinwarton which depicts St

Anne reaching forward to support her daughter, a very natural impulse when a child is climbing but entirely contrary to the traditional story of the miracle.[39] Further, unlike Lydgate's St Anne who faints for joy at the sight of Mary on the altar steps, the N-Town Anne refuses to leave the temple until she has seen her daughter safely at the top of the stairs: 'I wold not for al erthe se here fal.'[40] Even the priest appears to be not only doubtful that Mary will accomplish the task but seriously concerned for her safety:

> þu xalt be þe dowtere of God eternall
> If þe fyftene grees þu may ascende.
> It is meracle if þu do! Now God þe dyffende.[41]

The priest is almost as tender towards the child as her mother, whose words to her daughter are consistently convincing as a mother's to her child, full of gentle coaxing and encouragement: 'can ȝe gon a-lone lett se beth bolde'.[42] The author's stress upon this mother–daughter relationship is further exemplified by the parting of Mary and Anne in the Temple. Far from running up the steps without once looking back, her arms outstretched towards the priest, as in one illustration in a manuscript of the *Meditationes vitae Christi*, the N-Town Mary shows a child's reluctance in parting from her mother.[43] St Anne is very much affected by her child's obvious grief: 'Swete dowtyr, thynk on ȝoure modyr, An; / ȝoure swemynge smytyht to myn hert depe'.[44] The effect, while in no way diminishing the miraculous nature of the events, is to convincingly portray Mary as a child even though she speaks, to use Joachim's words, like a woman of twenty.[45] Pseudo-Matthew in fact gauges her maturity of speech to be consistent with that of a woman of thirty years, an age traditionally associated with the maturity of spirit of the Virgin.[46] It is a nice touch by the N-Town author, therefore, that he considers the maturity of twenty to be quite exceptional enough for his three-year-old subject.

The author of these N-Town plays goes much further then than most other medieval authors of accounts of the life of the Virgin in establishing the childlike qualities of his subject. The reason for this may merely have been a simple matter of devotion on the part of the author. However, it could conceivably have been intended to put an orthodox stress on the humanity of the Virgin. One of the main points about the *puer senex topos* is that the child miraculously transcends the normal levels of wisdom and virtue attributed to his age group. Christ, as has been said, was often depicted lecturing to the Doctors in the Temple, correcting St

Joseph and generally displaying the characteristic precocity of a *puer senex*. However, there was a theological danger in viewing the boy Christ purely in this way. In so far as he was God, there could be no limit to his wisdom and knowledge; but he was also man, and as such must be thought of as following (even if in exemplary fashion) the *cursus aetatis* natural to all men. It was his natural childhood and, more generally, the natural sequence of the ages of his life, which served to guarantee his true humanity. Thus, even though the Virgin is portrayed to some extent as a *puella senex* in that she displays astonishing virtue and great dexterity in climbing the stairs while reciting the gradual psalms, the stress laid upon her childlike qualities serves to emphasize her own humanity and subsequently that of Christ.[47] There was also another, less technical consideration. As Burrow points out, Christ's life was commonly held up, by preachers and others, as an example for all men to follow – a model for how the life of Everyman should ideally be. Hence it was necessary to show that his life's course was governed by the principle of *tempestivitas,* or seasonableness, which only saints could neglect with impunity.

The same could also be said of the Virgin herself, for like her Son she too was a model for humanity. Indeed, being completely human, *theotokos* but not herself divine, medieval society would appear to have formed more of a personal attachment to Mary.[48] Benedicta Ward's examination of the medieval miracles of the Virgin make this clear:

> John of Coutances urged that Our Lady of Coutances should not be confused with Our Lady of Bayeux. At Rocamadour, the Virgin was venerated as 'Our Lady of Rocamadour' . . . on one hand the popularization of the cult of the Virgin among the more simple people led to an acknowledgment of her ubiquitous powers, but on the other hand it domesticated her as the 'Lady' of certain areas.[49]

The Blessed Virgin of one town was not to be confused with the Blessed Virgin of the next. When Glutinus of Exeter prayed for ten days before the relics of the Virgin in Salisbury without receiving a cure for his lameness, the canons came to the conclusion that the Virgin would only cure him in his own diocese, upon which he was forcibly removed and cured by his local Blessed Virgin.[50] Thus, although the Virgin Mary's influence was regarded as universal, especially given that her bodily assumption meant that holy relics were rather few and veneration could not be so easily localized, people strongly identified with her, and the absence of important bodily relics in fact brought about a universal localization. In ·fact, her role as intercessor with the highest authorities is reminiscent of the role outlined by Jennifer Ward in this volume for the noblewomen who interceded with the king and others on behalf of individuals or their communities as a whole. The Virgin was the ultimate intercessor with the largest community and it is upon this personal interior devotion to and identification with the Virgin that the N-Town author draws, while simultaneously presenting her as an irreproachable model for his audience. Just as his ambiguous approach to the question of the Immaculate Conception had enabled the author to stress both the purity and humanity of the Virgin at the same time, this very humanity promotes an identification with the child who is, after all, uniquely pure. In this way N-Town's Mary is a child both like and unlike all others; both imitable and respectfully inimitable. In the words of Joachim:

> A, ho had evyr suche a chylde ?
> Nevyr creature ȝit þat evyr was bore !
> Sche is so gracyous, she is so mylde -
> So xulde childyr to fadyr and modyr evyrmore.[51]

The didactic aim of the English vernacular plays has often been emphasized, and the N-Town Mary plays do not differ in this respect. In a direct expository way they are only occasionally so, for example, Joachim's remarks to the audience: 'So xulde euery curat', 'so xulde childyr'.[52] As Peter Meredith points out, however, exemplary teaching is far more pervasive in the play. Joachim and Anne are presented as the ideal married couple, devoted to God and to one another, and loving in their treatment of Mary. Both Ysachar and the Bishop are stern but just and exemplary enforcers of the Lord's will. Even the shepherds with their dutiful concern for their master and mistress, are exemplary.[53] Mary, of course, is a model of perfection, all the more so because she is no longer the hazy figure of the gospels but is instead placed within a community where she functions as a real child and a real woman, even while she offers a medieval ideal of behaviour.

The tone of the N-Town drama is in fact often reminiscent of the *Ancrene Wisse* in the gentleness of its reproof and its encouragement of moderation in all things. It has even been suggested that this section of the N-Town cycle was written by someone with a practical knowledge and interest in religious communities of young women.[54] The Virgin was undoubtedly a central image for women mystics, both lay and religious, and also more generally for women's devotional lives. However, her appeal was wide and not merely confined to those interested in leading religious lives. As was illustrated by medieval response to the miracles of the Virgin, personal identification with Mary was strong. Further, she was capable of being almost literally many things at once. During a spate of apparitions of the Virgin in plague-ridden medieval Spain, Mary appeared as both mother and child, both tall and short, often within the one vision.[55] Thus, mothers who had lost children identified themselves with the Holy Mother while simultaneously seeing their children as the infant Mary.[56] The Virgin's ability to be all things to all women is further exhibited by the Feast of the Twelve Marys in medieval Venice. Throughout the festival social roles and age groups were precisely differentiated. Women considered the Festival to be their own and appeared in their roles as virginal daughters, devoted spouses, and pious mothers, all devoted to the Virgin. Poor girls received dowries from the rich; betrothals were solemnized; and there was a heavy emphasis laid on fertility.[57] Mary was the ideal young girl, the bride's model and guide, God's consort who had been mystically wed at the Annunciation, and the paragon of motherhood. She was also, of course, according to Augustine, the first voluntarily to vow her virginity to God and as such was a model for all virgins.

It is consequently no surprise to find in the young Mary of the N-Town plays the ideal model for all women. Even theatrical necessity facilitates this view. Mary, as already discussed, was three years old at the time of her presentation in the temple. At the time of her marriage to Joseph she was fourteen years of age.[58] She was consequently a child throughout the drama. It is not possible, however, that a child of three could have played the three-year old Mary. If it was a miracle that the Virgin, being so young, should ascend the stairs reciting the fifteen gradual psalms, it is highly unlikely that an equally gifted three-year-old would have been found for the occasion. Detailed records survive of one dramatic performance organized by Philippe de Mézières for the feast of the Presentation at Avignon in 1385. According to these, Mary is in fact played by a little girl three or four years of age. However, her role consists merely of being led everywhere and she was not expected to speak.[59] The child Mary in the N-Town play must consequently have been much older, a supposition supported by various pieces of iconography, depicting a child with very long hair, almost as tall as St Anne, climbing the stairs.[60] Similarly, at the time of Mary's betrothal the child could not be too old. Much is traditionally made of Joseph's old age, and a Mary who no longer looked like a young girl would have lessened the sense of disparity and most of the comic effect would have been lost. Therefore, the child Mary has the maturity of twenty and is played by a child considerably older than three; at the same time when she assumes the role of wife and mother it is her youth which must be stressed, factors which once more emphasize the universal appeal of the Virgin to any audience.

Therefore, the child Mary could appeal to and encompass all ages. She also traditionally encompassed all feminine virtues, a fact acknowledged by many Middle English courtesy books. Although there is an obvious reference to the *Regina Gratiae* of the theologians whenever Mary is referred to as Queen of Courtesy, the secular connotations of such phrases should not be dismissed. Mary may exhibit the purity of heavenly grace but the perfect courtesy of her human aspect is also evoked. The same theme is taken up by Nardon Penicaud (*c*.1470–1542). In this French work, the Virgin is depicted with the bouquet of perfect feminine virtues: obedience, poverty, patience, charity, compassion, praise (adulation), truth, humility, prudence, and purity.[61] These are all to some extent displayed by the Virgin in the N-Town plays. Her obedience, for example, is evident in her willingness to comply with the old law in presenting herself and her child in the temple in order to be purified. This, of course, was not the invention of the N-Town playwright but rather derived ultimately from an association with Matthew 5:17: 'Think not that I have come to abolish the law and the prophets; I have come not to abolish them but to fulfill them.' Traditionally much is made of Mary's willingness to comply with the law in spite of the fact that the Virgin Birth meant that she had in fact no need of purification. The situation is nicely summarized in one of the *Vercelli Homilies*:

> Since all women who gave birth sent themselves to the temple in accordance with the commandment, St Mary, the mother of Christ, waited in purity for the fortieth day – not at all because she had any need of that, because her body was so pure, which throughout everything was cleansed by divine dispensation and the merits of her life and through the grace of the Holy Spirit.[62]

N-Town's Joseph makes the matter similarly explicit: an undefiled body had no need of the ritual purification. However, this virtue, like all the others, is seen as more of a joy to the young Mary than mere obedience. While Joseph sighs and clutches the turtle doves which must be offered according to the law – and he makes it very clear that adherence to the law is his only reason for being there – Mary makes a true virtue of necessity and takes as much pleasure in the first offering of her son as in his first words or steps, delighted that his heavenly Father should witness this event:

> Receyvyth now þis lytyl offerynge
> Ffor it is þe fyrst in degre
> þat зour lytyl childe so зnge
> presentyth to-day be my shewyng.[63]

At a much more practical level, the N-Town author turns to the eating habits of the Virgin in order, apparently, to give warning to his audience. The Virgin is brought heavenly food daily by the angels. The author does not waste the opportunity, however, of describing what Mary does with the food that is brought for her from the temple. She gives it to the other girls who live with her, urging them to 'Fede . . . þerof hertyly . . . [and] nat spare'.[64] The tone of these passages is again similar to that of the *Ancrene Wisse* in which, although the anchoresses are encouraged not to eat meat and to accustom themselves to little drink, the views expressed on fasting and abstention remain very moderate: '. . . leoue sustren, зower mete ant зower drunch haue iþuht me ofte leassa þen Ich walde. Ne feaste зe na dei to bread ne to weattre bute зe habben leaue.'[65] There would appear to have been strong historical precedent for this warning. Caroline Walker Bynum, in her book *Holy Feast and Holy Fast*, argues convincingly that fasting was a particularly important element in the lives of women religious. In Tubach's *Index*, the longest fast made by any man is seventy-eight weeks. Mary Magdalene, on the other hand, fasted for thirty years, and it is women who provide both of the cases of fasting until death.[66] Allegorical portrayals of the Seven Deadly Sins, such as that in *Piers Plowman*, most frequently portray Gluttony as male, while giving a sin such as Pride a female form. In monastic circles in the high and later Middle Ages, we find further evidence that moralists associated vices pertaining to food with men more than with women. A short but popular anti-monastic parody, the *De monachis carnalibus* (*On Worldly Monks*), survives in three versions, one of which is an adaptation for nuns. Although the monks' versions focus to a large extent on the gluttonous monk, the nuns' version eliminates most of the food references, suggesting that vanity is a far greater temptation to women.[67]

One further direction is given by the Virgin with regard to their daily bread: '. . . if owght be leve, specyaly I pray зow / That þe pore men þe relevys þerof haue now.'[68] Mary was renowned for her acts of charity, and is depicted often surrounded by the poor as she distributes bread.

Lydgate describes her healing the sick too: '. . . euery wyght grevyde with sekenesse/ A touche of hir made hem hoole a noon.'[69] Once again, these are qualities expected of medieval women of adequate means, as shown in the papers both of Patricia Skinner and of Jennifer Ward. The implication in N-Town, however, is that the Virgin does not intend to visit the poor herself, but rather that her companions should do this work. J. Vriend has suggested that this supports his claim that the N-Town Marian cycle was written for women religious, who should not have too much contact with the outside world. Had this really been the case, however, it seems likely that the author would have devoted more time to the consideration of other such practical details. An obvious example would have been Mary's traditional weaving skills. Such a skill is found in almost all accounts of the girlhood of Mary, ultimately for a good, complex theological reason, for weaving was a traditional and frequent metaphor for the Incarnation. St Anthony of Padua, a principal Franciscan exegete, describes the Incarnation thus:

> Out of the sackcloth of our nature Jesus Christ made a tunic for Himself which He made with the needle of the subtle work of the Holy Spirit and the thread of the Blessed Virgin's faith.[70]

Of course, precise biblical references were often forgotten by authors anxious to convey firm belief in the various excellences of the Virgin, and subtle allusions to the Incarnation were often passed over in the excitement of proving that once again she far surpassed other women in skill as well as in virtue. In the *Protevangelium* Mary was chosen to spin the scarlet and the purple for the veil of the Temple, there being here a fairly clear reference to the Incarnation of the King of the World. By the time of Lydgate, however, this story appears to have lost much of its theological significance. Mary is now merely spinning her own clothes, and in an almost frivolous account, Lydgate describes how each girl reached out without looking (lest she be accused of vanity) and Mary's hand invariably fell upon the rich purple cloth.[71] The *Old English Martyrology* went even further, offering as proof of Mary's perfection the observation that she could weave far better than any of the older girls.[72]

The N-Town author chooses not to include Mary's well-known associations with cloth-making and sewing in his account of her life with her female companions. Had this cycle really been intended to instruct young nuns in their duties, the author would have missed an ideal opportunity to correct what had become one of the major problems in medieval nunneries. Nuns appeared not to have generally engaged in the spinning and weaving of their own clothes, and considerable bills to hired spinsters, fullers and weavers consequently figure in convent account rolls, a fact which was not relished by the Church. Even the author of *Ancrene Wisse* urges his audience not to waste their time on decorative work, but rather to make garments for themselves. Perhaps he had had practical experience of the kind which prompted the injunction sent to Nunkeeling, Yedingham and Wykeham in 1314 that no nun should absent herself from divine service 'on account of being occupied with silk work' ('propter occupacionem operis de serico').[73]

Perhaps the reason why the N-Town author did not include such details is that by so doing he would have equated the Virgin with one particular section of society more than he wished to do. The virtues she displays throughout are not particularly girlish, nor is she ever portrayed in particularly womanly terms. It would appear rather that while the author wished to stress the humanity of the Virgin by emphasizing her childlike nature, he did not wish her to appear childish, or as merely a model for children. She is, of course, a model for children but she is far more. The medieval world viewed her as a model for all people, and the N-Town Mary plays go far further than most accounts of the life of the Virgin in attempting to prove that this is so. The ambiguity displayed over the question of the Immaculate Conception enabled the author to fully stress both Mary's humanity and her perfect purity. The same ambiguity is the result of the Virgin's portrayal as a *puella senex*, for although she is a child she displays virtue, knowledge and even physical dexterity far beyond her years. The outcome then is a model which would touch all humanity, a polymorphous vision like that of the sixteenth-century Spanish peasant Francesca la Brava, in which the Virgin is seen at once as Holy Mother and Holy Child, Virgin and Bride. It is true, as this volume shows, that medieval communities are marked by exclusion as well as inclusion, but this textual community at least would appear to have included more than might have been previously realized. There may not be many women in the mystery cycles but the role of the Virgin in the early N-Town plays of her life is a complicated blend of theology and domesticity which would have brought together the different elements of the female community for the great communal festival of the drama.

Notes

¹ *N-Town Play,* ed. Spector, I, xvi.

² Gibson, *The Theater of Devotion,* 139.

³ Wickham, *The Medieval Theatre,* 182.

⁴ Aquinas, *Summa Theologiae,* 1a, q.98, art.2 (XIII, 154).

⁵ Jerome, for example, is adamant that Eden was a 'paradise of virginity' and that sexual union only occurred once Adam and Eve had been cast out from it. He even switches the order of verses in Genesis to make it appear that marriage followed sin: *Letter* 22, 18, *PL* 22:405; *Adversus Jovinianum* 1, 16, *PL* 23:235.

⁶ Eudes, *The Wondrous Childhood,* 90.

⁷ Lotario dei Segni (Innocent III), *De miseria* I, iii, 98–9; *PL,* 200: 703–7.

⁸ The *Parson's Tale* in *The Riverside Chaucer,* 318.

⁹ Augustine, *De civitate Dei,* xiv, 21, *PL* 41:429.

¹⁰ See for Isaac, Genesis 18, 21; for Joseph, Genesis 30; for Samson, Judges 13; and for Samuel, 1 Kings 1.

¹¹ *Legenda aurea,* ed. Graesse, cxxxi, 588: 'uterum claudit . . . ut mirabilius denuo aperiat, et non libidinus esse, quod nascitur, sed divini fore muneris cognoscatur'.

¹² *N-Town Play,* ed. Spector, 74, l.104.

¹³ *Ibid.,* 76, ll.149–50.

¹⁴ *Legends of the Holy Rood,* ed. Morris, 22–3, and 66.

¹⁵ See Clayton, *The Cult of the Virgin Mary,* 16. St Anslem of Canterbury, on the other hand, believed that the Virgin was purified from sin by a sanctification at the moment of her birth, but became completely pure only at the moment of the Annunciation: *De conceptu virginali et originali peccato, PL* 158: 431–64.

¹⁶ This idea had endured since its first recorded appearance in the *Protevangelium Jacobi.* See James, *The Apocryphal New Testament,* 40.

¹⁷ See Douhaire, *Cours sur les apocryphes,* 187–8. Another popular medieval account relates how St Anne springs from the thigh of Phanual and is suckled by a stag: James, 'Legends of SS Anne and Anastasia', 195–6.

¹⁸ See Wood, 'The doctor's dilemma', 710–27.

¹⁹ Paschasius Radbertus, *De partu virginis, PL* 120:1371–2: '. . . neque contraxit in utero sanctaficata originale peccatum'.

²⁰ Tischendorf, *Evangelia apocrypha,* 9.

²¹ Grabar, *Christian Iconography,* 130–1.

²² Mabillon, *The Life and Works of St Bernard,* II, 512–18.

²³ Gregory the Great, *Liber responsalis sine antiphonarius, PL* 78:731: 'Ingressus est per splendidam regionem, aurem Virginis, visitare palatium uteri; et regressus est per aurem Virginis portam'. Cf. *PL* 78:734: 'Introivit per aurem Virginis in regionem nostram, indutus stolam purpuream. Et exivit per auream portam lux et decus universae fabricae mundi'.

[24] *Cursor Mundi*, ed. Morris, II, l.10571.

[25] Lydgate, *The Life of Our Lady*, I, ll.120–6.

[26] Clayton, *The Cult of the Virgin Mary*, 245–6.

[27] *N-Town Play,* ed. Spector , 80, l.241.

[28] *Ibid.,* 79, ll.195–6.

[29] *Ibid.,* 81, ll.1–4.

[30] Burrow, *The Ages of Man*, 146.

[31] *N-Town Play*, ed. Spector, 205, ll.221–4.

[32] Horstmann, *The Early South-English Legendary*, 240–1.

[33] *Legenda aurea*, ed. Graesse, 439: 'aetatem puerilem virtute animi superavit'.

[34] *Cursor Mundi*, ed. Morris, II, ll.10593–4.

[35] Woolf, *The English Mystery Plays*, 162.

[36] James, *The Apocryphal New Testament*, 42.

[37] Tischendorf, *Evangelia apocrypha*, 61.

[38] *Legenda aurea*, ed. Graesse, 588.

[39] Reproduced in Anderson, *Drama and Imagery*, plate 7b.

[40] Lydgate, *The Life of Our Lady*, I, ll.196–7; *N-Town Plays*, ed. Spector, 85, l.93.

[41] *N-Town Play*, ed. Spector, 85, ll.96–8.

[42] *Ibid.*, 83, l.45.

[43] *Meditations,* ed. Ragusa and Green, fig. 4.

[44] *N-Town Play*, ed. Spector, 84, ll.80–1.

[45] *Ibid.*, 83, l.43.

[46] Assmann, *Angelsächsische Homilien*, x, ll.300–4: 'Ac heo wæs on gange and on worde and on eallum gebærum gelic wynsuman men, þe hæfde xxx wintra'.

[47] The lengths to which belief in and devotion to the actual childhood of Christ could be taken is exemplified by such stories as that told of Henry Suso who was in the habit of dividing his fruit into four parts: one part for Mary and three for the persons of the Trinity. The fourth part, which belonged to Christ, was always left unpeeled as children do not peel fruit. See Huizinga, *The Waning of the Middle Ages*, 137.

[48] The title *theotokos* (God-bearer) was defended by the Council of Ephesus and the Council of Chalcedon as the proper title for Mary.

[49] Ward, *Miracles and the Medieval Mind*, 145.

[50] *Ibid.,* 140.

[51] *N-Town Play*, ed. Spector, 85, ll.86–9.

[52] *Ibid.*, 73, l.54; 85, l.89.

[53] *The Mary Play*, ed. Meredith, 13–14.

[54] Vriend, *The Blessed Virgin Mary*, 48.

[55] Christian, *Apparitions*, 182.

[56] The phenomenon was not however, merely confined to the visions of grief-stricken mothers. It is a commonplace of medieval thought. When Margery

Kempe, for example, decides to think about her holy 'mother' what she actually thinks of is the birth of the Virgin: see Kempe, *The Book of Margery Kempe*, eds. Meech and Allen, 18.

[57] See Muir, *Civic Ritual*, 139–51.

[58] *N-Town Play*, Spector, 95, l.10. The *Protevangelium* actually cites the age of betrothal as twelve, as do some, but not all, of the manuscripts of Pseudo-Matthew. See James, *The Apocryphal New Testament*, 42 and 73. That a girl should be forced to leave the temple at either age echoes a Jewish taboo that at puberty she would defile the sanctuary. See Warner, *Alone of All Her Sex*, 32.

[59] Young, *The Drama of the Medieval Church*, II, 228: 'Primo namque erit quedam virgo iuuencula et pulcherrima circiter trium aut iiij annorum'.

[60] See, for example, the Kinwarton alabaster, referred to in n.39 above.

[61] Reproduced in Warner, *Alone of All Her Sex*, plate 24.

[62] Szarmach, *The Vercelli Homilies*, 51–2.

[63] *N-Town Play*, Spector, 187, ll.198–201.

[64] *Ibid.*, 94, l.288.

[65] *Ancrene Wisse*, Tolkein, 211, ll.17–19.

[66] Bynum, *Holy Feast and Holy Fast*, 79.

[67] Rigg, '*Metra de Monachis Carnalibus*', 134–42.

[68] *N-Town Play*, Spector, 94, ll.289–90.

[69] Lydgate, *The Life of Our Lady*, I, ll.274–5.

[70] Rohr, *Sacred Scripture*, 72.

[71] Lydgate, *The Life of Our Lady*, I, ll.786–9.

[72] Herzfeld, *An Old English Martyrology*, 165, ll.17–19.

[73] Power, *Medieval English Nunneries*, 255–7.

Bibliography

Ancrene Wisse. ed. J. R. R. Tolkein (London, 1962).

Anderson, M., *Drama and Imagery in English Medieval Churches* (Cambridge, 1963).

Aquinas, T., *Summa Theologiae* ed. T. Gilby (London, 1966–74).

Assmann, B. (ed.), *Angelsächsische Homilien und Heiligenleben* (Kassel, 1889).

Burrow, J. A., *The Ages of Man* (Oxford, 1986).

Bynum, C. W., *Holy Feast and Holy Fast: The Religious Significance of Food to Medieval Women* (Berkeley, 1987).

Chaucer, G., *The Riverside Chaucer,* ed. L. D. Benson (Boston, 1987; London, 1988).

Christian, W. A., *Apparitions in Late Medieval and Renaissance Spain* (Princeton, 1981).

Clayton, M., *The Cult of the Virgin Mary in Anglo-Saxon England* (Cambridge, 1990).

Cursor Mundi, ed. R. Morris (London, 1892).

Douhaire, P., *Cours sur les apocryphes* (Paris, 1838).

Eudes, J., *The Wondrous Childhood of the Most Holy Mother of God,* anon. trans. (New York, 1915).

Grabar, A., *Christian Iconography: A Study of its Origins* (London, 1969).

Gibson, G. M., *The Theater of Devotion: East Anglian Drama and Society in the Late Middle Ages* (Chicago and London, 1989).

Herzfeld, G. (ed.), *An Old English Martyrology* (London, 1900).

Horstmann, C. (ed.), *The Early South-English Legendary* (London, 1887).

Huizinga, J., *The Waning of the Middle Ages: A Study of the Forms of Life, Thought and Art in France and the Netherlands in the Fourteenth and Fifteenth Centuries,* trans. F. Hopman (London, 1924).

James, M. R., 'Legends of SS Anne and Anastasia', *Cambridge Antiquarian Society* 9 (1896–8), 194–204.

James, M. R. (trans.), *The Apocryphal New Testament* (Oxford, 1926).

Kempe, M., *The Book of Margery Kempe* ed. S.B. Meech and H.E. Allen (London, 1940).

Legenda aurea, ed. T. Graesse (Lipsae, 1850).

Legends of the Holy Rood, ed. R. Morris (London, 1881).

Lotario dei Segni (Innocent III), *De miseria condicionis humane,* ed. R. E. Lewis (Athens, Georgia, 1978).

Lydgate, J., *The Life of Our Lady,* ed. J. A. Lauritis (Pittsburgh, 1961).

Mabillon, D. (ed.), *The Life and Works of St Bernard, Abbot of Clairvaux,* trans. S. J. Eales (London, 1896).

The Mary Play from the N-Town Manuscript, ed. P. Meredith (London and New York, 1987).

Meditations on the Life of Our Lord, ed. and trans. I. Ragusa and R. B. Green (Princeton, 1961).

Muir, E., *Civic Ritual in Renaissance Venice* (Princeton, 1981).

The N-Town Play, Cotton MS Vespasian D.,8, ed. S. Spector (Oxford, 1991).

Power, E., *Medieval English Nunneries c.1275–1535* (Cambridge, 1922).

Rigg, A. G., 'Metra de Monachis Carnalibus: the three versions', *Mittellateinisches Jahrbuch* 15 (1980), 134–42.

Rohr, L. F., *The Use of Sacred Scripture in the Sermons of St Anthony of Padua* (Washington, 1948).

Szarmach, P., (ed.), *The Vercelli Homilies* (London, 1958).

Tischendorf, C., *Evangelia apocrypha* (Leipzig, 1876).

Vriend, J., *The Blessed Virgin Mary in the Medieval Drama of England* (Purmerend, 1928).

Ward, B., *Miracles and the Medieval Mind: Theory, Record and Event 1000–1215* (London, 1982).

Warner, M., *Alone of All Her Sex: The Myth and the Cult of the Virgin Mary* (London, 1976; repr. 1990).

Wickham, G., *The Medieval Theatre* (Cambridge, 1974).

Wood, C. T., The doctor's dilemma: sin, salvation and the menstrual cycle in medieval thought', *Speculum* 56 (1981), 710–27.

Woolf, R., *The English Mystery Plays* (London, 1972).

Young, K., *The Drama of the Medieval Church* (Oxford, 1933).

Index